Previous pages:

Frank Lloyd Wright in Administration Building, 1950. (Courtesy of Johnson Wax)

Herbert F. Johnson (left) and William Connolly (right) in Administration Building, 1939 (Photo by Torkel Korling, courtesy of David Phillips)

FRANK LLOYD WRIGHT
AND THE
JOHNSON WAX BUILDINGS

JONATHAN LIPMAN

INTRODUCTION BY KENNETH FRAMPTON

To John H. Mitchell

First published in the United States of America in 1986 by
RIZZOLI INTERNATIONAL PUBLICATIONS, INC.
300 Park Avenue South, New York, NY 10010

Designed by Abigail Sturges
Composition by Rainsford Type, Ridgefield, CT

Library of Congress Cataloging-in-Publication Data

Lipman, Jonathan.
Frank Lloyd Wright and the Johnson Wax buildings.

Includes index.
1. Wright, Frank Lloyd, 1867–1959—Contributions in innovative architectural design. 2. Wright, Frank Lloyd, 1867–1959—Criticism and interpretation. 3. Johnson Wax—Buildings. 4. Architecture, Modern—20th century—Wisconsin—Racine. 5. Racine (Wis.)—Buildings, structures, etc. I. Wright, Frank Lloyd, 1867–1859. II. Title.
NA737.W7L57 1986 725′.23′0924 85-43498
ISBN 0–8478–0705–3
ISBN 0–8478–0706–1 (pbk.)

Reprinted 1991

Printed and bound in Japan

CONTENTS

Published on the occasion of an exhibition organized by the Herbert F. Johnson Museum of Art, Cornell University, for presentation at

Renwick Gallery of the National Museum of American Art, Smithsonian Institution, Washington, D.C.
April 26, 1986–September 1, 1986

Herbert F. Johnson Museum of Art, Cornell University, Ithaca, New York
September 26, 1986–November 9, 1986

Milwaukee Art Museum, Milwaukee, Wisconsin
December 5, 1986–January 25, 1987

Grand Rapids Art Museum, Grand Rapids, Michigan
February 28, 1987–April 26, 1987

Cooper-Hewitt Museum, the Smithsonian Institution's National Museum of Design, New York
May 11, 1987–July 19, 1987

Farish Gallery, Rice University, Houston, Texas
August 15, 1987–October 11, 1987

Bell Gallery, List Art Center, Brown University, Providence, Rhode Island
November 21, 1987–December 18, 1987

Los Angeles Municipal Art Gallery
January 30, 1988–March 24, 1988

The Walker Art Center, Minneapolis, Minnesota
April 23, 1988–June 19, 1988

The High Museum, Atlanta, Georgia
July 16, 1988–September 11, 1988

Chicago Historical Society, Chicago, Illinois
October 8, 1988–December 31, 1988

PREFACE AND ACKNOWLEDGMENTS

I was first struck by the inner logic of Frank Lloyd Wright's Johnson Wax buildings, and their utterly original solutions to the design of the workplace, when I designed an addition to them as an architectural thesis at Cornell University. Adequate floor plans of the buildings had never been published, and on examining the complete drawings that the company sent me, my thesis adviser, Lee Hodgden, suggested the possibility of mounting a museum exhibition based on the material. Conducting subsequent research in the Johnson company and Frank Lloyd Wright Foundation archives, I discovered a fascinating story in the interchange between the parties as Wright persuaded his clients to build a radical, inspiring workplace. The interaction between Wright and Herbert Johnson emerges as one of the illuminating chapters in modern architectural history.

The Johnson Wax Administration Building and Research Tower complex is a *gesamtkunstwerk*, a total work of art. Although built ten years apart, the two buildings are conceptually and formally unified. Wright orchestrated every element in them; virtually all of the components—the delicate mushroom columns, wall system, glazing, detailing, and furniture—were newly invented. Sunlight is so transformed by the skylights and by its interaction with the curving shapes of the building that it also seems to be a newly created element.

Over the past decade Bruce Pfeiffer, Director of Archives of the Frank Lloyd Wright Foundation, has completed the enormous task of cataloging and photographing the 21,000 drawings at Taliesin. Consequently, it has been possible to thoroughly examine Wright's conceptual and developmental sketches of the Johnson buildings for the first time and to discuss photographs of the drawings with the former Wright apprentices who actually drew many of them. The eloquent correspondence between Frank Lloyd Wright, Herbert Johnson, and others further documents Wright's architectural decisions. In interviews retired Johnson company executives and former apprentices recalled many of the conversations Wright, Johnson, and others had as they debated the emerging form of the radical buildings.

This book was written while I was Guest Curator for the exhibition "Frank Lloyd Wright and the Johnson Wax Buildings: Creating a Corporate Cathedral," organized and circulated by the Herbert F. Johnson Museum of Art, Cornell University. My work was aided by receiving an appointment as Visiting Scholar in the Department of Architecture, College of Architecture, Art and Planning, Cornell University. I wish to thank both the college and museum director Thomas Leavitt for supporting the project. I also wish to acknowledge the receipt of an Eidlitz Fellowship from the College of Architecture, Art and Planning, Cornell University.

The project would not have been possible without the generous assistance and cooperation of Bruce Pfeiffer, to whom I extend my appreciation. For sharing their recollections, I wish to thank the late Olgivanna Lloyd Wright and Frank Lloyd Wright's former apprentices John Howe, William Wesley Peters, Robert Mosher, John Lautner, and especially Edgar Tafel.

Also for their recollections, I would like to thank current or retired Johnson company employees E. O. Jones, John Halama, Elsie Dostal, Robert Gardiner, Julia Jari, Elmyra Steinle, Charles Folwell, Edward Wilder, Richard Simon, Karl Moore, Eugene Kitzke, Winnie Manchester, Ed Sandle, Serge Logan, Richard Spinks, and the late J. Vernon Steinle and Raymond Carlson; members of the Johnson family Samuel C. Johnson, Henrietta Louis, and Karen Boyd; and David Hunting, Elmer F. Nelson, Jr., and Jacob Stocker for recollections of construction of the building.

I wish to acknowledge John H. Mitchell and Diane Heimer for critical early assistance in the project; Charles Montooth, Indira Berndtson, and Greg Williams for courteous assistance at Taliesin; Michael Dennis, Archie MacKenzie, Jerry Wells, the late Jason Seeley, Alexander Kira, Carolee Walker, Linda Johnson, and Carol Fields for assistance at Cornell University; National Air Survey Corporation, Fuhrman Photographic Laboratory, and Image Connection for excellent photographic printing; the archives of the Frank Lloyd Wright Foundation, S. C. Johnson and Son, the *Racine Journal-Times*, the *Milwaukee Journal*, Northwestern University, the Art Institute of Chicago, *Life* magazine, the Smithsonian Institution, the American Institute of Architects, and Corning Glass; and Gary Paul, Roger Sliker, David Phillips, Ken Vineberg, and Judy Cohen for their help. For bringing historical information to my attention, I thank Robert Sweeney, Jack Quinan, Wilbert Hasbrouck, Mark Heyman, and Richard Kinch.

For drafting new drawings for the book, I am indebted to Gerald Wilson, Francois de Menil, and Don Coles.

For the original suggestion to assemble an exhibit on the Johnson Wax buildings I wish to acknowledge Lee Hodgden.

For critical insights or criticism of the manuscript, I thank Kenneth Frampton, Edgar Kaufmann, Jr., Arthur Drexler, Neil Levine, Charles Pearman, Anne Rieselbach, Brian Stains, and Joel Lipman; and especially Diana Davies and Rizzoli editor Stephanie Salomon who enormously improved the book with their intelligent editing.

While gratefully acknowledging the above assistance I wish to claim sole responsibility for any errors.

INTRODUCTION

THE JOHNSON WAX BUILDINGS AND THE ANGEL OF HISTORY

And the texture of the tissue of this great thing, this Forerunner of Democracy, the Machine, has been deposited particle by particle, in blind obedience to organic law, the law to which the great solar universe is but an obedient machine.

This is the thing into which the forces of Art are to breathe the thrill of ideality! A SOUL!"

FRANK LLOYD WRIGHT
"The Art and Craft of the Machine," an address to Hull House, Chicago, March 6, 1901

It is one of the most intriguing and significant aspects of Wright's long career that almost all of his public buildings were introspective and virtually windowless while his private works were extroverted and integrated with the landscape. Where the one, the urban monument, was predicated on an internal semipublic realm, illuminated from above, the other, the private house invariably extended its enclosure, through continuous fenestrations, outriding terraces, and overhanging eaves, into the surrounding beneficence of nature. Where the urban environment was regarded as a fallen world, as an alienating occidental "nowhere" beyond redemption, the American landscape was seen as an Edenic promise, as an oriental paradise garden that was still imbued with the unspoilt ethos of aboriginal man. It was as though Wright, Romantic Emersonian to the last, could never bring himself to accept the often provisional and ugly reality of the late-nineteenth-century American city, the open-ended grid of which was usually too speculative in nature to provide any convincing sense of civic continuity. In a word, the American *civitas* was too insubstantial and physically ill-defined to engage even Wright's capacity for suspended disbelief. This being so, he invariably turned his back on it, preferring to encase his conception of the living spirit of democracy within four solid walls. It was as though the redeeming soul or *mécanique céleste,* naively alluded to at the end of his seminal address of 1901, could only survive if it were cultivated through a secret semisecular rite within a concealed space of appearance set in opposition to the newly and loosely urbanized vastness of the continent.

Like the Larkin Building in Buffalo of 1904, like the Unity Temple and Midway Gardens built in Chicago in 1906 and 1914, like the Imperial Hotel in Tokyo of 1922, like the Morris China Gift Shop of 1949 and the Guggenheim Museum of 1956, Wright's Administration Building for S. C. Johnson & Son, completed in Racine in 1939, was no exception to this rule. It was, in fact, a totally hermetic citadel; a compensatory semipublic realm within which the new industrial democracy could be brought to realize its essentially secular Protestant ethos through the daily sacrament of work.

Not surprisingly, a similar intent informs the monumental fountains and stone panels that flank the entries of the Larkin Building. These last, embellished with angels and inscribed with the aphorism, "Honest labor needs no master, simple justice needs no slaves," anticipate to the letter the ideological impulse behind the creation of the Johnson Wax buildings. Indeed, exactly the same mixture of Puritan idealism, social conscience, and moral sentimentality no doubt caused the second heir to the firm, Herbert (Hibbert) Johnson, to settle finally on Frank Lloyd Wright as his duly appointed architect. Jonathan Lipman shows us how Jack Ramsey and William Connolly, Johnson's trusted managerial and advertising executives, persuaded their patron, at the eleventh hour, to hire Wright for the job. All of this tends to suggest in retrospect how each man's individual ideology tended to converge about a single issue, for in one way or another they were all committed to the liberative potential of the machine. Like the Saint Simonians before them, they believed, in their different ways, that the machine could be brought to redeem the soul of industrialized society, and that Taylorized production, reduced working hours, increased welfare and benefits (S. C. Johnson & Son was an early American firm to introduce profit-sharing), together with improved environmental conditions, could be subtly combined so as to overcome the contradictions of capitalism and inaugurate a new golden age. Whether they chose to express this in terms of ergonomic management or through the mysticized machine-age aesthetics, the sociocultural goals were essentially the same. This perhaps explains why Johnson never disowned Wright despite all the anxiety and expense that he suffered at his hands. In fact the only juncture at which Wright and his clients came close to parting was, as Lipman reveals, in the dispute over where the building should be erected, with the corporation insisting, with sufficient reason, that the building should be built on its existing downtown site and Wright constantly trying to persuade them to move the entire plant into the backwoods, where, appropriately accompanied by workers' dwellings, the Usonian vision could have been more fully realized. As his ever-present guardian-wife, Olgivanna, was prescient enough to remark at the time, continuing with this advocacy beyond the briefing stage would have cost him the commission.

It may be argued that Wright's Administration Building for Johnson Wax is not only the greatest piece of twentieth-century architecture realized in the United States to date but also, possibly, the most profound work of art that America has ever produced. The grounds for such an assertion lie primarily in the fact that in this singular masterwork the sixty-seven-year-old Wright was to push himself to the very limits of his architectonic creativity, thereby producing a building that was not only suavely composed and brilliantly organized, but also one that employed a totally unprecedented structural device. It was a concept, in fact, that introduced an entirely new tectonic and spatial discourse into twentieth-century architecture; a work that, more than any other single influence, was to be the prime inspiration behind the career of Louis Kahn. Wright's architectonic invention of a top-lit hypostyle hall, made up of sixty reinforced-concrete, hollow, tapering, "lily-pad" mushroom columns, projects the Johnson Wax buildings into another historical class, comparable one might say, to Brunelleschi's building of the dome over Santa Maria dei Fiore in Florence in 1434 or, at the very least, to Henri Labrouste's building of a lightweight cast- and wrought-iron infrastructure over the reading room of the Bibliothèque Nationale in Paris between 1854 and 1875. It is significant in this last regard that where Labrouste was to conceive of his reading room as an open-air court, covered by a canvas *velarium*, Wright compared the experience of his Great Workroom to that of being ". . . among the pine trees, breathing fresh air and sunlight." Here, in this surprising metaphor, the underlying complexity of the concept becomes crystal clear. It is at one and the same time both *res publica* and unspoilt nature, both corporate cathedral and the original domain of God. It is instructive to have to acknowledge how this complex fusion of two essentially antithetical ideas is at the same time part of that still unfinished dematerializing trajectory of the modern world that Le Corbusier once characterized as the victory of light over gravity.

We tend to forget, largely because of his perennial Romanticism, that Wright, throughout his life, had a remarkably creative engineering capacity at his disposal. This was in large measure due to the fact that he constantly sought out engineers of exceptional ability, from Paul Mueller who devised and calculated the antiseismic raft foundations of the Imperial Hotel to William Wesley Peters who, before he came to Wright, had been thoroughly trained as an engineer. And, indeed, as Lipman shows us, it was Peters, in conjunction with the brilliant Mendel Glickman, who profiled and finally calculated the structural integrity and bearing capacity of these unorthodox lily-pad columns.

To all intents and purposes this was a stressed-skin, reinforced-concrete structure, since the columns were reinforced with steel mesh rather than rods, a key innovation when it came to reducing the wall thickness of their hollow stems to three and a half inches. The introduction of other unprecedented methods followed naturally from this use of mesh, above all the pumping of concrete into the formwork and the mechanical vibration of the mix. All of these are common techniques today but were certainly unusual fifty years ago. Each of the primary columns rose twenty-one feet in the air to support a circular, cantilevering concrete pad (or flat mushroom) some twenty feet in diameter. Thereafter the column tapered downward, in a reverse entasis of two and a half degrees to culminate in a nine-inch diameter, "hinged" metal point support. In addition, since the tangent points of all the circular pads were interconnected, the entire system was virtually a rigid frame. Wright's use of high-strength concrete, sustaining up to 7,000 psi, enabled him and his builder Ben Wiltscheck to fabricate and test a column that, in the event, was demonstrably capable of carrying 48 tons over the required 12-ton-loading capacity stipulated by the Wisconsin Industrial Commission.

Wright was to match this anticlassical Egyptoid forest of columns with an equally anticlassical approach to the fenestration and general modeling of the building—far more anticlassical, one might add, than the syntax adopted in the case of the Larkin Building. This inversion is surely never more pronounced than in the case of the clerestory that runs as a continuous antiparapet around the perimeter of the building and that, while occupying the place of the cornice, totally denies its traditional role from the point of view of profile and mass. In the first instance it recedes upward toward the inner body of the building instead of projecting outward; in the second it is translucent and ephemeral, aside from its capacity to glow mysteriously at night when illuminated from within. It is, in the last analysis, a conscious dematerialization of the elaborate concrete textile block, which constituted the deep Pre-Columbian cornice applied to the brick A. D. German warehouse that Wright built at Richland Center, Wisconsin, in 1915. As Wright was to put it later: "Glass tubing laid up like bricks in a wall composes all the lighting surfaces. Light enters the building where the cornice used to be. In the interior the box-like structure vanishes completely."

The A. D. German cornice, translated into glass and reduced in depth, was surely the model for the ingenious, interlocking glass-block clerestory initially designed for the Johnson Wax Administration Building in collaboration with Libbey-Owens-Ford. The textile block, dating in Wright's work from the Avery Coonley House of 1908, is here replaced by a similar crystalline element that is now projected to occlude the gap between the recessed concrete roof slab and the brick perimeter walls. Its canted and crystallized profile, would have been comprised of two hollow glass-block membranes separated by an insulating void and stiffened by a cranked iron rod armature, linked by wire ties to each of the lap joints between the blocks. The reason for abandoning this technically watertight clerestory system in favor of stacked lengths of butt-jointed Pyrex glass tubes still remains somewhat unclear; although aesthetic considerations (above all the impossibility of rounding off corners with glass construction) seem to have dominated Wright's final decision to risk the installation of a more vulnerable and totally unproven clerestory of caulked glass tubing. It is ironic that this tubing should be the crowning glory of the Administration Building (the building is unthinkable without it), since it was the one element that was to be the source of innumerable failures, above all, the spot leaking due to the repeated expansion and contraction of the tubes and the accompanying rupture of the caulking, as well as a certain amount of unexpected incidental glare that led to the hanging of Aeroshades along the inside perimeter. It worked sufficiently well, however, for the tube fenestration to be retained for the first twenty years of the building's life, with Wright and the company never abandoning their search for an ideal caulking compound, which finally arrived with the development of flexible silicone. The tubes themselves failed here and there over time, especially in the flat skylight of the hypostyle hall, and were replaced by sections of ribbed translucent plastic sheet, which simulated the bonding pattern of the original tubes. This, plus the demand to introduce artificial illumination between the two layers of the top-lighting, has long since transformed the original subaqueous quality of the light remarked on by Henry-Russell Hitchcock. Nevertheless it is to the company's great credit that they continued to persevere with the tubing, proving once again that outstanding architecture demands exceptional clients as well as gifted architects. In fact, glass tubing was still to be used as the first layer of fenestration when Wright added the fifteen-story laboratory tower in the late 1940s.

It is remarkable that the sixty-seven-year-old Wright could modify his Shangri-la vision to bring it into accord with the emerging modern discourse of the 1930s. As he was to put it, with characteristic irony, it was "high time to give the hungry American public something truly streamlined," and in this regard it is possible to see the Johnson Wax buildings as the *Twentieth Century Limited* translated into bricks and mortar. At the same time Wright kept that feeling for a glistening, seamless continuity, which first appears in his Doheny Ranch project of 1923 and which emerges as a crystalline ambiguity in the National Life Insurance Building projected for Chicago in 1924; ambiguous in the sense that one can longer clearly differentiate between glass fenestration and copper sheathing. A similar ambiguity is surely intended when Wright first envisages using green brick for Johnson Wax in an obvious effort to fuse the masonry with the color of the glass. A comparable motive appears in the furnishing of the interior, where the tubular stretchers of the purpose-made desks are not only painted Cherokee red, to match the brickwork, but are also spaced so as to accord with the rhythm of the coursing.

The idea of covering a building in a continuous fabric has its origins in the work of Louis Sullivan, in structures such as the Guaranty Building, Buffalo, of 1895, where the terra-cotta revetment assumes the form of a tattoo covering the entire surface. This almost Islamic sense of continuity anticipates Wright's concrete (textile) block houses of the late 1920s. It is equally close to Louis Kahn's vision of the mid-1950s wherein he imagines a building, "flowing endlessly, seamless white and gold," and the same impulse is surely present in the crystalline high-rise city hall for Philadelphia, which Kahn designed with Ann Tyng between 1952 and 1957.

The Johnson Wax Administration Building is the apotheosis of Wright's lifelong desire to transform the workplace into a sacramental structure. This much is patently evident from his rendering of the office cafeteria as a theatrical space and from his efforts, as in the Larkin Building, to incorporate a pipe organ within the mezzanine overlooking the workroom. While Johnson totally rejected the organ, Wright still conceived of his hypostyle hall as "an interpretation of modern business . . . as inspiring to live and work in as any cathedral ever was to worship in."

Despite this Nietzschean promise of redemption—reminiscent of the Bauhaus *Zukunftskathedrale*—the Administration Building remains a characteristically modern work, above all in its postulation of an introspective world. Like Pierre Chareau's Maison de Verre of 1932, it resembles the closed room in J. K. Huysmans's novel *A Rebours*; a strange twilight compound removed from the ruined world of uprooted men and divided labor; a translucent limpid light momentarily separated from the storm of progress and the angel of history.

KENNETH FRAMPTON
January 1986

FRANK LLOYD WRIGHT AND THE JOHNSON WAX BUILDINGS

CHAPTER 1

INCEPTION OF THE ADMINISTRATION BUILDING

Let's not try to build only a bigger business—let's not let mere size be the goal of our ambitions—let's build a finer, more perfect corporation, so as to make our chosen life's work fine, and more enjoyable.

HERBERT FISKE JOHNSON

Fig. 1. Herbert F. Johnson (1899–1978), circa 1936. (Courtesy of Johnson Wax)

By the spring of 1936 S. C. Johnson & Son, a highly successful wax and paint manufacturer in Racine, Wisconsin, had outgrown its office facilities. A number of the firm's executives were working in a wood-framed house next to the company's warehouses and factory buildings, while other officers and clerical employees worked in two additions to the house and an adjacent larger office building. Herbert F. (Hibbert) Johnson, the company's president and grandson of its founder, recalled, "At first we had no thought of building an office nor of commissioning [Frank Lloyd] Wright to do the work."[1] Rather, Johnson planned to have the office remodeled, and expanded at another time. He and his employees calculated the amount of space needed and contemplated adding to one end of the main office building, extending a wing, or adding another story. Finally, they decided instead to build one new office structure to house the scattered clerical workers and executives. The firm was prospering, and Johnson felt that he ought to do something to improve his employees' working conditions.

Herbert Johnson's daughter Karen Boyd recalls that her father wanted a beautiful, pure, and completely American image for his company. Above all, he wanted it to be a place where his employees would be happy to work. "That was something that he told me his own father had spoken about—to be sure that the people who worked for him felt a part of everything that the company was trying to do."[2] The younger Johnson was also artistic—he enjoyed drawing and he had the desire, in his words, "to eliminate the drabness and dullness we so often find in office buildings." Seeking ideas for the new facilities, he visited other companies.

Johnson was especially attracted to the Hershey Chocolate Corporation's buildings, in Pennsylvania. Like the Johnson company, the Hershey organization was privately held, and the founder, M. S. Hershey, took a broad interest in the welfare of his employees. He had built a planned, picturesque town for his workers and in 1935 erected a windowless limestone office building that featured indirect lighting and air-conditioning. Air-conditioning was uncommon in the early 1930s and the modern amenity intrigued Johnson, since whenever a temperature of 90 degrees was reached in his factory buildings he ordered the company closed for the day.

On his return from Hershey, Johnson commissioned J. Mandor Matson, a prominent local architect, to design an office building that was air-conditioned, artistic, and uplifting.[3] As no large vacant parcel of land remained on Johnson's sprawling two-block complex, the company bought up half a block of houses across the street to the east and began clearing the site. Matson proposed a three-story brick Beaux-Arts building. Air-conditioned and windowless, it was to be lit by skylights. The building filled the entire site and, in the Beaux-Arts style, was entered through the center of the main street facade. In response to Johnson's request for topical art, Matson proposed three niches on either side of the entrance that were to hold bas-reliefs representing the history of wax and wax products, including a boy waxing a table and a woman waxing a floor.

Fig. 2. Aerial view of S. C. Johnson & Son Company headquarters and factory, Racine, Wisconsin, 1929. View from southeast, with old administration building in center foreground. Site of Frank Lloyd Wright's future Administration Building is to the right of vacant lot in lower right. (Courtesy of Johnson Wax)

Fig. 3. Old administration building in 1939. (Courtesy of Johnson Wax)

Neither Johnson nor his general manager, Jack Ramsey, were satisfied with the building design. Ramsey told Johnson, "It isn't good enough, it's just another building."[4] Since neither Ramsey nor William Connolly, the company's advertising manager, could suggest how to improve the design, Johnson suggested that they widen the search for an architect. Johnson's brother-in-law, Jack Louis, was a partner in Needham, Louis & Brorby—a Chicago public relations firm that the company used. They showed Matson's drawings to Melvin Brorby and Brorby's art director, E. Willis Jones. Connolly reported the results of the meeting to Ramsey, whose notes have been preserved:

> Jones and Brorby reacted to the sketches as we have—just "common", uninspired, etc. Mel said he knew just exactly the man they ought to talk to and knew him well enough to lay the problem before him frankly without any obligation. It was a Mr. Raftery, very fine architect, winner of a lot of contests on just this type of modern design, highest standing, etc., etc.
>
> Bill and Mel went to see him. Reaction to present sketches polite but just like everyone else's reaction. Said he himself would like a crack at the problem but if he understood the Johnson Company and its desires and ideals there was only one thing in the world to do. We have right here under our noses a native Wisconsonian who was the absolute father of all modern architecture, who is the outstanding architect of the world today (not excepting Paul Cret or anyone else), and it would be a crime not to talk to him—Frank Lloyd Wright.[5]

Earlier that summer, a friend of Wright's, William Kittredge of the Lakeside Press in Chicago, had suggested that his fellow members of the Chicago Art Directors' Club spend a weekend at Taliesin, Frank Lloyd Wright's home in Spring Green, Wisconsin, and in late June the members of the club gathered there for a conference. It was a social occasion. Former Wright apprentice John Howe recalls that the directors gathered in the Hillside garden dining room with Wright while the apprentices served their meals. In the course of the gathering, E. Willis Jones, who was a member of the club, mentioned to Wright that the Johnson company was planning

Fig. 4. Frank Lloyd Wright and apprentices. Rear row: John Lautner, second from left; John Howe, third from left; Edgar Tafel, first from right. Front row: Robert Mosher, first from right, William Wesley Peters, second from right. Each of these apprentices had a large role in the Johnson commissions. (Photo © Bill Hedrich/Hedrich-Blessing)

to build a new office building, and Wright showed an interest in the project.[6] The Johnson company was known in Wisconsin for its enlightened treatment of employees. Such a commission might give Wright an ideal chance to design a project expressing his recent theories.

During the first decade of the twentieth century Wright had developed a philosophical foundation for his work. His vision of man's place in nature shaped his highly influential Prairie style, which established him as a world-famous architect.

After leaving Chicago in 1909, the number of commissions he received declined. The Depression robbed him of his remaining work, and between the years 1928 and 1936 Frank Lloyd Wright built just two buildings for clients. As he had few buildings through which to express his philosophy of architecture, Wright devoted much of his time to writing, giving lectures, and preparing museum exhibits of his projects. In debt and without commissions, Wright and his wife, Olgivanna, founded the Taliesin Fellowship in 1932, opening their home and studio to apprentices, who would divide their time between farming Taliesin's fields, restoring the dilapidated buildings, and learning architecture by working under Wright's eye in the drafting room.

Wright mailed a circular to friends and newspapers, and in August 1932, nineteen-year-old John H. (Jack) Howe arrived as one of the first apprentices. While still in high school in Evanston, Illinois, Howe had visited Wright in his Chicago office. Howe spent over three decades as Wright's chief draftsman. In the autumn of that year the early apprentices repaired and enlarged buildings for the expected additional recruits. By Christmas the Taliesin Fellowship numbered twenty-three, among them Robert Mosher, William Wesley (Wes) Peters, and Edgar Tafel.

Wright and his apprentices farmed the fields below Taliesin and achieved a degree of self-sufficiency. Contemplating the urban unemployment of the Depression, Wright had recently proposed a social reordering of the nation which would bring dignity to the American worker. The program involved allotting one acre of land to each adult and child in the United States, hence its name, Broadacre City. Far more than simply a proposal for the redistribution of land, it outlined major changes in urban design, political institutions, economics, transportation, and buildings.

In the spirit of Henry Ford's corporate experiments on the Rouge River, Broadacre City was predicated on the notion that every family would have at least one car, and land would be distributed so that each family could raise a substantial portion of its food. All building designs, monitored by the watchful eye of county architects, would harmonize with the larger city, schools would be decentralized, and utilities concentrated in the hands of state and county governments. Monorails would crisscross the nation, providing high-speed long-distance travel, and highways would be built throughout the country for short- and medium-distance travel.

In 1886, the same year that nineteen-year-old Frank Lloyd Wright left the University of Wisconsin to begin his career in Chicago, another Wisconsin resident, fifty-three-year-old Samuel Curtis Johnson, embarked on a new career. Earlier, Johnson had closed an unsuccessful stationery store in Kenosha, Wisconsin, and moved to nearby Racine to sell parquet flooring for the Racine Hardware Manufacturing Company.

Parquetry—composed of patterns of small, geometrically shaped pieces of multihued wood—was a popular choice for floors in Victorian America. Johnson was a successful salesman and in 1886 he purchased the flooring business from his employer. His factory staff initially numbered four, with Johnson himself doing the selling and bookkeeping as well as managing the business. In its first year, the S. C. Johnson Company made a profit of $268, on gross sales of $3,148.

Johnson believed strongly in product promotion, and in 1888, he began placing advertisements for his flooring in national magazines. His strategy was successful, and the business grew. Within a few years, the Johnson company was selling parquetry to customers as far away as New England and Colorado.

Customers who were accustomed to wide pine-board floors found that their former practice of scrubbing the floors with lye, strong soap, and hot water loosened and warped the small wood blocks. Some asked Johnson how to preserve their new floors. Seeing an opportunity to expand his business and offer an additional service to his customers, Johnson resolved to solve the problem. He knew that parquet floors in Europe survived for hundreds of years and that it was the custom in Europe to protect floors with wax. He investigated waxes and experimented with one produced by the leaves of the Brazilian Carnauba palm tree, learning how to process the substance into a paste wax. He began to ship cans of Johnson's Prepared Paste Wax along with each new floor he sold. Promoting the product in national advertisements, Johnson oversaw the birth of a new industry. By 1898 the company's income from the sale of wax, wood fillers, and finishes exceeded its income from flooring, and at the turn of the century "Johnson's Wax" was becoming a household word throughout the United States.

The beginning of the twentieth century also witnessed a change in architectural taste. In Chicago, thirty-three-year-old Frank Lloyd Wright and several other architects from the Midwest came to be known collectively as the Prairie School. This group favored an architecture that stressed horizontality in houses—the line of the prairie—and evolved a style in which rooms opened onto each other and extended the spatial enclosure into the site. Emphasizing space as the reality of a building, Wright and his contemporaries urged an end to the cluttered rooms and agitated surfaces of Victorian architecture. Nationwide shifts in taste, encouraged in part by Wright and the Prairie School, caused the market for the Johnson company's intricate flooring to fall sharply, until in 1917 Johnson and his son discontinued the sale of parquetry entirely.

Aggressive innovation continued to characterize the company under Johnson's son Herbert Fiske Johnson, who joined the firm in 1888. Although Samuel Johnson believed in promotion, he was a conservative man, and his foremost concern was to maintain the high quality of his products. Herbert was an effective salesman and original marketer, and it may well have been he who initiated national advertising for the company. In 1906 Samuel made his son a full partner in the firm, and changed its name to S. C. Johnson & Son. The two men diversified the business into related areas, such as brushes, varnishes, wood dyes, and enamels and began exporting products, establishing a British subsidiary in 1914, followed by plants in Canada and Australia.

The elder Johnson was remembered as strongly religious, with a sense of civic responsibility, contributing one-tenth of his income to religious organizations and serving as president of the Racine YMCA. His son also was generous and looked for ways to improve the working conditions of his employees, who worked the fifty- to sixty-hour week common at the turn of the century. He introduced paid vacations, and in 1917, after installing time-saving assembly lines, asked his factory supervisor whether his workers could do in nine hours the work they were doing in ten. Assured that they could, the company initiated a nine-hour workday with no reduction in wages. Within three months, hours were further reduced to eight, again with no change in pay.

That same year, with the business prospering, Herbert Johnson decided to share the company's prosperity with the workers. Shortly before Christmas he distributed $31,000 of the company's profits among all the employees, making S. C. Johnson one of the first companies in the nation to institute profit sharing. It has continued its annual Christmas custom ever since.

Samuel Johnson died in 1919, three years after he had given his sixteen-year-old grandson, Hibbert, his first summer job with the company. Hibbert Johnson studied chemistry at Cornell University and joined the company full time after graduating in 1922.

In the 1920s, seeing a large potential market open up as the American public began to view the automobile as a necessity, S. C. Johnson & Son introduced a line of automobile care products, and the chemists in its fledgling research and development department created lacquers, paints, and liquid wax. As the company entered into the new markets and expanded sales nationally and internationally, it required more facilities. Located at the junction of an industrial and a residential section of town, the company was forced to purchase additional residential lots to its east since a major thoroughfare to the west blocked further expansion into the industrial zone. It built new warehouses and factory buildings every few years, as well as an office building for clerical workers. Over time the company remodeled newly acquired houses to serve as additional offices.

As it expanded, the company continued to install the latest assembly-line technology in its industrial buildings. In 1925 a magazine article noted that "although the company is doing 100 percent more business than it did a few years ago, the work is being done with fewer employees, and the explanation is evident to the visitor who goes through the factory. Everything is done with machinery that can be done, for it is the pride of the Johnson Company that it is up to date in every respect." The article also observed that the company's Racine floor finish plant was the largest in the world.[7]

Herbert Johnson, Sr., died in 1928, and at the age of twenty-eight, young Hibbert, who had changed his name to Herbert, became president of the company. He echoed his father's attitude toward employees, later saying, "My father had the idea of bringing the employer and worker together. Call it enlightened selfishness if you like, for when people get proper wages and proper working conditions they don't feel the need to organize to fight for what they want."[8]

The following year, the United States entered the Great Depression. During this time business declined drastically for the company. In response the younger Herbert Johnson made two important and unusual decisions: unlike most employers he decided not to lay off any employees and, to keep them working, he encouraged the company to look for opportunities to expand without waiting for the Depression to end.

During the first three years of Herbert Johnson's presidency, the company's annual sales dropped from $5 million to $3 million. With no earnings, the company skipped its annual profit sharing in 1931 and 1932. Johnson cut workers' hours and created make-work projects for some of them, avoiding what must have appeared to be inevitable layoffs. In the spring of 1932, when Depression sales were at their lowest, the firm took a gamble. A competitor had just introduced a self-polishing floor wax. The Johnson company's research chemists were able to improve on it, and the company named its new product "Glo-Coat." Immediately, the company planned a major national advertising campaign, and without waiting for orders, shipped a carton to each of its 90,000 dealers. Two months from the day the company decided to produce the product, a half million pints of Glo-Coat were in stores across the country. Almost all the dealers decided to keep the product, the company marketed it vigorously, and Glo-Coat quickly became a nationwide success. Prospering again, the company put its employees back on a forty-hour week and hired more workers. In 1936, in the middle of the Depression, Herbert Johnson hired J. Mandor Matson to design a new administration building for the now overcrowded Racine plant.

Interviewed years later, Needham, Louis & Brorby art director E. Willis Jones recalled William Connolly showing him the drawings of Matson's proposed office building for the Johnson company. Connolly asked him to recommend a sculptor for a frieze at the top of the building, but Jones urged him to reject the entire building design and hire Frank Lloyd Wright to make a fresh start. Connolly was unfamiliar with Wright, so Jones showed him copies of the Wasmuth and Wendigen publications of his work, noting that Connolly was entranced. Jones called in his firm's vice president, Melvin Brorby, and architect Howard Raftery, and the three men convinced Connolly to pursue Wright.[9]

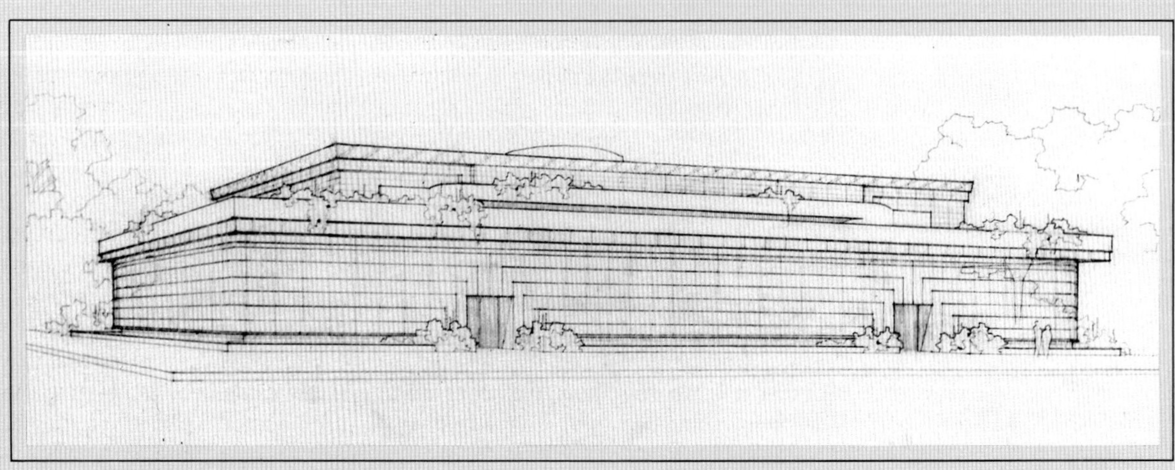

Fig. 5. Perspective. Capital Journal project, Salem, Oregon, 1931. Pencil and color pencil on tracing paper. 31″ × 17″. (Courtesy of the Frank Lloyd Wright Foundation)

CHAPTER 2

AWARDING WRIGHT THE COMMISSION

Ground was to be broken on Matson's new office building in July 1936, but Connolly and Ramsey were willing to speak to Wright. It had been only two weeks since Jones had been to Taliesin and interested Wright in the Johnson company's plans for the new building. Jones telephoned Wright and arranged for Connolly, Ramsey, and himself to drive to Taliesin Friday in mid-July.

In 1936, Wright's practice was just beginning to revive. When Jones's telephone call came, Wright was at work on three residences: the first Usonian project—the Lusk house in Huron, South Dakota; the Hanna house in Palo Alto, California; and Fallingwater—a summer home in Pennsylvania for the parents of recent apprentice Edgar Kaufmann, Jr. Wright recalled, "When the sky at Taliesin was dark, the days there gloomy . . . Hib [Johnson] and Jack [Ramsey] were the ones who came out to Taliesin . . . to see about that new building. They came, you might say, like messengers riding on white steeds trumpeting glad tidings."[1] Edgar Tafel wrote years later, "When we heard that the Johnson people were coming to interview Mr. Wright, we apprentices went to work: windows were washed, the grounds raked, floors cleaned and waxed, the cases were filled with foliage."[2] Connolly and Ramsey drove from Racine, while Jones drove from Chicago and beat them by an hour to brief Wright. When Connolly and Ramsey arrived, Wright showed them the grounds and theater, and lunch and tea were served elegantly as Wright made a proposal. "The pitch that he gave them was masterful and a shocker," Jones recalled later. "In brief, it was not to build on the site adjacent to the ugly old factory, but to raze everything and get out of town four or five miles west, run in a railroad spur, plan a Johnson Village around a new factory and office building, homes for employees, their own shopping center . . . the works."[3] Edgar Tafel remembered, "Mr. Wright was trying to get them to move out in the country where there is room to breathe . . . and have an open building, [but] they wanted it right there."[4]

Wright very possibly showed drawings he had made five years earlier for an urban newspaper plant, the facilities for the *Capital Journal*, in Salem, Oregon.[5] Ideas in the unbuilt project seemed applicable to the Johnson project. The Capital Journal design was composed of a two-story-high room filling half an entire city block. Inside the glass-enclosed room, mezzanine offices overlooked the printing presses on the ground floor. The room was filled with mushroom columns that supported the roof slab, and on the roof was a garden and duplex apartments for employees. Like Le Corbusier's highly publicized Villa Savoye of 1929, the building celebrates movement through space, using the free plan and a prominent ramp. As in Villa Savoye, an enclosed garden is located on the roof, and in both designs the outer curtain wall is lifted off the ground, emphasizing the fact that it is non-loadbearing, while the transparency of the skinlike wall allows the loadbearing columns to be visible from the outside.

The project typified Wright's ability to transform existing architectural concepts and apply them to wholly original purposes. In this case Wright's structural strategy

Fig. 6. First-floor plan. Capital Journal project. Sepia print. 33″ × 34″. (Courtesy of the Frank Lloyd Wright Foundation)

Fig. 7. Roof garden level and mezzanine floor plan. Capital Journal project. Sepia print. 33″ × 34″. (Courtesy of the Frank Lloyd Wright Foundation)

Fig. 8. West elevation, Capital Journal project. Sepia print. 33″ × 34″ (Courtesy of the Frank Lloyd Wright Foundation)

Fig. 9. Section, looking south. Capital Journal project. The lower half of the Capital Journal design was a single, vast space in which printing presses were to be located. Some glazed offices shared the floor, while others were located on a mezzanine that encircled the space. A ceiling slab over the great space was supported by mushroom columns—common factory construction practice at the time, and the exterior walls were glass, set in copper screens hung from above. The translucent walls would have allowed light to flood the space, and, as shown in Wright's elevations, would have made the columns visible from the street. Two circular stair towers were located near the front of the building and a circular service ramp in the rear enclosed a smokestack. Above were located two-story apartments, surrounding a garden court for the owner and employees of the firm. Sepia print. 33″ × 34″. (Courtesy of the Frank Lloyd Wright Foundation)

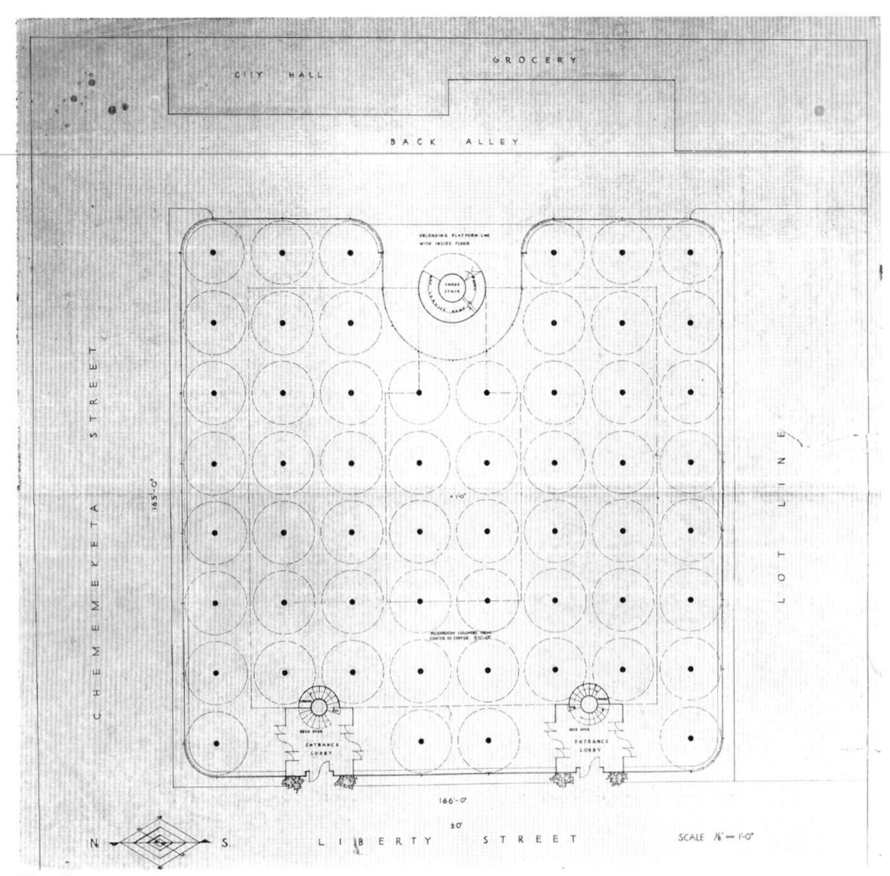

Fig. 6.

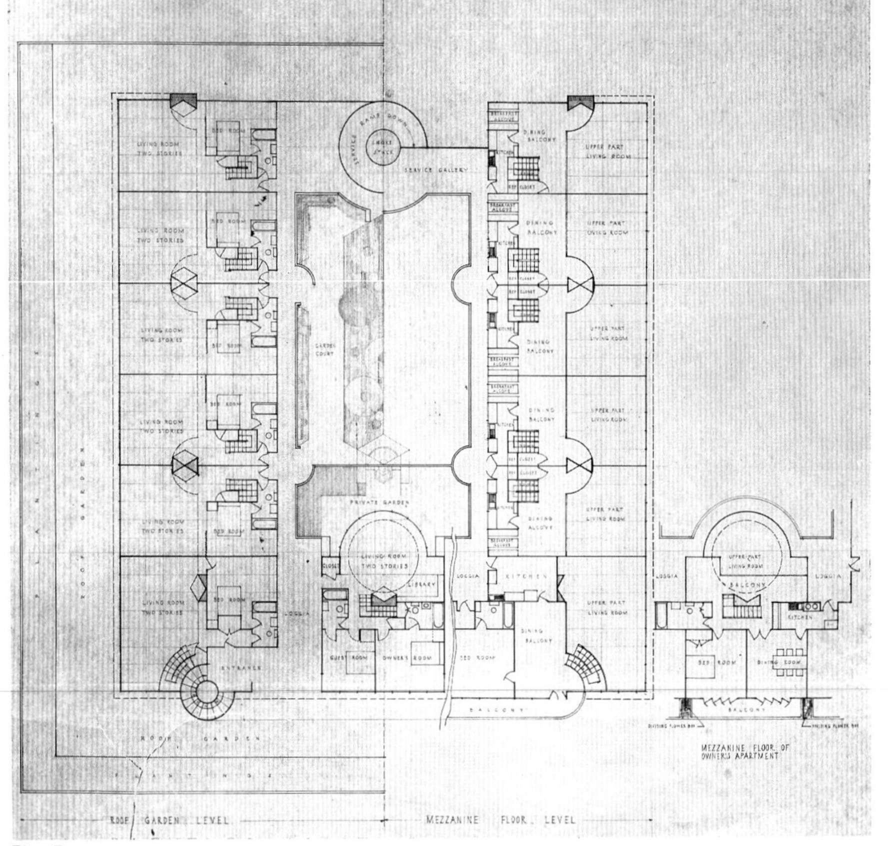

Fig. 7.

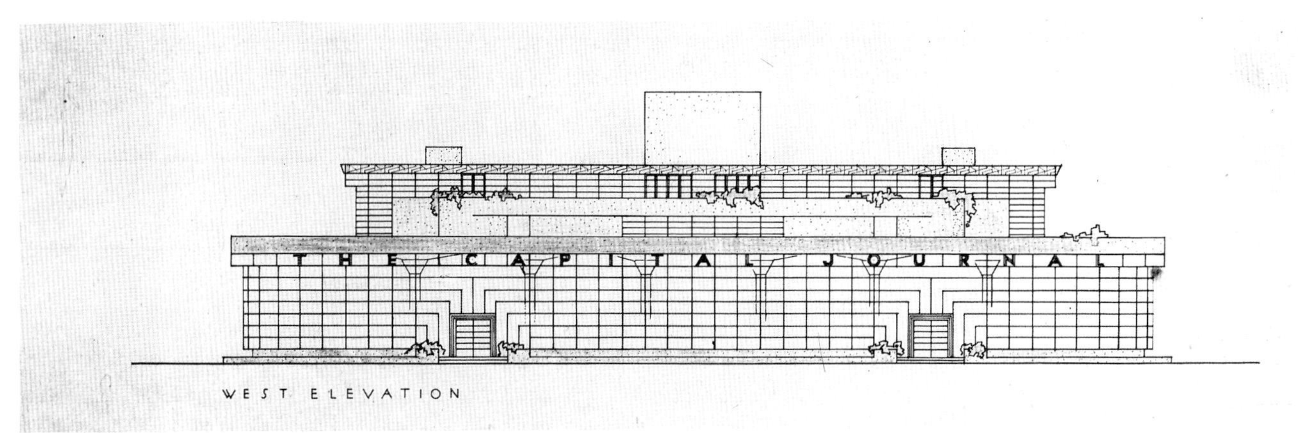
THE CAPITAL JOURNAL
WEST ELEVATION
Fig. 8.

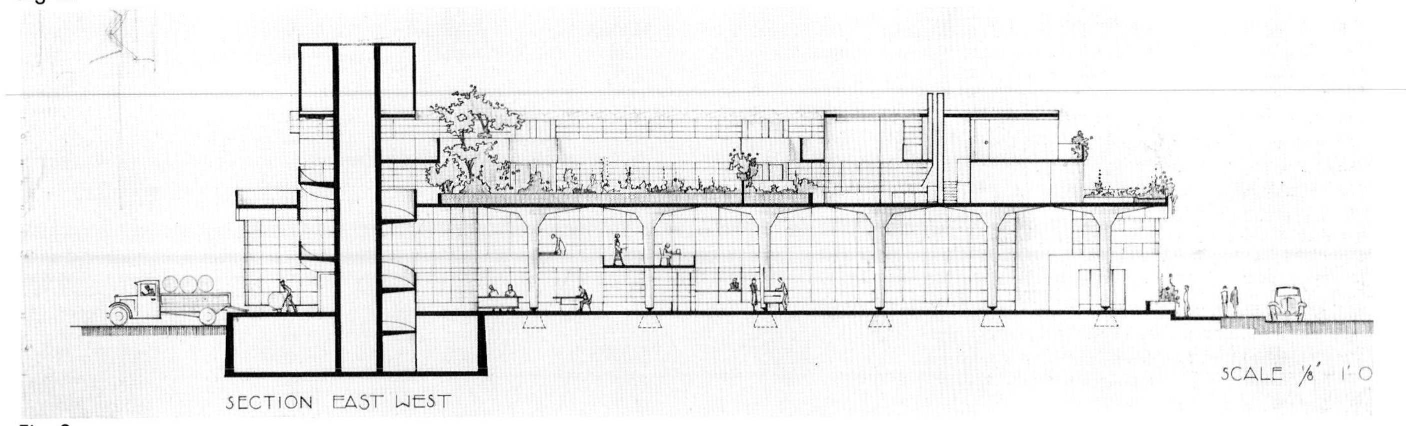
SECTION EAST WEST
SCALE 1/8" 1'-0
Fig. 9.

cleverly solved the program's critical problem: how to isolate the apartments from the noise and vibrations produced by the printing presses. The downward tapering columns sat on tiny metal shoes,—almost points—which in turn rested on footings separate from the floor slab on which the presses sat. The shoes served to prevent the vibrations in the floor from being conducted up the columns; hanging the exterior wall from the isolated ceiling slab was intended to prevent vibrations from being conducted up the wall.[6]

Though Ramsey was considered a practical businessman, he found himself excited by Wright's architectural ideas. He confessed to Wright that he hated buildings with face brick on the front and common brick on the back, as Matson's design called for, that he found the idea crude—he would prefer common brick all the way around the building. Wright's ardent agreement helped convince Ramsey that there would be no aesthetic problems if Wright were hired. By the time they had finished tea with Mr. and Mrs. Wright, Ramsey and Connolly were convinced that Wright should design the new building.

However, Herbert Johnson was a single-minded man, and they were at a loss as to how to suggest to him that the company discard Matson's idea and start over with Wright. Ramsey pondered his next step all day Saturday. Before going to church Sunday morning, he came to the office and set down his thoughts in a hand-written letter to Johnson, who was at his summer cottage in northern Wisconsin:

Regarding the new building, I had a day Friday that so confirmed and crystallized my feeling about Matson's present offering and that at the same time so inspired me as to what can be done that I was on the point of sending you wild telegrams Friday night when I got home, or getting you out of bed on the telephone. . . . Honest Hib I haven't had such an inspiration from a person in years. And I won't feel satisfied about your getting what you want until you talk to him—to say nothing of not feeling justified in letting $300,000 be clothed in Matson's designs.

He's an artist and a little bit "different" of course but aside from his wearing a Windsor tie, he was perfectly human and very easy to talk to and most interested in our problem and understood that we were not committing ourselves, but gosh he could tell us what we were after when we couldn't explain it ourselves.

About Matson's sketch, he was decent but honest. About the strongest remark he made was a bit of gentle sarcasm concerning the niches, something to the effect that they "memorialized the defunct windows," meaning that Matson evidently could not forget that windows had to be in a building whether it were windowless or not.

I believe he got the greatest kick, and understanding of our desires, when I showed him a copy of that note you wrote Matson about what you would like to symbolize on those niches and medallions, telling him it was not definite but would probably give him an idea of the "flavor" of your thought on the building. He wants to talk to "the young man." The young man has some sentiment he wants expressed, but he'll never get it that way by adding isolated details to such a plan, etc. . . .

And he asked about what we thought this building would cost us. I said, when we got through with building, landscape, furnishings, etc. we'd be investing around $300,000. He asked how many people it would house. I said about 200. He snorted and said it was too damn much money for the job and he could do a better functional job in more appropriate manner for a lot less. . . .

. . . He is very easy to talk to, much interested in our job whether he has anything to do with it or not because it hits his ideas of modern building, because it is a Wisconsin native proposition, and because it seems to hurt his artistic conscience to see so much money spent on anything ordinary. . . . Will you see him?[7]

One can only speculate what Herbert Johnson knew about Wright. In 1905 when Johnson was a child, the Hardy house, an important example of modern architecture, was built by Wright several blocks from Johnson's home. Undoubtedly, Johnson was familiar with it as he would have passed it frequently when driving from his home or the company to downtown Racine. It stands in a prominent location at the edge of a park, on a cliff overlooking Lake Michigan. His sister, Henrietta Louis, recalls,

"It's a kooky house—every room is on a different floor. That was crazy in those days. . . . We thought Wright was kooky. Frank never went over in Racine very much." Ironically, she notes that their father laughed at the house.[8]

Wright's successful Prairie period, in which he built the Hardy house and other buildings, largely ended when Johnson was ten years old. In the twenty-five following years, press coverage of Wright tended to focus on his personal life. Johnson was familiar with the stories, and Ramsey felt compelled to warn him. "Don't think of newspaper publicity on his matrimonial troubles and all that right away, as I did. That all means nothing in regard to architecture, of course."[9]

Johnson made an appointment to see Wright the following day. John Howe recalls, "Whenever Mr. Wright talked to his clients or potential clients, he never liked having anyone of us around. It had to be a one-to-one thing. So it would have been there: Mr. Johnson just had lunch with Mr. and Mrs. Wright."[10] Johnson, Wright, and Olgivanna Wright each had dominating personalities. Sparks flew almost as soon as Johnson arrived.[11] Johnson showed Wright Matson's plans, and recalls that Wright insulted him over them:

He insulted me about everything, and I insulted him, but he did a better job. I showed him pictures of the old office, and he said it was awful. I came back from Spring Green and said, "If that guy can talk like that he must have something." Everything at Spring Green was run down. He had a Lincoln-Zephyr, and I had one—that was the only thing we agreed on. On all other matters we were at each other's throats.[12]

Wright described Matson's plan as "a fancy crematorium," telling Johnson that thirty years earlier he had designed a far better office building: a completely original, highly successful administration building for a soap manufacturing firm in Buffalo, New York—the Larkin Company. Olgivanna said that Johnson pleaded, "Please don't make the building too unconventional!" Laughing, Wright said, "[Then] you came to the wrong man. You'd better find yourself another architect. The Johnson administration building is not going to be what you expect. But, I can assure you of one thing—you'll like it when it is put up." Olgivanna recalled sensing a bond forming between the two men as Johnson replied, "It's okay with me then, if you think so. We'll have your kind of building, not the kind of building I had in mind."[13]

It would be difficult to overestimate the significance of the Johnson commission to Wright. During the past six years he had formulated his vision of an ideal America, and now he had an opportunity to build a prototypical piece of it. The Johnson company was nearly an ideal Broadacre City client. The business was largely decentralized, with plants in five countries; its headquarters were not in New York but in a small midwestern city. The company's business principles conformed to Wright's notions: it avoided introducing a product simply to follow a competitor's lead. Rather, it marketed new products when they contained some significant innovation and would benefit their users; and the company conducted its own product research. Most important, the company's owners had an unusual degree of respect for their employees. With a "no layoff" policy, profit sharing, and a forty-hour work week since 1919, it was a model for the humane economy Wright advocated. Herbert Johnson himself was the perfect Wright client. He was imaginative and willing to take risks. He also had a vision of the possibilities that architecture could offer and had faith that Wright could realize them.

Ensuring himself the commission, Wright told Johnson that he could design a building that would cost $200,000—well under the projected cost of Matson's design, but a small fraction of the ultimate cost of the Administration Building. Howe notes, "From the start, the money they were talking about wouldn't have done the most ordinary kind of building. Mr. Wright always started doing what he thought was right for the building. He didn't burden himself with undue considerations of cost."[14]

Two days later Johnson wrote to Matson that the company had decided not to build his scheme, and in a second letter offered Wright the commission:

Although we have invested $4640 in the work of Architect Matson to date, I am today instructing him to discontinue his work and:

I am now asking you to proceed with plans and sketches of a $200,000 office building for us in Racine on the basis of 2½% or $5,000 to be paid you when sketches and plans are submitted. . . .

It is my understanding that the remaining commission of 7½% or $15,000 will not be paid you unless your plans are used wholly and under your supervision. Also, that we are free to use any or all of the ideas you offer—either ourselves, or other architect.

It is also my understanding that you will develop for us your conception and plan of what our plant might be in the future.

. . . I want to take this opportunity of expressing my appreciation, as well as Mr. Ramsey's, for your gracious hospitality, and for the inspiration and education we received.[15]

During this time Wright's office was just off the drafting studio at Taliesin. Howe remembers that as Wright sat in his office opening his mail he would make comments on it to the apprentices. When Johnson's letter arrived, Wright shouted, "It's all right boys, we got the job!" and he displayed the enclosed $1,000 check. Tafel recalled, "What elation we felt . . . our first big, solid commercial project." Wright immediately responded:

My dear Mr. Johnson: You have a way of putting yourself in on the ground floor with your architect. I appreciate your business like way of attaching him to you.

You shall have the best he has.

While I did say you were free to fire him after preliminaries were submitted I did not say you were free to use the plans I would make for you with another architect. But you have taken punishment enough already and inasmuch as I wish only to be of real help to you I will concede that point also.

Of course I want to build your building and intend to do so. I believe you will want no one else to do it when you see how well equipped in engineering and building experience we are—here. And how much money our method will save you. Let that however appear as we proceed.[16]

That evening Johnson picked up his daughter Karen from Kemper Hall, her boarding school in Kenosha to bring her home for the weekend. In a recent interview with the author she recalled, "My father asked me on the way home who I considered to be the leading architect in the world—he knew I'd been studying art history—and I said that I thought Frank Lloyd Wright. He gave me this astonished look and said, 'Well, I think so, too! In fact, I have decided to have him build an office building for the company!' I was so proud of him—and astonished too. We were rather pleased with each other that day."[17]

Early the next week Wright came to Racine driven by Tafel for his first visit to the plant. The two men examined the already cleared site, and Wright was determined to talk the company into moving its facilities into the country. To the west of the site was a two-story bar and grill, destined to serve as construction headquarters when Tafel became the job's supervisor. Beyond the bar and grill were the company's office and factory buildings. To the south, up and down Sixteenth Street, were located a movie theater, small shops, and triplexes. Two-story, undistinguished, circa-1905 wood-frame houses on tiny lots filled the blocks to the north and east. The site itself occupied half a block. More two-story frame houses, situated close together, filled the north half of the block.

Johnson was out of town, and Wright and Tafel met with Ramsey and Connolly. Wright again attempted to convince them that the Johnson company should build its new office building several miles out in the country. Ramsey, however, was adamant about staying in Racine.

Ramsey probably gave Wright the program for the new building at this meeting. The program listed fifteen departments then containing 130 employees, plus department heads. The largest departments were collections, billing, bookkeeping, costs, sales records, files, accounting, and general. The smaller departments were mail room, Addressograph, and branch records, statistical, stock room, Multigraph, and tabulating. The new building was to allow for expansion of 50 percent in most of the departments, for a total of 200 employees. There was also to be a director's conference room, cafeteria, and loading dock. By compiling such a program, Ramsey may have assumed that Wright would design a building with separate offices for each department—certainly the custom at the time, but not one that Wright would follow.

To acquaint him with the particular needs of the company Ramsey and Connolly had Wright consult with each department head. As Wright had proposed to eventually redesign the entire plant, Ramsey also gave him and Tafel a tour through the manufacturing buildings, where they observed wax and paint being made.

As manager of operations, Ramsey would oversee construction of the new building for the company, but Tafel notes that Wright resolved to deal as much as possible with Johnson. Perhaps he felt that the younger man would be more responsive to his ideas, or perhaps, as Tafel believes, he wanted to be in touch with the man who ultimately controlled the firm's finances. Tafel recalls "Mr. Wright romanced Hib; he turned on the charm."[18] Johnson appreciated Wright's attention. Not only was Johnson to become, in Wright's mind, one of his most enlightened clients, but in the coming months Taliesin became Johnson's favorite weekend retreat.

Two days after Wright's visit Johnson returned to Racine from a trip to New York. He wrote to Wright:

> On my way back from New York, I stopped at Buffalo for a few hours to visit the Larkin office building. I was impressed with its beautiful exterior, efficient arrangement of offices, etc., also the pipe organ; I was not impressed by the use of stone masonry material throughout the interior, crowding of desks on all floors, discontinuance of fountain arrangement in entrance, and fireplace installation in lobby.
>
> I though I would write you my impressions, even though it may not have any bearing on our building.[19]

The next week Wright and Tafel returned to Racine. Wright again proposed his Broadacre City scheme for the company to Johnson and Ramsey. Successful as the Johnson company was, Wright's ideas were extravagant. Tafel remembers that the point caused a major disagreement between architect and clients. Johnson and Ramsey wanted their new office building to be built near the company's existing plant, and they refused to accept Wright's proposal. Unwilling to accede, Wright, Tafel recalls, may have been near the point of losing the commission.

Johnson, Wright, and Tafel drove to Johnson's house for lunch. On the way, they passed the Hardy house, which Wright pointed out to Johnson. Johnson took them through his own conventional house and proudly showed them his formal gardens. Tafel notes that Wright nodded cordially as they walked, though he undoubtedly disliked the Gothic-revival style of the house.

Wright and Tafel returned to Taliesin with blueprints of Matson's scheme for site information. When Wright discussed the trip with his wife and reported that his clients were adamant over not moving their business into the country, she responded, "Give them what they want, Frank, or you will lose the job."[20]

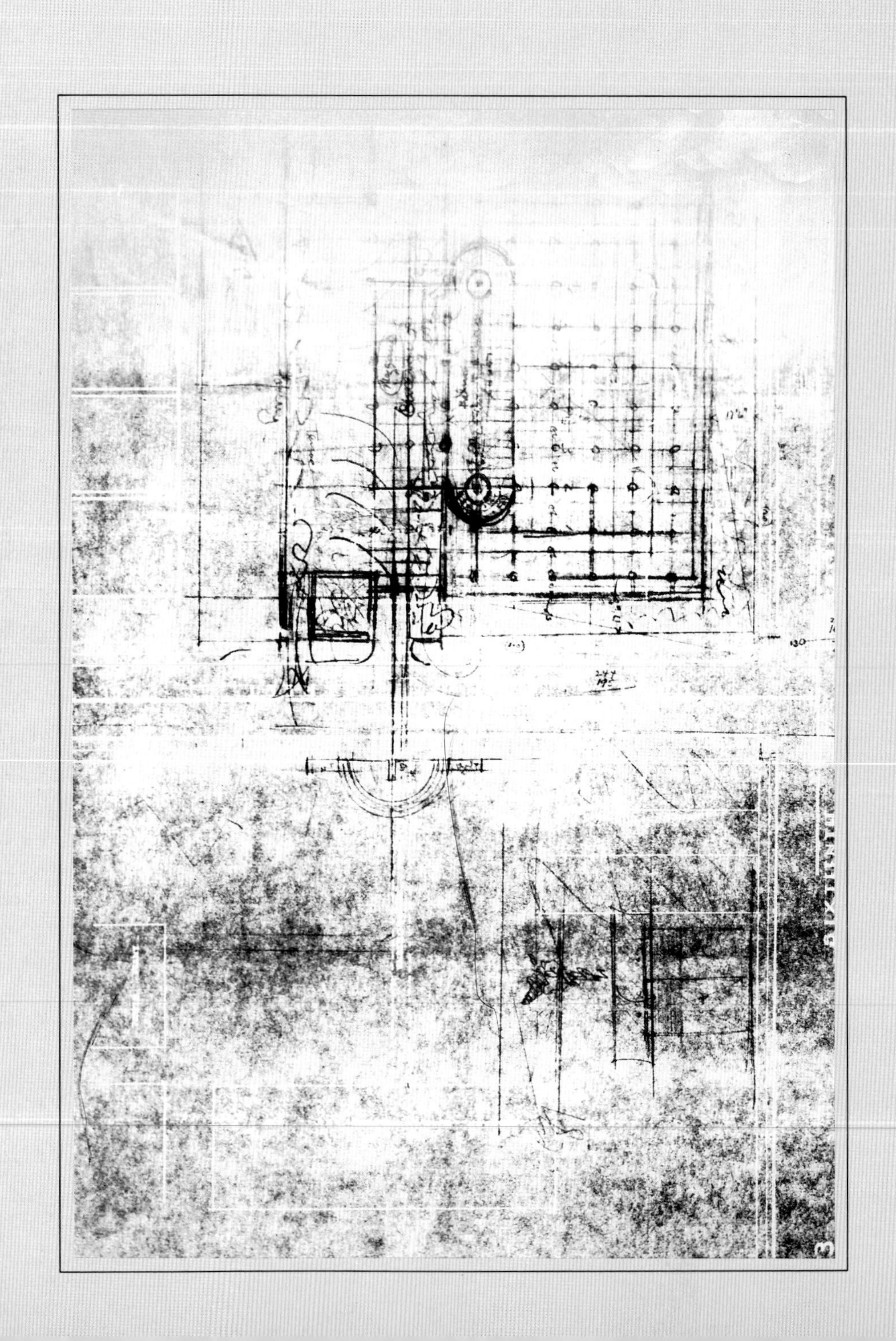

CHAPTER 3

DESIGN DEVELOPMENT

Fig. 10. Parti of floor plan of Administration Building. Next to Wright's plan is a barely legible small drawing that appears to be a simple conceptual sketch of the design. It may well be Wright's first drawing of the building. The Great Workroom is at one end of the drawing, the carport at the other, and a shaded zone for pedestrian and vehicular circulation is in the center. Drawn in yellow pencil over blueprint. Faded photograph of drawing; original drawing missing. (Courtesy of the Frank Lloyd Wright Foundation)

Wright conceded to Olgivanna's point of view and decided to design a scheme on the urban site; but it was to be a solution that would not sacrifice his ideas regarding the importance of integrating man into nature. He proposed to wrap a wall around the plot to block all views of its surroundings, and, since nature was hardly present, he would recreate nature on the site—in his own vocabulary. The problem, and his solution, were similar to those of the Larkin Building, which was also in an urban industrial setting, across the street from that company's factory complex.

Former apprentices John Howe, William Wesley Peters, Robert Mosher, and Edgar Tafel recall Wright's early work on the Johnson office building. From their recollections and from Wright's conceptual drawings, preserved in the Taliesin archives, we can reconstruct Wright's act of creation. Just as in Matson's scheme, he would design a windowless box but it would be based on two of his own earlier urban office designs: the Larkin Building and the Capital Journal project.[1]

In his autobiography, Wright wrote:

> What a release of pent-up creative energy—the making of those plans! Ideas came tumbling up and out onto paper to be thrown back in heaps—for careful scrutiny and selection. But, at once, I knew the scheme I wanted to try. I had it in mind when I drew the newspaper plant at Salem, Oregon, for Editor George Putnam, which he had been unable to build. A great simplicity and grace—organic.[2]

From the Capital Journal project he repeated the idea of a large workroom, filled with columns supporting a U-shaped upper story (*see* figs. 5–9). As in both of the earlier projects, the large room for the Johnson company would be ringed by a mezzanine suitable for semiprivate office space. As in the Capital Journal building, the floors would be connected by two large circular stair towers near the entrance. As in the Larkin Building, an auxiliary space—in this case a carport—would be separated from the workroom by an entry circulation area[3] (figs. 14–16).

Wright refined his design for the next several months; indeed he continued to refine details until construction was complete, but almost all of the building's ideas are present in Wright's first drawing, done in yellow pencil directly on Matson's blueprint (see fig. 10). Tafel recalls that Wright immediately decided to use the twenty-foot column grid of the Capital Journal project, and to surround a columnar hall with a seventeen-foot-deep mezzanine. Fourteen feet of it would project beyond the outermost row of columns—a satisfactory width for an office, and three feet of it would cantilever in from the columns—suitable for an aisle. Wright chose to use an even number of columns, presumably to avoid giving inappropriate significance to one bay of columns falling on the axis of symmetry.

On the site, 245 feet wide from sidewalk to sidewalk, nine twenty-foot bays of columns enclosed by fourteen-foot mezzanines left roughly eighteen feet six inches for a zone of plantings outside the building to the east and west. Wright continued this spatial sequence on the south side as well. To the north of the great room

Fig. 11.

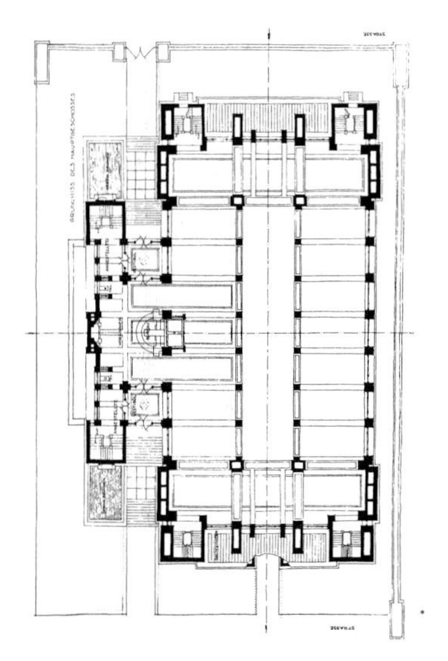

Fig. 12.

Fig. 13.

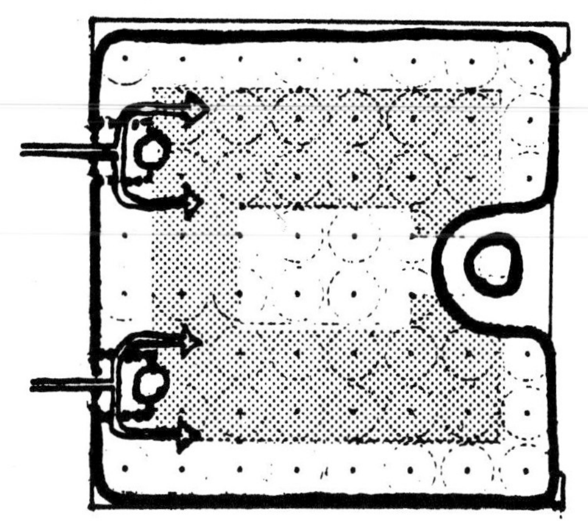

Fig. 14.

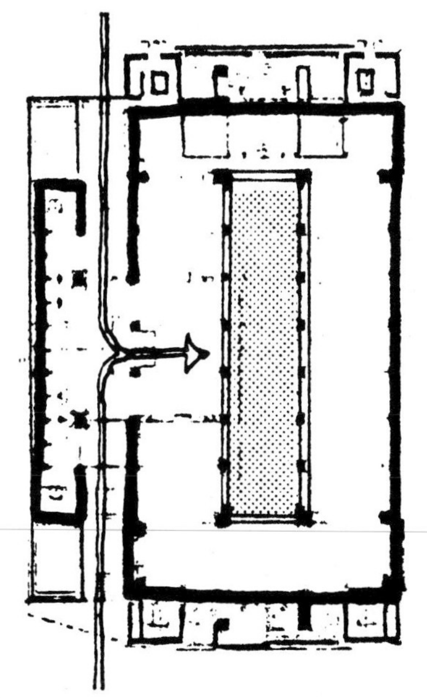

Fig. 15.

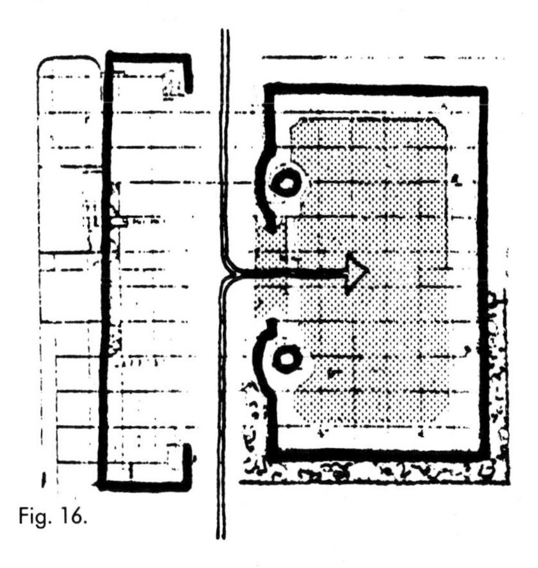

Fig. 16.

Fig. 11. Larkin Building, Buffalo, New York, 1903. Demolished 1950. Presenting a stark, closed exterior to the industrial site, the Larkin Building was made up of two masses: a large, main work area and a smaller three-story mass containing lockers and washrooms. Lithograph. (Courtesy of the Frank Lloyd Wright Foundation)

Fig. 12. First-floor plan of Larkin Building. The two masses of the symmetrical structure are separated by a circulation zone containing two entry vestibules. Lithograph. (Courtesy of the Frank Lloyd Wright Foundation)

Fig. 13. Central court of the Larkin Building, circa 1908. The main mass of the building is composed of rectangular mezzanines ringing a five-story, top-lit central space. The open interior stands in contrast to the austere exterior. (Photo courtesy of the Frank Lloyd Wright Foundation)

Fig. 14. Parti of Capital Journal project.

Fig. 15. Parti of Larkin Building.

Fig. 16. Parti of Johnson Administration Building. A comparison of the three conceptual sketches gives convincing evidence that the idea for the plan of the Johnson building was derived by superimposing the Capital Journal project's columnar structural system and circular geometry onto the layout of the Larkin Building.

Fig. 17. Aerial view of Johnson Administration Building, 1939. The building comprises a single, large room (right) and a carport (left). Spanning the two are a second-story theater and third-story executive offices. The massing derives from the Larkin Building, although the proportions and detailing differ. Wright called the Larkin Building the masculine sire of the more feminine Johnson building, contrasting the former building's angularity and verticality to the latter's low curves. (Courtesy of Johnson Wax)

Fig. 18. Choisy drawing of the Great Workroom and lobby. With a large mezzanine-enclosed, skylight office space for the company's clerical workers, the Johnson Administration Building resembles the Larkin Building conceptually. The mushroom-column-and-slab structural system and the two-story space are based on the Capital Journal project. (Drawing by Gerald Wilson)

Fig. 19. Reconstruction of original parti of Administration Building. Wright visualized his designs very clearly before he began to draw. Consequently, every line on most of his sketches is significant. The diagrams in figures 20–24 have been prepared to analyze the information in figure 10. (Drawing by Gerald Wilson)

Fig. 20. Axes generated by columns. The potentially infinite column grid is bound by enclosing walls. (Drawing by Gerald Wilson)

Fig. 21. General disposition of the Administration Building program on-site. The site is zoned along its north-south axis: at the south end is the large workroom for clerical employees. A lobby is located at its north end, followed by a porte cochere and carport. At the north end is a service entrance, and the residential lots to the north of the site are earmarked for future factory expansion. (Drawing by Gerald Wilson)

Fig. 22. Circulation. Three distinct circulation routes are indicated for pedestrians, employee parking or passenger loading, and service vehicles. (Drawing by Gerald Wilson)

Fig. 23. Relative density of spaces. (Drawing by Gerald Wilson)

Fig. 24. Plantings used as space definers. (Drawing by Gerald Wilson)

Fig. 25. Figure/ground drawing of south Racine, showing outline of Wright's first plan of Administration Building superimposed on-site. (Drawing by Gerald Wilson)

Wright located a carport, the roof of which would be supported by more columns, also on the twenty-foot grid.

Next, Wright drew a south elevation of the scheme directly on top of the blueprint of Matson's elevation. That drawing is missing, but Howe remembers that Wright outlined a blank wall concealing the columns, with a continuous band of glass at the top. Whenever Wright drew, the occasion was a lesson for his apprentices. As Howe watched, Wright explained that in the Capital Journal project employees could gaze outside, but for the Johnson building, he would design an opaque screen wall around the outside, blocking the view of the dreary surroundings. Only a high skylight running around the top of the wall would provide sunlight.

As Wright began to design the building Howe recalls that he talked many times about the Johnson design as an excellent example of the destruction of the "box."[4] The confining nature of traditional rooms was contrary to Wright's vision of an architecture that would elevate the freedom of the individual. Apprentice Robert Mosher irreverently provoked an impromptu lecture from Wright when he asked how one got into "this box." The word *box* connoted the essence of what Wright disliked in Victorian architecture. In a later talk, Wright explained that he first consciously began to try to destroy the "box" in the Larkin Building, by making the stair towers into freestanding, individual features that pushed out from the corners of the main building. In Unity Temple (1905) Wright continued, he achieved his first real expression of the idea that the space within was the reality of the building—the antithesis of the box.

> ... If in a building [such as Unity Temple] you feel not only protection from above, but liberation of interior to outside space ... then you have one important secret of letting the interior space come through.
>
> ... I knew enough of engineering to know that ... a certain distance in each way from the corner is where the economic support of a box-building is invariably found. ... When you support at those points you have created a short cantilever to the corners that lessens actual spans and sets the corner free or open for whatever distance you choose. The corners disappear altogether if you choose to let space come in there, or let it go out. Instead of post-and-beam construction, the usual box building, you now have a new sense of building construction by way of the cantilever and continuity. ... [In] this simple change of thought lies the essential of the architectural change from box to free plan and the new reality that is space instead of matter.
>
> ... These unattached side walls become something independent, no longer enclosing walls. They're separate supporting screens, any one of which may be shortened, or extended or perforated, or occasionally eliminated.
>
> ... To go further: if this liberation works in the horizontal plane why won't it work in the vertical plane? No one has looked through the box at the sky up there at the upper angle, have they? Why not? Because the box always had a cornice at the top. It was added to the sides in order that the box might not look so much like a box, but more classic. ...
>
> Now—to go on—there in the Johnson Building you catch no sense of enclosure whatever at any angle, top or sides. You are looking at the sky and feel the freedom of space. The columns are designed to stand up and take over the ceiling, the column is made a part of the ceiling: continuity.
>
> The old idea of a building is, as you see, quite gone.[5]

According to Mosher, Wright may have shown the apprentices his drawings of the column-filled Capital Journal project, indicating that it was the inspiration for the new building's layout. But when Mosher again asked how one got into the building Wright replied that one entered from the rear as it should be done—not from the front.[6]

Wright handed Howe the blueprints with his two yellow sketches, and Howe laid out the floor plan on a clean sheet at a scale of ⅛-inch to 1 foot (fig. 26). Wright almost always designed on a grid, and presumably Howe began by laying out the 20-by-20-foot grid of the columns, marking their bases and dotting in the circles

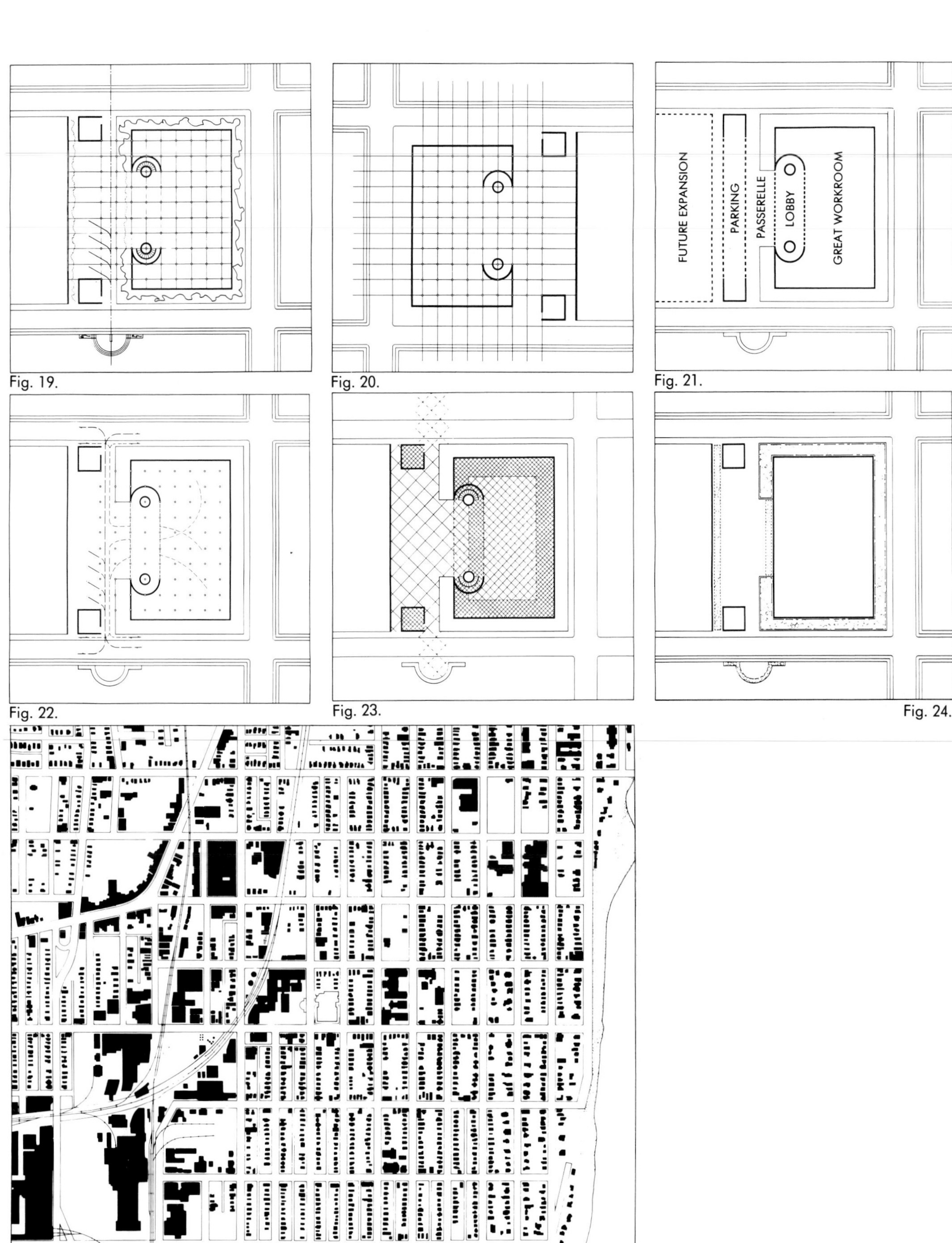

Fig. 19.

Fig. 20.

Fig. 21.

Fig. 22.

Fig. 23.

Fig. 24.

Fig. 25.

Fig. 26. Parti of first-floor plan, the Great Workroom. The outermost layer of the space is partially divided into offices, and a zone of file cabinets is adjacent to it. A mezzanine running above portions of that layer is alluded to, apparently becoming a balcony over the entry area into the space. Two zones of basement lockers extend south from the two vertical circulation cores; between them a reflected ceiling plan indicates skylights illuminating the center of the space, four bays wide. Lightly drawn green lines (not visible in reproduction) may denote a U-shaped upper floor of executives' offices, which Wright called a penthouse. To the left is a roofed carport, which is separated from the great room by a porte cochere. Pencil on tracing paper. 31″ × 32″. (Courtesy of the Frank Lloyd Wright Foundation)

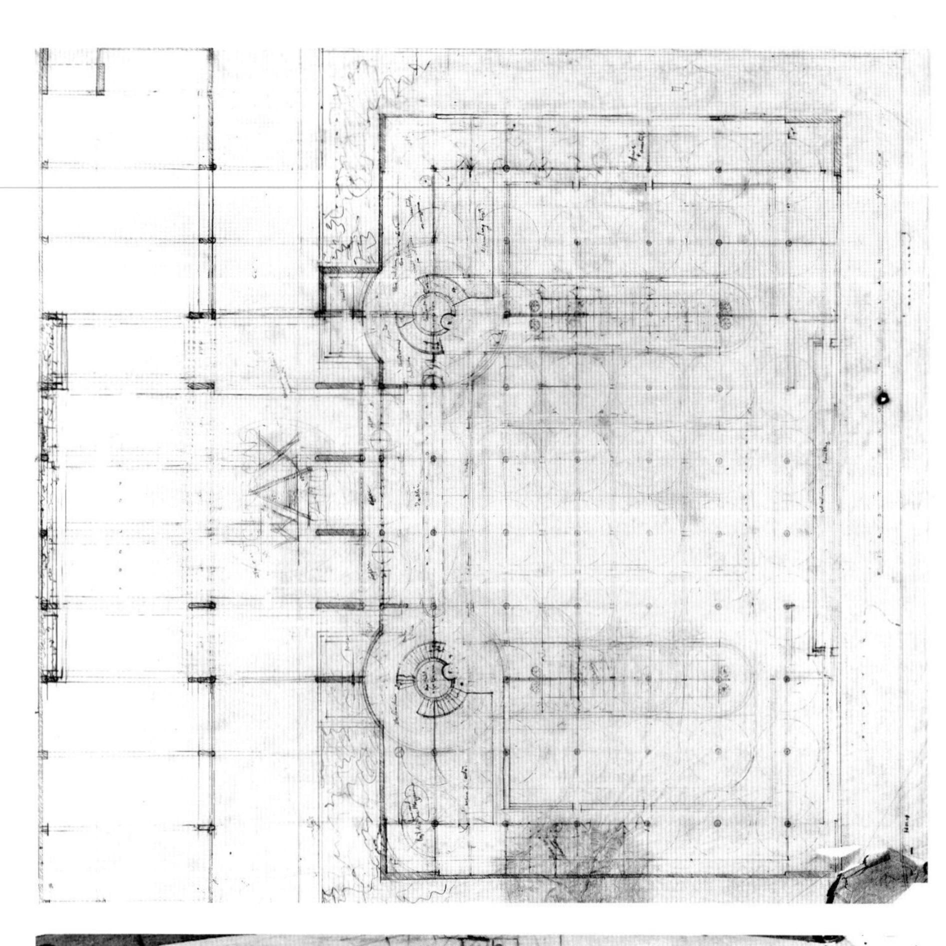

Fig. 27. Partial section of the Administration Building showing the profile of the exterior wall of the Great Workroom, the mezzanine, and three columns, and the penthouse in elevation. To the left of the section is a corresponding partial elevation. A first sketch of a master plan for an entire new company complex may be seen above the section, depicting two bands of buildings that stretch one and one-half blocks north of the proposed administration building. A stack is marked near the far northeast corner. The two bands appear to enclose a courtyard, all forming a "body" extending from the figural "head" of the design—Wright's building. Characteristic of Wright's response to urban sites, the scheme is inwardly oriented. The borders of the existing plant are outlined at the left of the drawing. Aside from one later perspective drawing, Wright developed his master plan for the Johnson company property no further than this sketch. However, the strategy remained with him and he followed it seven years later when he was hired to design a building for research and development for the company. Pencil on tracing paper. 22″ × 17″. (Courtesy of the Frank Lloyd Wright Foundation)

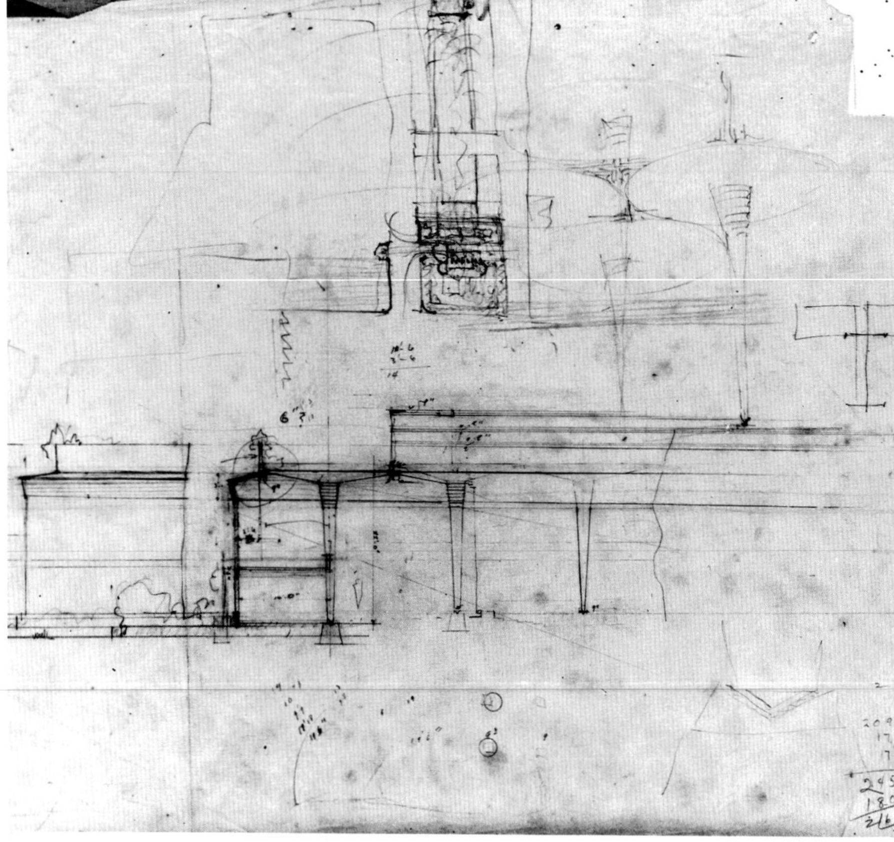

described by their upper edges. After Howe began to lay the drawing out, Wright worked on it. Forty-five years later, Howe could still distinguish between the lines he and Wright drew in the plan. Howe remembered that he drew overly precisely, while Wright, in a hurry to get his ideas on paper, worked more fluidly. Wright occasionally sat at the board and drew, and then, getting up, gave further verbal instruction to Howe.[7] Apprentice William Wesley Peters, today Senior Architect in the Taliesin Fellowship, watched as Wright drew. He recalls that although the original ideas for the Johnson building came quickly, Wright spent an enormous amount of time on details to clarify the building's basic geometry.[8]

Perhaps the most time was spent on the first drafted first-floor plan (see fig. 26). Ideas were drawn, erased, and redrawn. In the drawing the basement, first floor, mezzanine, reflected ceiling, and upper level are all visible as Wright simultaneously shaped the five levels of the building. His struggle to integrate the circular geometry of the column with the orthogonal geometry of the grid is one of the primary themes running through the series of progressively refined drawings he produced over the following months.

Wright's next drawing was the partial section and elevation shown in figure 27. In these early drawings, Howe notes:

> Mr. Wright was establishing what he called the grammar of the building. He always quoted Louis Sullivan, who said, "Just take care of the terminals, and the rest of the building will take care of itself," which means the corners of the building. The profile and the corners are the grammar; for instance, in Mr. Wright's Prairie houses, it's the overhanging eaves. With any building, Mr. Wright designed in plan, first and foremost. Then he moved [to] a section, and then the elevations were the result of the plan and the section. His buildings really were designed from the inside out . . . Mr. Wright would establish the grammar of the buildings from working on the elevations.[9]

In the Capital Journal project, Wright had used the word *penthouse* to describe the two stories of apartments on top of the building. Initially, the third floor of the Administration Building had almost the same formal configuration as the top floors of the Capital Journal project, and Wright retained the name *penthouse* to describe it, although it contained offices. Peters remembers that Wright was not satisfied with the U-shaped penthouse and also briefly considered a simpler I-shaped penthouse (see figs. 32 and 34). According to Peters, Wright was discontented with both versions—they were "blocky" and the main portion of the building was not joined fluidly to the carport. That struggle and its resolution are apparent in Wright's subsequent drawings. In the penthouse plan in figure 35 Wright replaced the U-shaped penthouse with a far more plastic form that acknowledges the circular shape of the mushroom-column petals and links the carport to the main mass of the building. It is perhaps with this move that the design for the Johnson Wax Administration Building becomes the pure expression of an idea quite unlike that of the Capital Journal project design. The Johnson building's profile is no longer static, but rather that of a sinuous creature—its skin stretched over living organs. An intimate fit has been established between the building's interior spaces and its external form.

As the Johnson building scheme emerges in these drawings, it is clear that Wright was designing his first curving, streamlined building, a major departure from the earlier Capital Journal project. The concept of streamlining was originated by airplane and ship designers who attempted to create forms that would meet with the least resistance in air and water. In the mid-1930s streamlining became the symbol of the future, as the public associated its elegantly curved, clean forms with man's increasing technological conquest of the elements. By 1937 all mass-produced U.S. automobiles had streamlined detailing, and the look was also being applied to such rather less mobile objects as radios and tea services. In the mid-1930s the style was also grafted onto utterly immobile buildings. The Streamlined Moderne style was usually applied by architects to nonresidential buildings, perhaps because

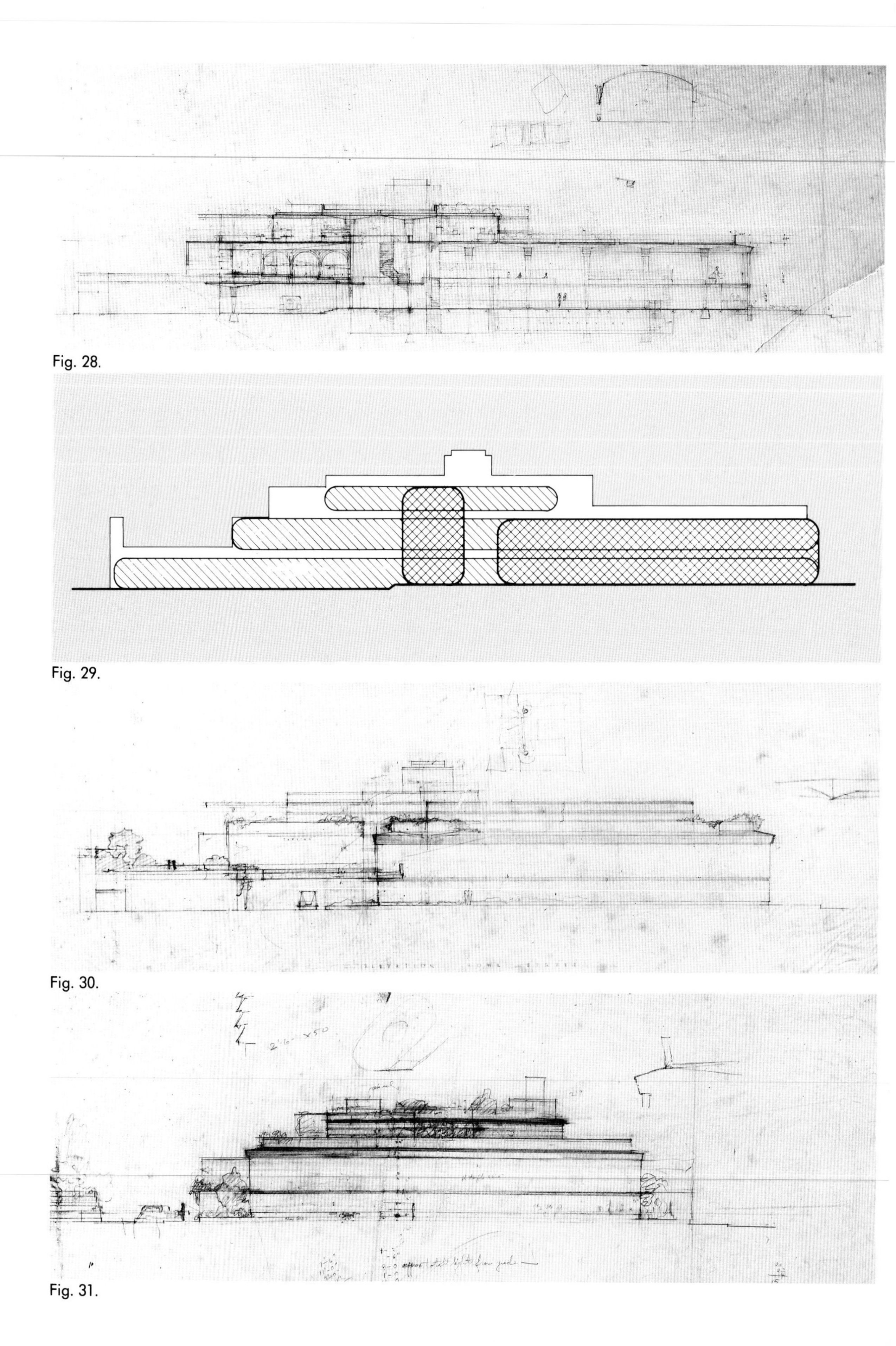

Fig. 28.

Fig. 29.

Fig. 30.

Fig. 31.

Fig. 28. Longitudinal section. The organization is clear in this early section. On the upper, or penthouse, floor, a conference room (right), and cafeteria (left) overlook a three-story reception well. On the second level to the left is a theater. This level becomes a mezzanine in the Great Workroom (right). The carport is to the left on the ground floor. The three-story lobby is in the center, and the Great Workroom is to the right. Pencil on tracing paper. 36″ × 18″. (Courtesy of the Frank Lloyd Wright Foundation)

Fig. 29. Analytic section, showing the interlocking arrangement of the Administration Building's interior spaces.

Fig. 30. West elevation. The penthouse is above the Great Workroom on the right. One of two large, round ventilating stacks projects above the building in the center, and a theater is located over the carport, near left. Pencil on tracing paper. 42″ × 15″. (Courtesy of the Frank Lloyd Wright Foundation)

Fig. 31. South elevation of Johnson Administration Building. A major distinction between the Capital Journal and the Johnson designs is made clear in early elevations. In contrast to the Capital Journal project, in which space is boxed by strong horizontal planes and rusticated curtain walls, a reading especially strong in the west elevation (see fig. 8), in the first elevations of the Johnson Wax project roof planes have disappeared, concealed by a parapet. As in the Capital Journal design, exterior walls are articulated as non-loadbearing, but by interrupting the brickwork with thin horizontal bands of glass. The bands of glass also have significance for the building's interior. Three of them are located at cornices—those lines at which walls meet ceiling. A band of sunlight, rather than the customary corner, at these points has a strong liberating effect upon the experience of space inside the rooms. Pencil on tracing paper. 42″ × 15″. (Courtesy of the Frank Lloyd Wright Foundation)

Fig. 32. Conceptual roof plan of Administration Building. The sketch indicates that the penthouse floor was originally conceived as a U-shape. At this stage the massing of the building, excluding the carport, was almost identical to that of the Capital Journal building. Pencil on tracing paper. 42″ × 15″. (Courtesy of the Frank Lloyd Wright Foundation)

Fig. 33. Roof plan of Capital Journal project. (Drawing by Don Coles)

Fig. 34. Roof plan of Administration Building with I-shaped penthouse. (Drawing by Don Coles)

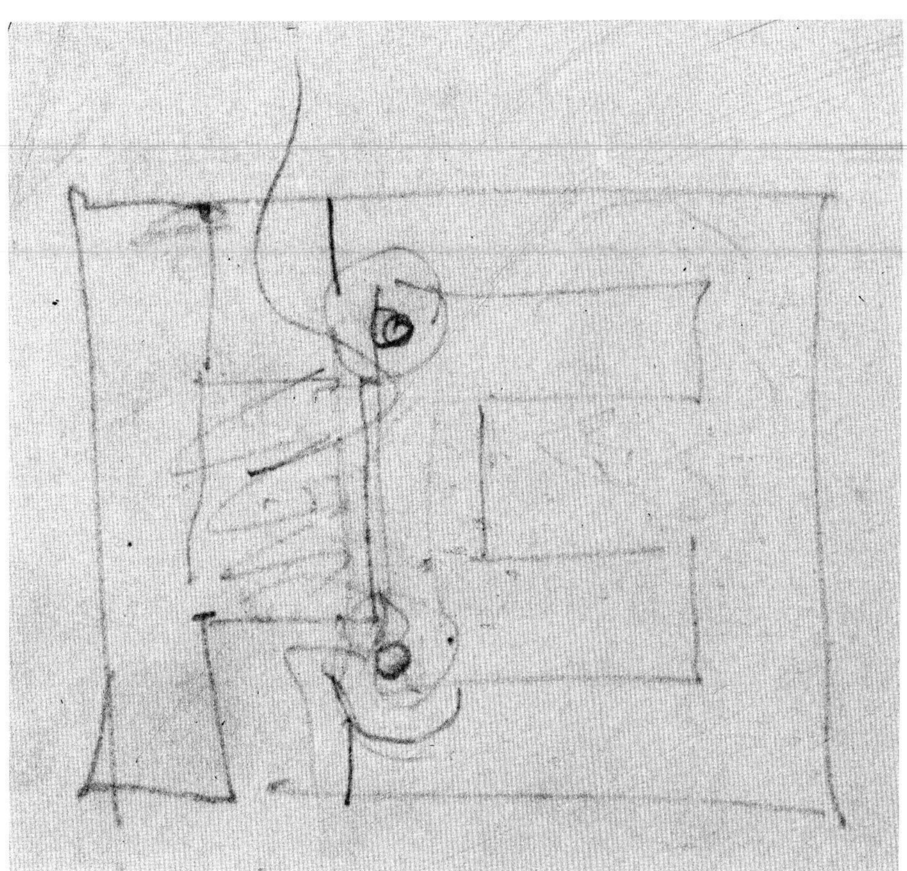

Fig. 32.

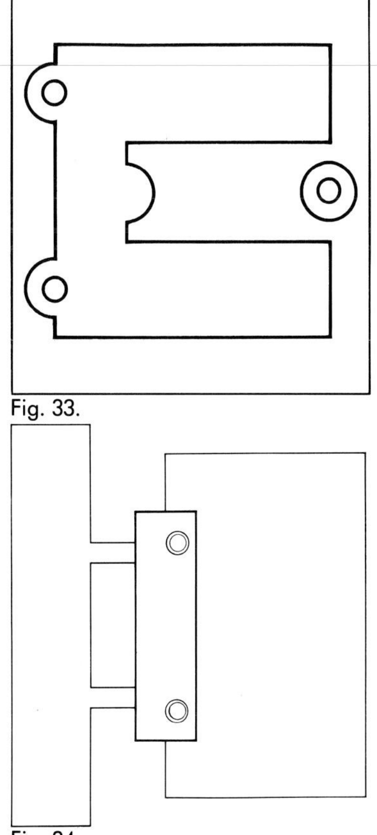

Fig. 33.

Fig. 34.

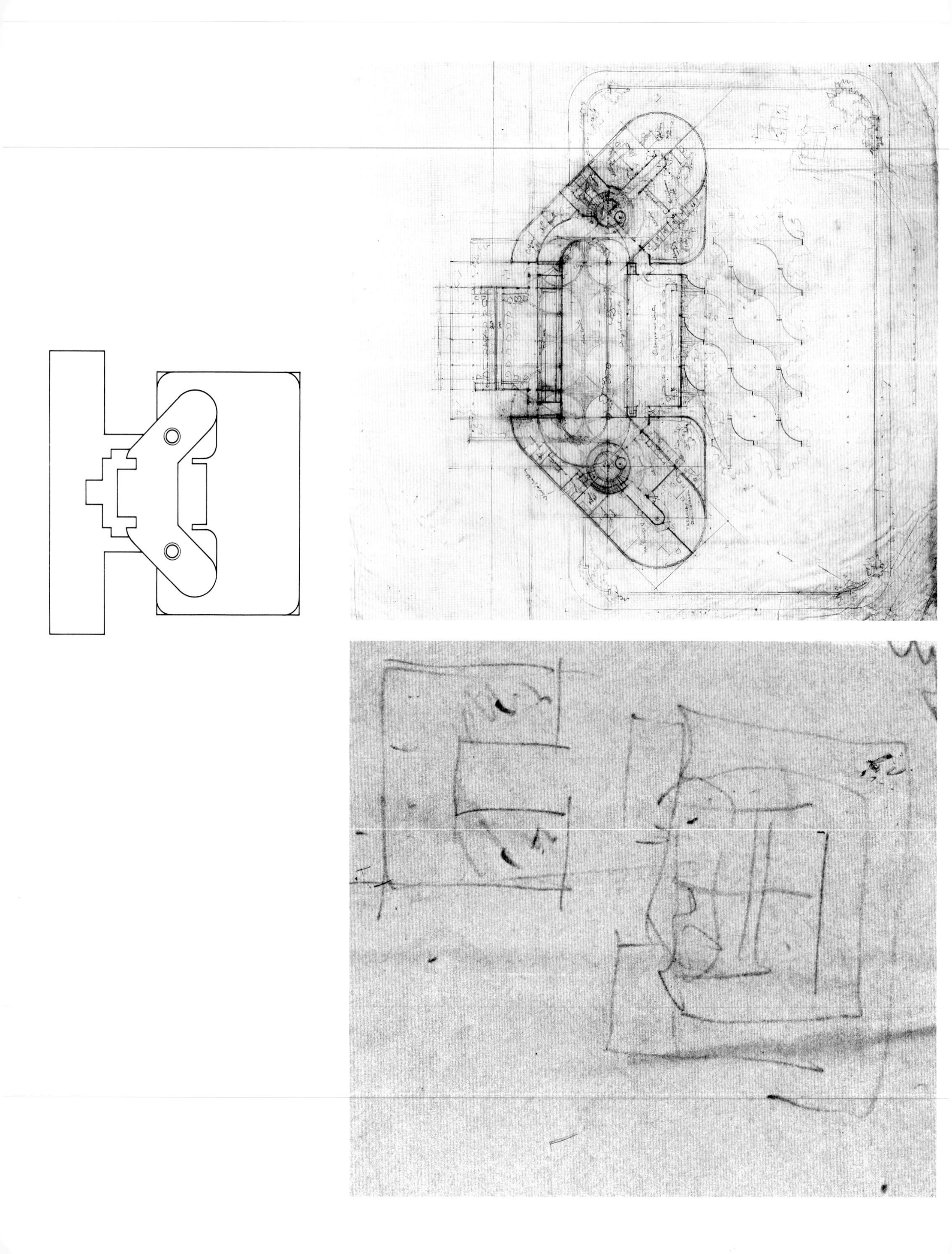

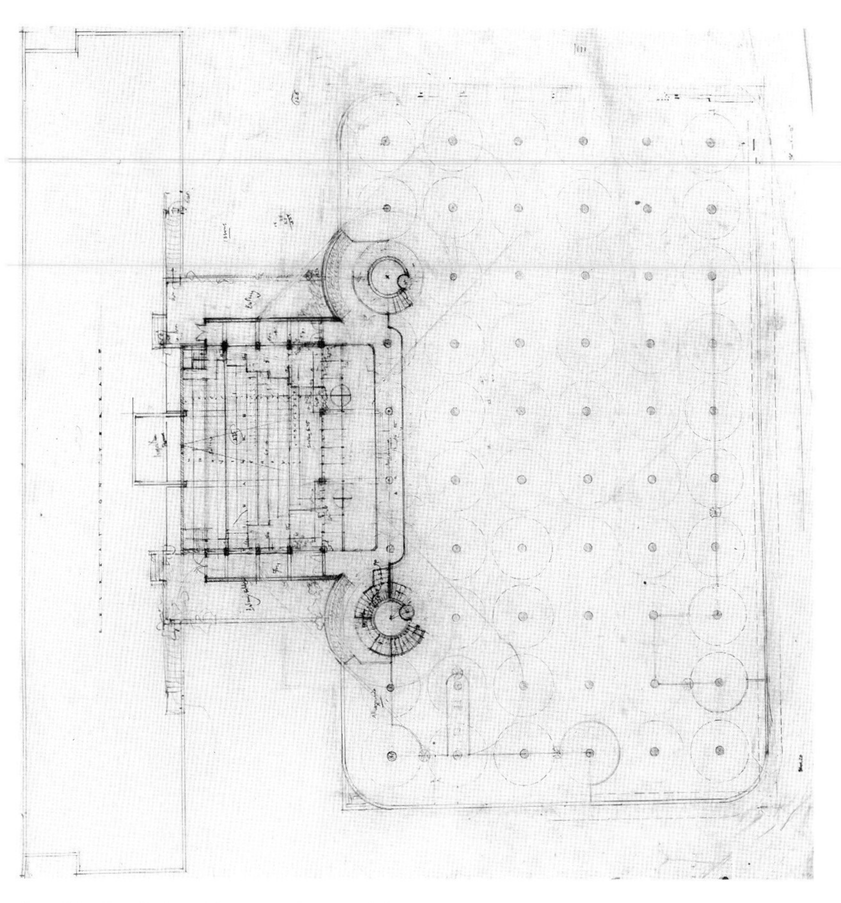

Fig. 35. Roof plan. The new shape of the penthouse unites the two masses of the building. (Drawing by Don Coles)

Fig. 36. Penthouse plan for Administration Building. A small sketch in the upper right of the plan shows the U-shaped penthouse above the mezzanine-ringed Great Workroom space. Erasures on the penthouse-level drawing remain from this scheme, but, what has been redrawn is a far more plastic form. At the center of the third floor is a court open to the lobby below. To the front of the court is a food bar, seating area, and dining terrace. To the court's rear is a directors' conference room, and to its sides are two wings of executive offices and meeting room. Plantings are indicated on some of the mushroom columns on the roof of the Great Workroom. Pencil on tracing paper. 32″ × 36″. (Courtesy of the Frank Lloyd Wright Foundation)

Fig. 37. Plan sketch showing old U-shaped penthouse. Detail of figure 36. Pencil on tracing paper. 32″ × 36″. (Courtesy of the Frank Lloyd Wright Foundation)

Fig. 38. Mezzanine plan. Two mezzanines extend asymmetrically into the workroom. Beneath the third-floor dining terrace the mezzanine joins a theater. A recreational terrace straddles the theater over the carport. Pencil on tracing paper. 31″ × 32″. (Courtesy of the Frank Lloyd Wright Foundation)

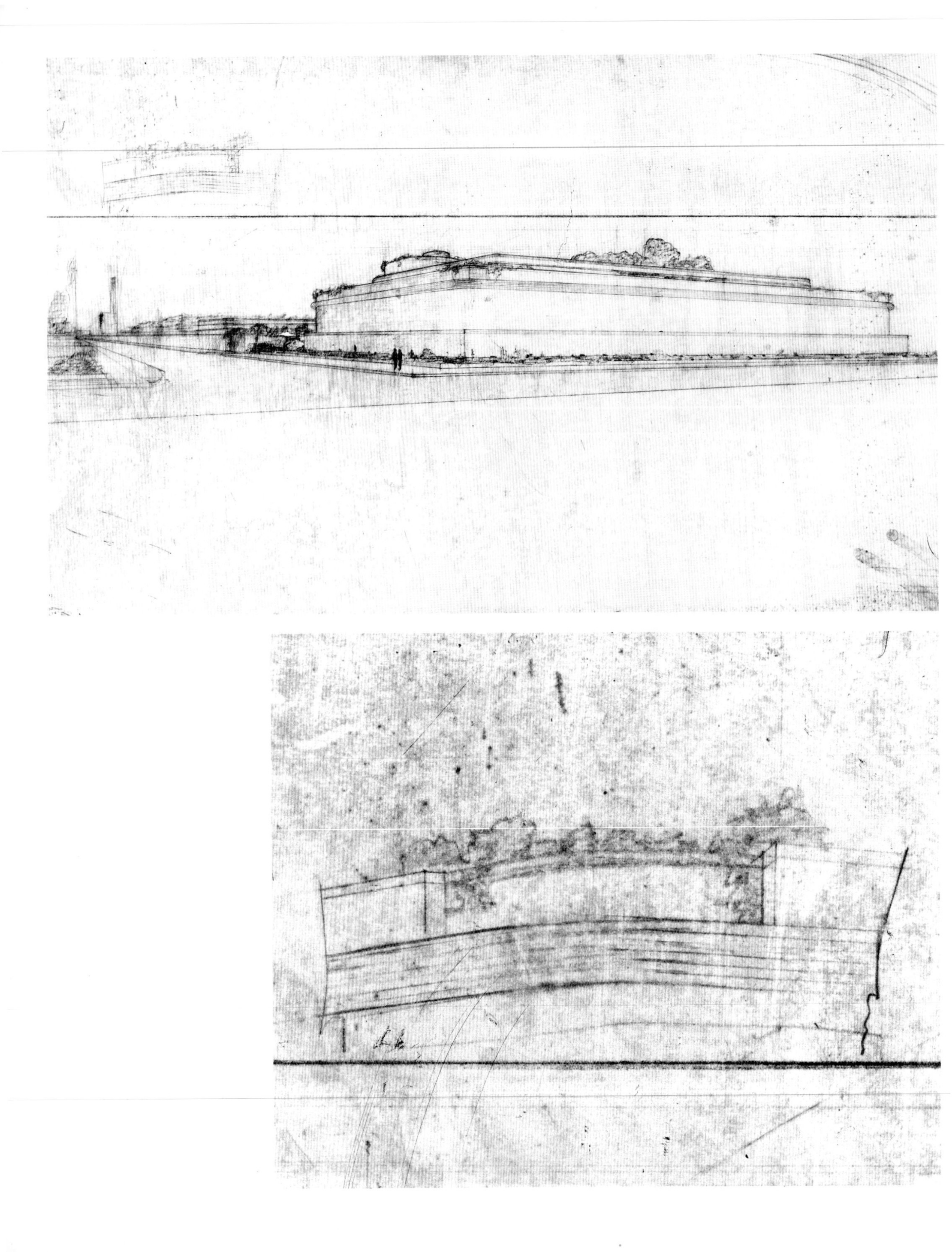

Fig. 39. Perspective. This may be Wright's first perspective of the Administration Building. It is of particular interest because it also depicts his contemplated future expansion of the Johnson company's facilities, apparently as a walled garden-development—a private world contained within two city blocks. Pencil and colored pencil on tracing paper. 37″ × 20″. (Courtesy of the Frank Lloyd Wright Foundation)

Fig. 40. Detail of figure 39. This sketch shows a refinement of the parapet corner that adds plasticity to the building's profile and expresses the support of the mushroom column beneath. Wright has created an illusion, in which a small portion of the exterior wall seems to be peeled away, permitting the inside of the building to be visible. (Courtesy of the Frank Lloyd Wright Foundation)

Fig. 41. Iowa State Bank and Trust Company. Fairfield, Iowa. Contemporary photograph of typical example of the nonresidential Streamlined Moderne style.

corporate clients considered it good business to be associated with the "future." Wright's first and most ardent champion at Johnson Wax, William Connolly, was in charge of the company's advertising. If Wright saw the building as advertising for the company it would have been logical to design it in the newest popular style—as long as he could demonstrate his mastery of it. Throughout his career it was Wright's habit to demonstrate (often just once) that he could produce a masterful work in the current style, and the Johnson building was his first nonresidential commission since the streamlining trend had arisen. Wright wrote about the Johnson building: "High time to give our hungry American public something truly 'streamlined'. . . . " Commonly, streamlined buildings feature arbitrarily curved walls and applied ornament to achieve their effect. The Johnson building's streamlining is more profound. Its sinuous horizontal detailing represents a complete integration of structure with natural and artificial lighting systems. The elegant streamlined desks were remarkably practical, and the curved walls seem to be logical containers of efficient curved spaces within. As Wright produced his early drawings of the Administration Building, Peters recalls, "I remember clearly his great struggle to make space flow. It was a gradual transition. . . . Part of [his] effort [at] streamlining is understood in the sense of making [the building] a great plastic space enclosure."[10] Wright's design for a carport to be integrated with the building merged the concept of streamlining with his Broadacre City notion. The act of entering the building from a carport celebrated the automobile, which was the most essential element of Broadacre City, allowing human society to decentralize without suffering isolation.

Howe, Tafel, Peters, and others worked on the drawings day and night, and through the weekend. When Wright was unsure of a detail he circled it. When he thought of a solution he sketched it on a piece of paper and handed it to the apprentice working on the drawing, who erased the circle and drew in the correction. Frequently, Wright went to bed puzzling over an unresolved detail and awoke before dawn with a solution. When the apprentices came into the drafting room to begin their work day, they found the circle erased and the new detail drawn in by Wright.

Barely ten days since Wright had begun, he was ready to show Johnson his scheme. With plans, two elevations, and a section, Tafel drove Wright to Racine on August 9, 1936, where they were met by Johnson and several executives. Tafel recalls, "Wright's presentation was very dramatic and right to the point. He described the site—wax and paint factory building to the west, movie houses, stores, houses on the other sides. It was all mediocre architecture. There was nothing to look out to, no views. So [the solution was to] turn everything inward."[11]

Unrolling the floor plans, Wright pointed out Johnson, Ramsey, and Connolly's offices at the top of the building, together with other administrative and advertising offices. He described the air-conditioning systems of the sealed building in which all the air would enter through two large "nostrils" that would extend above the structure. Tafel notes, "He made one of these beautiful presentations in such a way that they knew that this was an idea, and that the details would follow. They were in any case not expecting details at that time." The Johnson executives received the project enthusiastically.

When questioned about cost, Wright insisted that the building be built on a "cost-plus" basis—that is, the contractors would charge their actual costs and then add an agreed-upon percentage for overhead and profit. Wright had been utilizing innovative construction techniques for over three decades and he knew that contractors were unable to accurately estimate the cost of an unorthodox building. Consequently they would either refuse to submit bids, or submit ones that were too high. The only way to get the building built was to hire a competent contractor and remove his financial fears by allowing him to work on a cost-plus basis.

Johnson told Wright that he already had a general contractor in mind, his close friend Ben Wiltscheck. Wiltscheck had been educated as an architect at the University of Pennsylvania, but instead of practicing, entered the construction business and built houses in Racine. Some were for executives at Johnson Wax, members of his social circle. John Howe believes that it was preordained that Wiltscheck would build the new office building.

While Wright often thought of contractors as enemies, Howe remembers that Wiltscheck, who turned out to be a careful and precise builder, would not allow Wright to think of him as an adversary. Their first meeting was a cordial one, in which Wiltscheck took Wright and Tafel to see a house he had just built for one of the Johnson employees. A humidifying system in the house had become stuck after the home was finished, and to Wiltscheck's embarrassment, the wallpaper had fallen off of the walls. However, Wright did not seem to hold that against him and wrote, "[Wiltscheck] has never done anything this big, but he does seem like a fine man."

That weekend Wiltscheck spent a day at Taliesin. Over the drafting board, Wright described the proposed building to him. Wiltscheck was enthusiastic over the design, and he in turn received cautious approval from Wright. By this time Wright and Johnson had become closer than mere business associates. In correspondence they now referred to each other as "My dear Mr. Johnson" and "My dear Mr. Wright." Among other things, the two men shared a passion for music, both live and recorded. Their tastes, however, were quite different: Wright favored Beethoven and Bach and played the piano, while the younger man preferred jazz and ragtime and played the saxophone. Responding to the events of the week, Wright wrote to Johnson:

> We are proceeding with the preparation of the working plans. . . . I am calling, in consultation, air conditioning people and if you know anyone you would like in on it—let me know. I am calling in Pittsburgh Plate Glass and Libbey-Owens-Ford also on the glass.
>
> Wiltscheck spent Sunday with me and so far as I can see he will be good help for us in getting the building properly built. He is cautious and has had some experience although none with this sort of building.

Of course in this structure all depends upon the experienced working out of every detail to the smallest, and upon the closest supervision by ourselves. This, continuously, from the beginning to end no matter what the builder or who he may be. The building is simple but so distinguished that a false decision or a bad interpretation of even a seemingly minor part could seriously mar the whole. If you will stand by, however, and stand back of your architect you will have a result of which you will always be proud because I am more than interested to get the building, so well conceived, just as well planned in detail and well built.

. . . [accept my thanks for] your fine decision to build immediately without vexatious delays.[12]

Three days later Johnson responded:

I was very favorably impressed with your words as to how the plans will be worked out. The building cannot help but be right if we carry on as you have put it.

I am glad you think Wiltscheck will do. Certainly he is willing to do what we want, and he should be because the opportunity is great in a building such as the one you have planned. He goes around with a sort of silly grin on his face, and acted a bit cagy when we were talking about the building the other day, but I cannot see that that will make any difference as long as he builds well.

Sometime ago the Directors approved a sum of $200,000 for a new office building. No mention was made of furnishings, fees, etc. At the next meeting I will advise them of your goal—the building complete at $250,000—which I feel will be acceptable to them, considering the plus value we will receive by having you do it for us. Our meeting will not be held until September 15, but this should not delay the progress on the working drawings. . . .[13]

In a letter to Wright written the previous day, Johnson requested two substantive changes in the design. He wrote, "Positions of Directors' Room + Lunch Room should be reversed, I think," and ". . . arrangements [should be] made to have handball and racquet courts on the garage floor."

Frequently a client's request for changes in an already designed building's program can force alterations that blur the clarity of the architect's original intentions. However, in responding to these two requests Wright caused some of the building's underlying ideas to read more clearly, unarguably strengthening its design.

Herbert Johnson and several other company executives played handball and raquetball. Some time earlier the firm had built a playing court nearby. Wright may have suggested that the new building include a court. It certainly was compatible with his notion of the Broadacre City architect as shaper of a complete environment for work and leisure. As the squash court was only for the use of the company's executives, Wright located it on the carport and designed a bridge directly linking it to the penthouse. Wright intended the remaining roof of the carport to serve as a recreation terrace for employees.

Johnson's other request did not offer an immediate answer. The proposed location for the lunchroom was in the apex of the design—the point from which a viewer could survey almost the entire building. Perhaps Johnson felt the directors' conference room was more appropriate there than a cafeteria. Later, however, Johnson also requested that Wright design a single space to serve as both cafeteria and theater. In earlier drawings Wright included a two-hundred-seat theater beneath the conference room. Apparently the theater was Wright's suggestion: he recently had built a new theater at Taliesin, and Howe remembers Wright was then especially enthused over the idea of a theater in the Johnson building. He called such spaces "cabarets"—places for performances, at which refreshments could be served. According to Howe, Wright felt that this could be the social center of the Johnson company. Johnson, however, vetoed the separate theater.

Wright redesigned the theater on the mezzanine level to also serve as a dining room. A kitchenette, projection booth, and dishwashing area line the north wall of the room, and a rostrum is located at the center of the south end. Directly above on the penthouse level, Wright placed Herbert Johnson's own office. The directors' conference room remained in its earlier location (see figs. 42–44).

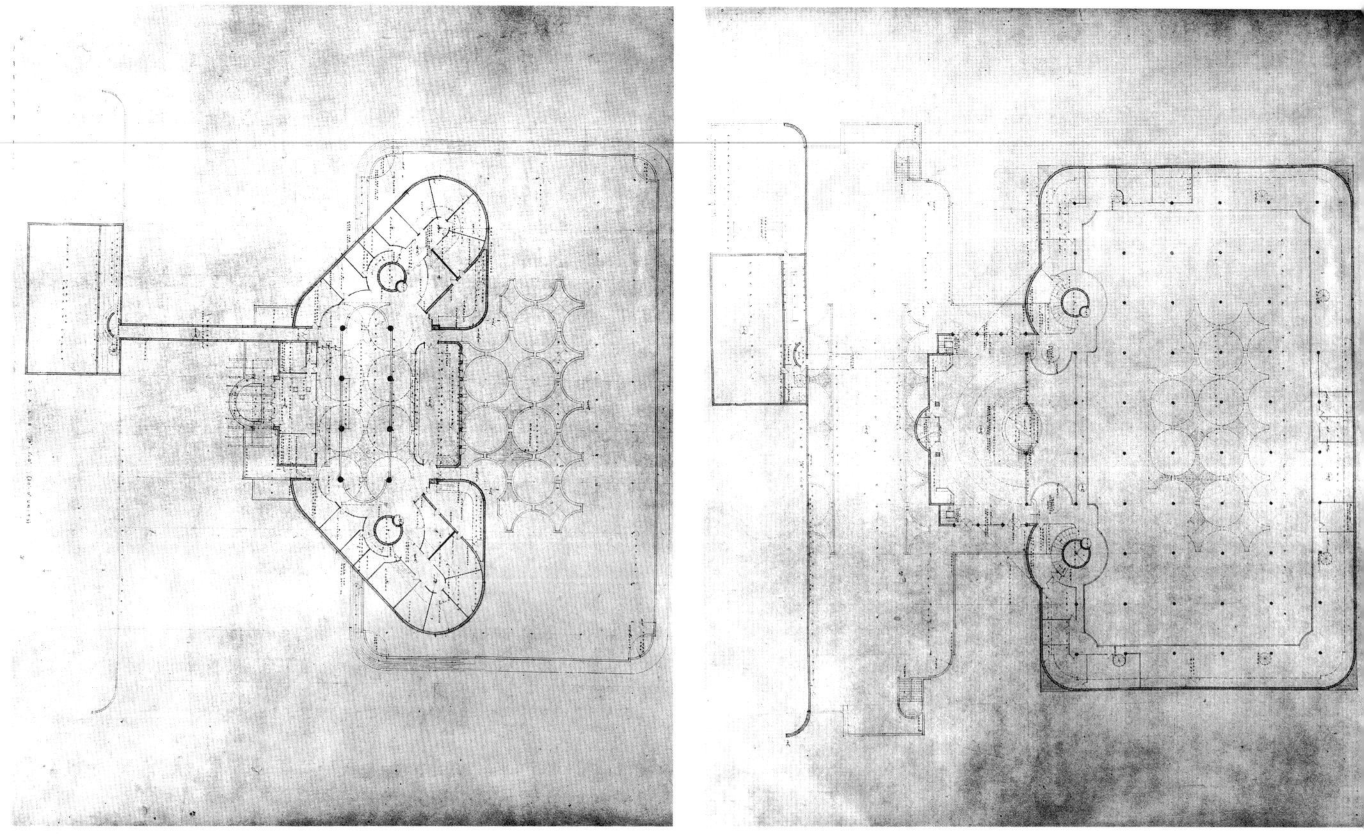

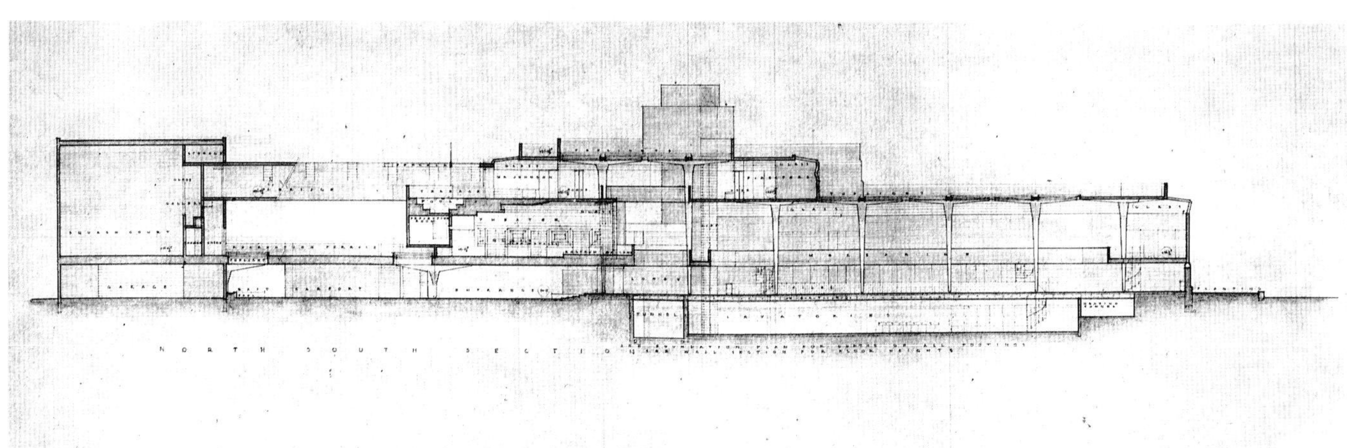

Fig. 42. Penthouse plan. In this drawing Wright clarified the building's internal hierarchy to such a degree that the scheme became a three-dimensional flow chart of the company's personnel relationships. At the top and center, jutting forward from the main mass of the building, is Johnson's office. The executives of the company's two divisions—operations, and advertising and public relations—are located in wings on either side. The offices of the managers of the two divisions are situated at the tips of the wings, and between the two wings is the conference room. Blueprint. (Courtesy of Johnson Wax)

Fig. 43. Mezzanine plan for Administration Building. Middle-level managers are located on the continuous mezzanine, ringing their subordinates on the floor of the workroom. Blueprint. (Courtesy of Johnson Wax)

Fig. 44. Section of Administration Building. Blueprint. (Courtesy of Johnson Wax)

Fig. 45. Lobby viewed from Great Workroom, 1939. Visible in the foreground is the back of the reception desk and telephone switchboard, with the narrow mezzanine bridge above it. The two rectangles on the side of the bridge are supply vents from the air-conditioning plenum, which fills the lower portion of the bridge. Sound-absorbent cork is placed on its underside, and joints are concealed behind metal strips. Two strips of glass tubing on the ceiling, at the upper right, conceal the artificial lighting sources. (Courtesy of Johnson Wax)

Fig. 46. Apprentice Hulda Drake constructing model of Administration Building, 1936. (Photo by Edmund Teske)

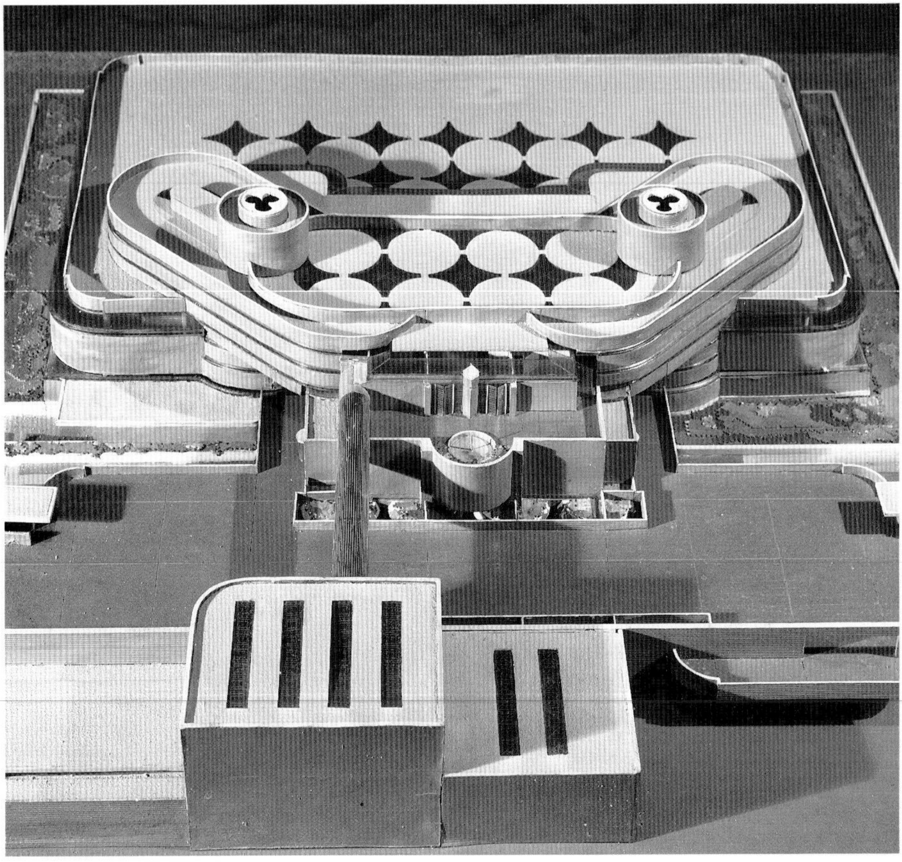

Fig. 47. Frank Lloyd Wright's model of Administration Building. (Courtesy of Johnson Wax)

With these design revisions, Wright clarified the building's internal hierarchy to such a degree that the scheme became *architecture parlante*, a three-dimensional flow chart of the company's personnel relationships. Johnson's office jutted forward from the main mass of the building at the top and center. In two wings on either side were the offices of the executives of the company's two divisions: advertising and public relations, and operations. At the tips of the wings, framing Johnson's office, were the offices of the heads of the two divisions, Ramsey and Connolly. Behind Johnson and between the two wings was the conference room. Isolated from the rest of the employees, executives on the penthouse level could nonetheless view the Great Workroom from the reception well. Middle-level managers could be located on the mezzanine ringing their subordinates on the floor of the workroom, or in glazed offices beneath the mezzanine.

Howe recalls the inception of the mezzanine: the company required noisy duplicating machinery in a central location. Wright placed it against the rear, south wall of the Great Workroom and enclosed it beneath a low ceiling, intending that the space over the ceiling—a mezzanine—could be used for storage or additional office space. However, it was suggested that the mezzanine might continue around the room, creating extra office space that might be needed later on. According to Howe, Wright preferred a discontinuous mezzanine, to allow the tall screen wall to be more clearly expressed, but it was not of major importance to him. In the revised plans the mezzanine is one continuous surface (compare figs. 38 and 43).

In another modification, the mezzanine bridge connecting the stair tower was narrowed. Earlier Wright had proposed a bridge wide enough to contain a pipe organ. Suspending an organist above the Great Workroom, to perform for productions in the theater and employees below, may have appealed to Wright's theatrical sense and emphasized his ecclesiastic vision of the building. Johnson, however, vetoed the pipe organ, although he liked the one he saw in the Larkin Building. In the mezzanine plan, Wright removed the organ and narrowed the bridge to a mere three feet six inches. Extremely narrow, and with a parapet only two feet high, the bridge inspires acrophobia in some users, but as a spatial device it is breathtakingly effective, magnifying the exhilarating impact the lobby and Great Workroom have on their viewers (fig. 45).

In the final response, Wright's plans included Johnson's requested squash court, to the north of the carport, with a maintenance garage beneath it. An enclosed bridge connecting the squash court to the executive offices is visible in the penthouse plan and section (see figs. 42 and 44). Only design refinements and small programmatic alterations distinguish this proposal from the design of the built work.

Johnson and Wright also discussed including a tower in the complex, although they did not decide what the tower should contain. Johnson could not convince his board that a tower was worth the cost so Wright let the idea go for seven years.[14] Howe verified this, recalling that when he drew a smokestack in the perspective drawing (see fig. 39) Wright told him that they really should include a tower in the drawing.[15]

At the end of August Wright guided three of his apprentices, Blaine and Hulda Drake, and Eugene Masselink, in the construction of a large, detailed model of the Administration Building that could be separated into two halves, allowing one to peer into a miniature Great Workroom. Although he originally inquired whether Wright would make one, Johnson hesitated over paying the additional expense for a model, writing, "Never mind about the model. . . . " But Wright wrote back, ". . . we will mind about the model." Apparently it was valuable to him for refining his design of the buildings: Edmund Teske, photographer at Taliesin in the late 1930s, recalls Wright entered the room as the Drakes were completing the model. Referring to the shape of the squash court, he said, "Let's just change this." With a curving gesture of his hand he indicated that one of the corners of the cubelike squash court was to be rounded.[16] This detail is visible in the center foreground of figure 47.

In their correspondence, by mid-August Johnson and Wright were concerned primarily with minor accommodations of the design to programmatic requirements, working out the building's heating and air-conditioning systems, and selecting materials and suppliers. Wiltscheck and Johnson visited a brick factory near Racine to locate a source for the gray-green Racine brick Wright and Ramsey had discussed in their first meeting. On August 17, Johnson wrote, "[This factory] would be out of the question as the source of our brick supply. Their production is very small, and the color does not run uniform." Wiltscheck sent Wright samples of bricks from several other midwestern firms over the following two weeks; Wright selected one made by the Streator Brick Company in Streator, Illinois. With a hard, smooth finish, it had a maroon-orange tint that Wright dubbed Cherokee red. He used the color so often in his buildings during the next two decades that it came to be associated with him.

In his autobiography, Wright recounts that while he was in Japan overseeing construction of the Imperial Hotel, one room of his dinner host's otherwise chilly home was warm. His host explained to Wright that the room was heated in a traditional Korean manner: air heated by a small sunken fire was vented through ducts beneath the floor, warming the room. Wright was taken by the idea: it eliminated radiators and allowed one to feel comfortable in an ambient temperature lower than in a convection-heated space. He tested the system, using electrically heated elements in the bathroom of the Imperial Hotel, and was pleased with the result. He resolved to use the system on a larger scale, and years later the Johnson commission gave him the opportunity.

His intention in Racine was to lay drain tile on the gravel bed beneath the Great Workroom floor, which would be composed of plywood over a concrete slab. The ducts would be connected to a boiler, and steam forced through them would warm the floors. Johnson was hesitant, and wrote to Wright, "I do not understand how heating through the floors is going to work out. If the floors get too hot the girls with their thin leather soles will be uncomfortable; if the temperature outside drops fifteen to twenty degrees in a short time, it would take quite a while to heat the main office building through the floors."[17] In response, Wright wrote:

> The effect of such heating as I have observed it in the orient is more that of "climate" than heating. You make a natural climate instead of an artificial condition. While there is yet no data on the subject we will find out just what will be necessary by experiment, and provide ways of speeding up the heating otherwise, to be used in emergency to make us safe enough.
>
> Changes in temperature outside (if we do our building properly) will hardly affect the air of the interior room very much as all air introduced would be checked and lifted in temperature at the intakes by direct contact with radiation. And there is no exposed glass surface. The floor cooled in summer would have the same effect in summer as the reverse in winter.[18]

Johnson and Ramsey remained unconvinced, and asked Wright to work out the idea in more detail and obtain the endorsement of a heating company. Also, they feared that the floor heat would loosen the glue in the plywood, and they advocated newly available rubber tiles as flooring. After several exchanges Wright grudgingly acquiesced:

> Concerning the floor as a heating surface: the temperature to which the floor need be raised would be no more than blood-heat and have no appreciable effect upon good glue or materials. . . . When I spoke of plywood I had in mind the new resin-glue which enables the laminations to be welded together with the result that the plywood is stronger than any solid wood would ever be and permanently so. . . . We could then have any width of surface or flower of grain we wanted. These fine extensions of quality-surfaces are modern just as rubber tile is modern. But rubber tile is all right too for that matter.[19]

Wright's plans to air-condition the building were more conventional. The two nostrils on either side of the lobby would rise a story above the penthouse roof where they would draw air cleaner than that on street level of the industrial area. The fans, compressors, and filters would be located at the base of the nostrils, and plenums within the mezzanine floor would spread the conditioned air through the Great Workroom. The use of integral plenums would almost eliminate the need to use sheet metal in the building. Ceiling ducts would circulate the air through the penthouse level.

Wright and Ramsey contacted air-conditioning and heating companies to solicit reactions to Wright's proposals. On September 9 Ramsey cabled the Carrier Engineering Corporation: "Planning new office building and architect Frank Lloyd Wright has very interesting but decidedly different heating ventilating idea. Want opinion from practical expert but one with enough imagination not to condemn plan because unusual and to advise sincerely even if does not call for standard Carrier equipment." The Carrier engineers proved open to Wright's ideas, although the York Company later received the contract.

Countless programmatic, structural, material, and design decisions remained to be made, but by locating the column grid, exterior wall, and the small basement, which connected to the Johnson factory buildings across the street through a tunnel, Wright was ready to begin construction just thirty days after this first meeting with his client. On August 24 he wrote to Johnson, "I can give Wiltscheck enough data to enable him to put in the foundations of the building right away." Wright's projected timetables on the job were highly optimistic, but site preparation did begin one month later.

Providing Wiltscheck with the drawings he needed was to prove a struggle throughout the many months of construction, but the job began unusually quickly. Wiltscheck began making test borings of the site at the end of August and sent Wright a soil survey on September 3. He noted, ". . . there is about a two feet layer of sandy clay under the top soil, sloping toward Lake Michigan. Below this is a blue clay quite suitable for the foundation."

Official company approval necessary for construction to begin had to wait for the September 15 board meeting at which Wright and Johnson were to submit their proposal. There had been a controversy among the board members as to whether it was wise to build a new office building in the middle of the Depression. When Johnson hired Wright, there was further resistance, because, as Johnson already knew, Wright was a controversial figure, the subject of various unpleasant stories.

It is difficult today to know how much control the board had over the company. Johnson's family did hold the firm's stock. Two retired senior company executives claim that Johnson became fully involved in the company when he graduated from college, and that after his father died, the twenty-eight-year-old assumed active control of the firm. Committed though he was to the company and his employees' welfare, the firm was hardly his entire life. In 1936 the members of the board of the company may have debated his future degree of involvement with the firm, and that may have contributed to their hesitancy to approve his desire to hire the controversial Wright. Henrietta Louis recalls that the project was extremely important to him, perhaps because he was tired of living in the shadow of his father's successes and wanted to make his own mark.

Wright prepared a strong visual presentation for the board meeting, working with Howe and Tafel for more than a week as they drafted interior and exterior perspectives of the building (figs. 48 and 49). The meeting was successful. Strongly supporting each other, Wright and Johnson won the approval of the board, and construction was set to start almost immediately.

That night Wright told his wife that he had made a toast at the meeting, proclaiming that Johnson possessed a degree of understanding that few of his clients had.[20] Olgivanna Wright recalled that after every visit with Johnson, Wright would say with pleasure, "If only all of my clients were as enlightened as Hib Johnson is, I would have no trouble."[21] This statement may have been self-fulfilling. Wright

ig. 48. Exterior perspective of Administration Building. Ink on tracing paper. (Courtesy of the Frank Lloyd Wright Foundation)

Fig. 49. Interior perspective of Great Workroom. Ink on tracing paper. 36" × 11". (Courtesy of the Frank Lloyd Wright Foundation)

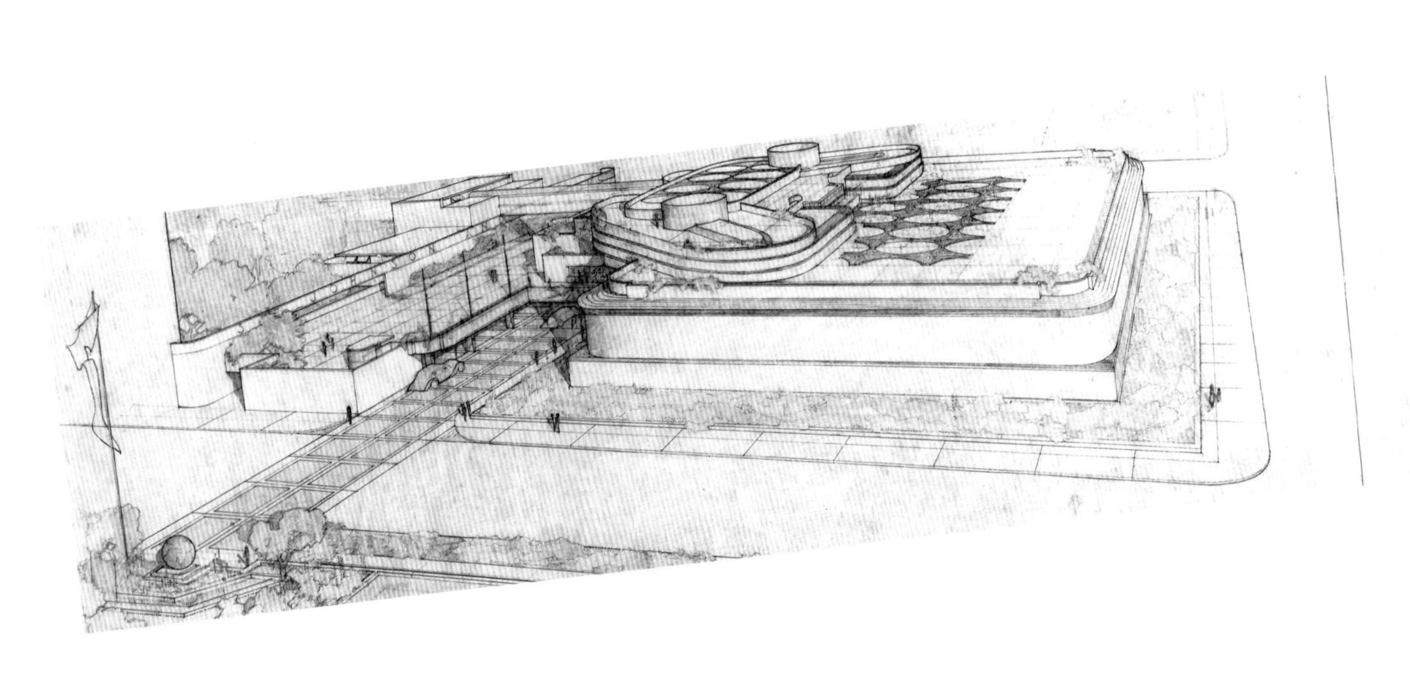

said about himself not long afterward, "Do you hypnotize your clients? Yes. Nothing so hypnotic as truth, so I hypnotize them with the truth."[22] However, he was more successful with Johnson than he was with most of his clients.

The relationship between Johnson and Wright grew to its closest at this time. Tafel and Lautner recall that Johnson began to spend weekends at Taliesin. Olgivanna Wright described:

The two men got along. There was some kind of tie that probably Hibbert Johnson couldn't even explain. But, they were close friends, and what can be better to a young man, as Mr. Johnson was at the time, than to accept this magnificent flow of ideas and never put up any . . . obstacle . . . ? Some special kind of closeness untied Mr. Wright completely so he could soar with the ideas exactly as he found [them, based] on what Mr. Johnson wanted. . . . They talked all the time about the building. It was wonderful to hear it because of the harmonious relationship. The younger man was completely absorbing the ideas which are so beyond . . . ordinary business status. [Johnson said] "I would like to have a beautiful building, I don't want just a business building." "Hibbert, you will get it, it is exactly what I had in mind—to give you a beautiful building so that whoever will work there will feel as though he were among the pine trees breathing fresh air and sunlight." "Oh! That is exactly what I want. I don't like the feeling of people cooped in without sun, without light. I am happy. You'll go [the] full length [with] your wish in your project."[23]

In a lecture delivered three years later, Wright may have had Johnson in mind when he said, "No man can build for another who does not believe in him, who does not believe in what he believes in, and who has not chosen him because of this faith, knowing what he can do. That is the nature of architect and client as I see it. When a man wants to build a building he seeks an interpreter, does he not? He seeks some man who has the technique to express that thing which he himself desires but cannot do. So should a man come to me for a building, he would be ready for me. It would be what I could do, that he wanted."[24]

CHAPTER 4

CONSTRUCTION BEGINS

Fig. 50. Exterior wall under construction, 1937, showing two rows of bricks, cork insulation, and reinforcing bars. (Courtesy of Johnson Wax)

Under Wright's direction the apprentices began to prepare working drawings at the end of August of 1936 and drafted a set of eighteen or twenty drawings—very few for a 54,000-square-foot building, because Wright wanted the set to convey the underlying simplicity of the building's concept. Floor plans, two pages of column details, and a single typical partial section were sufficient to explain most of the Great Workroom. The dimensions of the plan were based on the twenty-foot column grid, and four- or five-foot divisions, and most heights were determined by the three-and-one-half-inch height of a brick course.

Wright intended all walls to be of brick on both sides, except for those that were to transmit light or to be removable. To him the issue was more than one of superficial aesthetics. He wrote, "The exterior enclosing wall material appears inside wherever it is sensible for it to do so in order to make the structure as monolithic as possible."[1] Howe recalls, "That's part of what he called being a thoroughbred. If a [building] was brick it was entirely brick."

Johnson, however, had not appreciated the use of brick throughout the interior of Wright's Larkin Building. The walls of the Larkin building were massive, orthogonal piers, dividing recessed horizontal bands—a powerful treatment. The brick walls Wright envisioned for the Johnson building were to be neutral curtain walls. Acting strictly to define space, they would not interact with the interior space as did the masonry piers of the Larkin Building. The elements in the Johnson building that would interact with space comparably to the Larkin piers were the highly refined concrete mushroom columns. Wright's use of masonry as an interior material would not be jarring. On September 3 he wrote to Johnson, "I wish we might let the brick show inside on the walls of the big room. Won't you give this some consideration?"

Undecided, on October 2 Ramsey wrote to Wright, "Visualizing a small office such as Easson's under the mezzanine, the rough brick wall with mortar raked out deeply seems a bit harsh and incongruous. . . . We appreciate your arguments on appearance of this wall, but please think of it down to small places like that one office, and give us your reaction as to whether it should be smoother throughout the interior, or specially covered in such offices (that might look 'spotty'), or what you think best." Wright's response is not recorded, but his desire for all brick walls prevailed.

Wes Peters and Mendel Glickman began working out the building's structural details by early September. Glickman, a structural engineer, and his family had stayed at Taliesin for several years exchanging his engineering knowledge for Wright's architectural knowledge, and Howe recalls he was one of the few engineers Wright respected. Peters had studied civil engineering before he came to Taliesin in 1932 and soon did most of the structural calculations for Wright's projects.

Electrical, mechanical and fabrication drawings, as well as hundreds of field and shop drawings were not yet begun, but the Johnson Company wanted to get the new building's foundation in before winter, when the ground would become frozen.

the state Industrial Commission had to approve Wright's plans and specifications. The commission was unwilling to give its approval to a design with foundations, walls, structural columns, heating, and ventilation that did not meet codes. Wright, however, refused to hold up construction for a permit. Mosher notes that Wright said if the state wanted to halt construction, "Let them call out the militia!" When Johnson returned to Racine, he and Wright made plans to confront the commission together.

Wright and Johnson met with a building inspector in Madison to file applications requesting code modifications on November 4. The inspector, C. J. Caddell, told them that they might proceed with construction until the commission had an opportunity to study the applications. Two weeks later, on November 17, the commission held a hearing in Madison to consider their requests. Again, Johnson accompanied Wright, who wrote in his autobiography that Johnson "stood up at the board meeting beside me and squarely told the commission that he wanted that building that way and he was damn well prepared to stand back of it to the hilt—no limit."

Four days later the commission informed Johnson of its decisions. One waiver request concerned fire exits from the building. There were no exits on the east, south or west sides of the building. Wright had convinced the commission members that the building would never catch fire, and they accepted his layout. The commission also accepted, with slight modification, Wright's design for the exterior walls.

Thirteen years earlier, Wright had designed a series of concrete-block buildings in California about which he wrote, "The walls would thus become thin but solid reinforced slabs and yield to any desire for form imaginable."[3] The California block system was intended to be fast and cheap to build and require no skilled labor, but it was a crude system. For the Johnson building, Wright devised a more sophisticated version. Double rows of bricks, specially designed by Wright, were laid either five or eight inches apart. Three-inch thick slabs of insulating cork were placed between the rows of bricks. Steel reinforcing rods were put in place, and the gaps between brick and cork filled with concrete. The interior profiles of the bricks were jagged, to bond firmly with the concrete (figs. 50 and 53). The mortar in the flush, vertical joints was to be tinted almost the same color as the bricks, while the continuous horizontal joints were to be left untinted and raked deeply, leaving shadows running parallel to the ground.

Wright intended that the jagged bricks would bond with the concrete forming a unified mass, which he described as "monolithic." The Industrial Commission, skeptical of the structural value of Wright's innovation, declared that it would accept the proposed construction, "providing substantial copper ties are furnished every sixth course in height with a sufficient spacing to insure proper rigidity."[4]

A more serious problem was the commission's refusal to accept Wright's request for changes in the allowable unit stresses in steel and concrete needed to build the extraordinarily slim mushroom columns, and it asked for copies of Glickman's structural calculations. In the meantime, though, it permitted construction to continue on nonstructural portions of the building.

Finally, the commission noted that Wright had never received an architectural license and that he would have to obtain one before the building would receive final approval. Former apprentice John Lautner recalls that Wright never bothered to get one because he did not respect the state board—nor any other architectural institution, proclaiming that they were doing nothing useful. Though Wright practiced intermittently in Wisconsin for five decades, the commission had never insisted on his registration before he began his first large, publicity-attracting building. Considering himself vastly more qualified than any member of the board, Wright humorously replied that he would take a public oral examination at the state capitol. Lautner remembers that the board, imagining a public tongue-lashing from the eloquent Wright, backed down.

Professional interest in the project was growing, and in November the editor of *Architectural Review,* a journal that had published occasional articles by Wright for many years, asked Wright for the privilege of publishing the new building. Connolly, wishing to obtain the maximum exposure for the Johnson Company, investigated the *Review* and its two competitors, *American Architect* and *Architectural Forum.* After learning that the *Forum* had the highest circulation and subscription price, and was considered the most forward looking of the three journals, he offered the story to *Forum* associate editor Cameron Mackenzie, who in a telegram promised to do the best job that paper and ink would permit.

Wright agreed to select the *Forum,* which in turn proposed to devote an entire issue to him. Fourteen months later, in January of 1938, the special issue, written and designed almost entirely by Wright, assisted by George Nelson, was released. Its title page featured an abstract elevation by Wright of the Johnson building, and inside, 13 of the 104 pages on Wright were devoted to the Johnson building, with drawings, photos of the model, construction photos, and text drawn largely from the release Wright had written in October of 1936. Surprisingly, only three publications devoted entirely to Wright's work had previously been published in the United States: the March 1908 issue of *Architectural Record,* and *The Disappearing City* and *An Autobiography,* both published by Wright in 1932. The copy of *Architectural Forum* enhanced the Johnson Company's image as a progressive firm, but the issue probably did more for Wright, announcing his renewed career to the nation.

One day, while overseeing construction on the building, Mosher was called before the company's board of directors. They and Johnson were worried that the building would not be identified, as Wright had not designed a sign for it. They informed Mosher that they wanted a neon sign on the front of the building reading, "S. C. Johnson & Company, Wax". Mosher was confident Wright would dismiss the suggestion, so he responded, "When this building is finished it is going to be such a contribution that you won't need any sign. After all, there's no sign on the Washington Monument!"[5] Wright did put the company's name on the building, in discreet letters mounted on the wall above the north end of the carport.

Mosher and Wiltscheck worked in a temporary office and drafting room in the former bar-and-grill-turned-squash-court across the street from the site. At the beginning of December the Streator Brick Company informed them that it was ready to send the first shipment of special bricks Wright had designed. However, the bricks were not needed until the foundation walls were complete, and those awaited additional details from Wright. Mosher recalls that Wright had been visiting the site two or three times a month, but in early December a cold he had contracted turned into a serious case of pneumonia.

Later that year a result of his illness was the founding of Taliesin West, in Arizona, in response to his doctor's recommendation that he seek a milder winter climate. More immediately though, the pneumonia prevented Wright from answering questions Mosher and Wiltscheck were accumulating. Work on the site slowed and, by the time of Wright's partial recovery in mid-January, construction had come to a halt. Then, however, Wright was able to guide his apprentices in the preparation of new detail and structural drawings, and in late January Wiltscheck continued pouring column footings, started the exterior walls, and began the brickwork around the nostrils.

The decision earlier to include a squash court connected by a bridge to the penthouses also cost the project dearly in time, as well as money and headaches. Some of the column footings had already been poured before the decision had been made, and the additional weight of the bridge and court meant that fourteen footings had to be torn out and enlarged. Wright had not designed the new elements sufficiently before his illness for Peters to calculate their weight—and the corresponding sizes of the new footings. Delaying the footings held up additional work. On February 25, Wiltscheck wrote to Ramsey, "Mr. Wright's prolonged illness brought about an unavoidable delay. Now, if he is able to work again it would be advisable that the

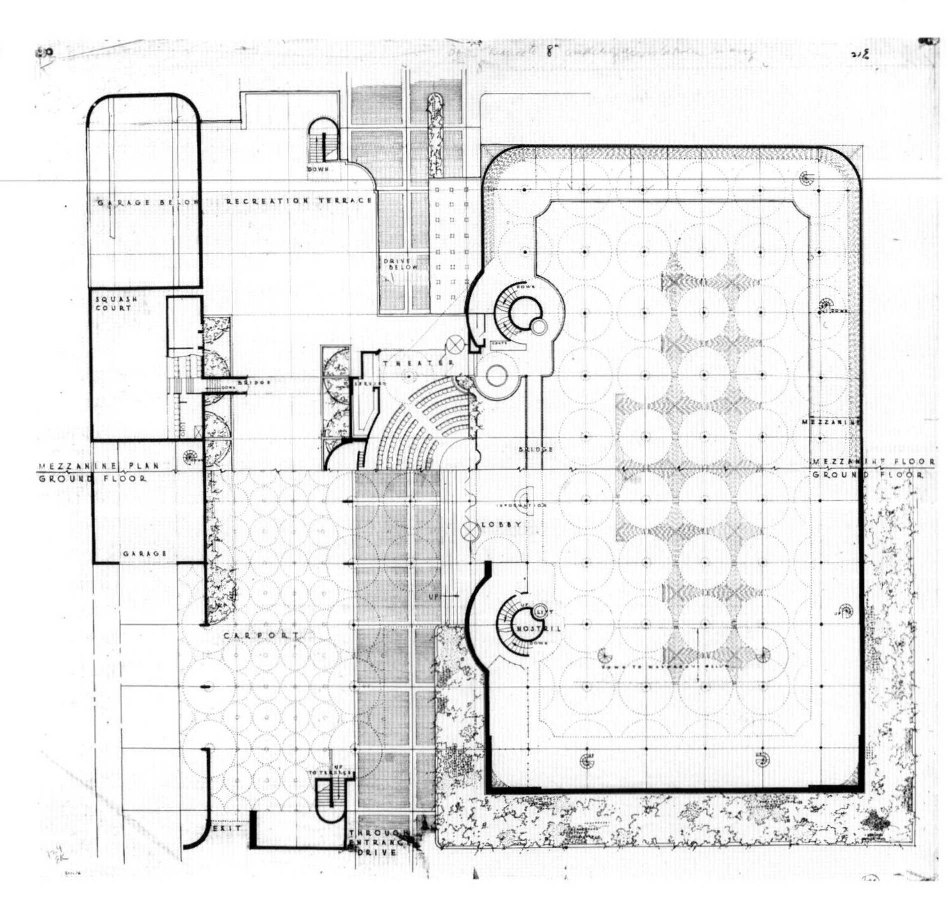

Fig. 54. Split plan of ground and mezzanine floors of Administration Building. Ink on tracing paper. (Courtesy of the Frank Lloyd Wright Foundation)

three of us sit down together to discuss plans for better progress of the work. . . . Let us bear in mind that we have now been operating nearly six months and we haven't even completed the foundations."

Meanwhile, cracks began to appear in the second-floor cantilevers of Fallingwater, and Tafel was ordered to return to Spring Green. Wright sent Mosher back to Pennsylvania to take his place, and consequently, in late January Tafel was dispatched to supervise the job in Racine. He spent much of the next two years serving as the Johnson project's "clerk of the works," making needed drawings on the spot, and sleeping on a cot in the back of the temporary construction office. Howe recalls that he also joined him eagerly a few times when Tafel had too many drawings to do. By that time Howe was in charge of the drafting room in Spring Green. The late 1930s were a busy time for the Taliesin draftsmen as Wright worked on nearly forty commissions—primarily Usonian houses.[6] Occasionally, Tafel drove to Taliesin for short visits when he needed detailed instructions from Wright to solve construction snags. Several times when problems arose and Wright was in Arizona during the winters of 1937–38 and 1938–39 Johnson paid to fly Tafel to Phoenix to clear them up.

The Johnson company bought the odd lot to the immediate northwest of the Administration building site on January 22, 1937. Wright had urged Ramsey to purchase the parcel since Ramsey had informed him of its possible availability three months before. The company had purchased the lot to the east of the new parcel in November to provide room for the squash court and a vehicle-waxing station, and Ramsey wished to place a garage large enough to repair trucks on the new northwest lot. However, the narrow residential lot could fit a garage only thirty-seven feet wide. Ramsey considered this too small for large trucks, so he proposed encroaching upon the north ten feet of the carport, which he felt was too extravagant.

Wright was not pleased with the suggestion. He wrote Ramsey: "Of course the parking area is a luxury—and an extended entrance feature. It would be a pity to find our wish to make a generous architectural interior-entrance landing us in a garage? . . . A carport is spacious and may have, in our case—should have—style. A garage—well, a garage is something else again?"[7] Wright explained his reasoning in more detail to Ben Wiltscheck later that week when Wiltscheck visited Taliesin. On January 29, Ramsey responded, "Ben tells me that you do not particularly like our suggestion about the garage, for architectural reasons. Before we settle this one way or the other, suppose you study the problem from our angle in an attempt to see if our practical consideration cannot be reconciled with the architectural principles. And I, at the same time, will try to visualize the architectural side as far as I can—I think I understand vaguely what you mean from Ben's explanation, but having bought the lot for the definite purpose of the garage my first reaction is that it is 'wasted' if we do not carry through for that purpose. Put yourself in my place and see if you can work out a scheme that will satisfy both of us."

Wright replied the next day:

I didn't realize that the extra lot depended upon building a garage there. We needed the lot badly to complete the back wall of our building group and to free our entrance from too close proximity of the incongruous. In fact we had to have it. I should like to see nothing there but a mass of tall green trees.

The greenery would add importance and beauty to our main issue: the new building—and be worth more than the lot cost by a good deal.

A truck garage with its inevitable noise and gaping front right next door to our stylish entrance-way could possibly be managed but isn't good—is it?

There is a lot of ground across the street for that slightly terrible purpose? However, think it over, bearing in mind that we don't want to be penny wise and pound foolish just yet. That "wisdom" has ruined more fine things than any kind of human ignorance, I know.

Two weeks later Wright met with Johnson in Racine, and the two men reached a compromise. The new lot would contain a narrow garage, and the existing carport would not be altered. By cantilevering a portion of the carport deck over the new driveway, Wright contrapuntally reasserted the circular geometry of the column at an end of the site which was previously dominated by the orthogonal geometry of the twenty-foot grid. The west edge of the deck was semicircular, reflecting the petal of the column below it. This proved to be the last substantial alteration to the plans of the Administration Building (fig. 54; see also fig. 47).

During the dispute over the garage, as well as during several heated exchanges over the building's budget and construction timetable, Ramsey displayed frequent irritation and occasional anger at Wright. He emerges as a deeply perceptive and appreciative client, however, and in a letter to Wright of January 29 he wrote, "I find myself just as enthusiastic as the day I saw the first sketches of the proposed building. I suppose I will continue to argue like the devil about various details but the underlying reason for such arguments is really pride in the building. You see, some day when it is finished I have a delightful vision of busting some carping critic in the nose with the joyful exclamation 'You're nuts, our Frank Lloyd Wright not only built the best looking office building in the world but it's the most workable and practical, and I know it.' "

CHAPTER 5

INNOVATIONS: COLUMNS AND GLASS TUBING

Fig. 55. Lobby of Administration Building. (Courtesy of Johnson Wax)

In one of his early conversations with Herbert Johnson, Wright had promised to give him a beautiful building in which a person could "feel as though he were among pine trees breathing fresh air and sunlight." In the Administration Building Wright created a private, air-conditioned working area nestled within a man-made forest, and though he screened out the surrounding environment, one element of the universe outside entered his forest—light, which poured in, bathing every surface and silhouetting the columns above. So rich that it appeared to have substance, the light seemed to be the matter of which the great room was made.

This quality of light, enveloping the columns, lends a greater reality to the enclosed space. The columns generate the space; the light makes it tangible. Space, the stuff of architecture, is nowhere more available to human experience than it is in this building. Wright's use of the columns, both technically and spatially, was a major innovation in twentieth-century building.

In the Great Workroom and the lobby the columns virtually are the ceiling. Discrete round slabs rest on each column, and the space between adjacent columns is open to the sky, filled only with a network of glass tubing (figs. 55, 56, 60).

Wright called the columns "dendriform"—tree-shaped—and he borrowed from botany to name three of their four segments: stem, petal, and calyx (fig. 57). The base of each column is a seven-inch-high, three-ribbed shoe, which he called a crow's foot. On it rests the shaft, or stem, nine inches wide at the bottom and widening two and a half degrees from the vertical axis. The taller columns are mostly hollow, the walls being only three and a half inches thick. Capping the stem is a wider hollow, ringed band, which Wright referred to as a calyx.

On the calyx sits a twelve-and-a-half-inch-thick hollow pad Wright called a petal. Two radial concrete rings and continuous concrete struts run through it. Both stem and calyx are reinforced with expanded steel mesh, and the petal is reinforced with both mesh and bars.

A slab rests on each petal of the twenty-one-foot Great Workroom columns and the thirty-foot-eleven-and-a-half-inch lobby columns. Each slab is circular, the same diameter as the petal beneath it.

The material of the columns—reinforced concrete—was used masterfully by builders in ancient Rome, where it was reinforced with iron, but knowledge of the medium was lost during the Middle Ages. Experimentation began again in nineteenth-century France, and in the 1880s engineers used reinforced concrete in bridge abutments and other nonarchitectural applications. As steel became widely available it replaced the weaker iron, and in 1908 C. A. P. Turner in Chicago and Robert Maillart in Switzerland independently pioneered similar methods of designing buildings from steel-reinforced concrete. Cast-concrete floor slabs were supported by concrete posts, which came to be known as mushroom columns because they flared outward at the top to reduce shearing stresses that would otherwise tend to cause them to punch through the slabs.

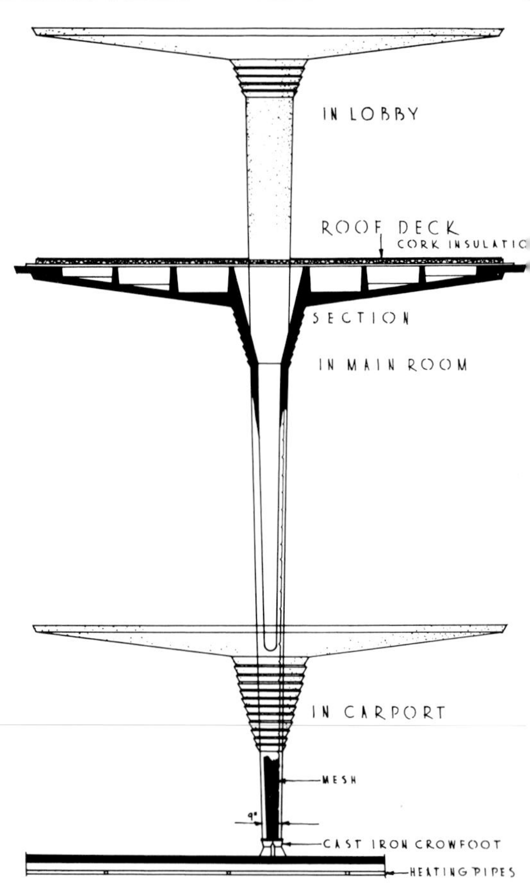
IN LOBBY
ROOF DECK
CORK INSULATIO
SECTION
IN MAIN ROOM
IN CARPORT
MESH
9"
CAST IRON CROWFOOT
HEATING PIPES

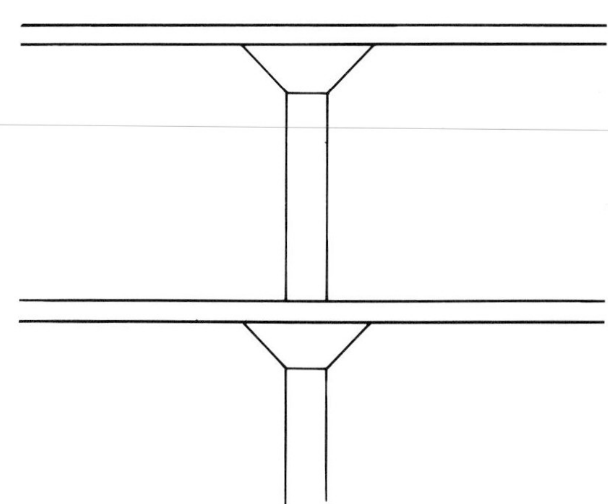

Fig. 56. Great Workroom, viewed from south mezzanine, circa 1959. (Courtesy of Johnson Wax)

Fig. 57. Presentation drawing of dendriform column. Ink on tracing paper. 13″ × 22″. (Courtesy of the Frank Lloyd Wright Foundation)

Fig. 58. A two-foot-thick reinforced concrete slab with domed coffers rests on the eight-foot-six-inch columns of the carport of the Administration Buiding. (Courtesy of Johnson Wax)

Fig. 59. Typical early twentieth-century mushroom column.

Fig. 60. *Overleaf*. Ceiling of Great Workroom, 1939. (Photo by Torkel Korling; courtesy of David Phillips).

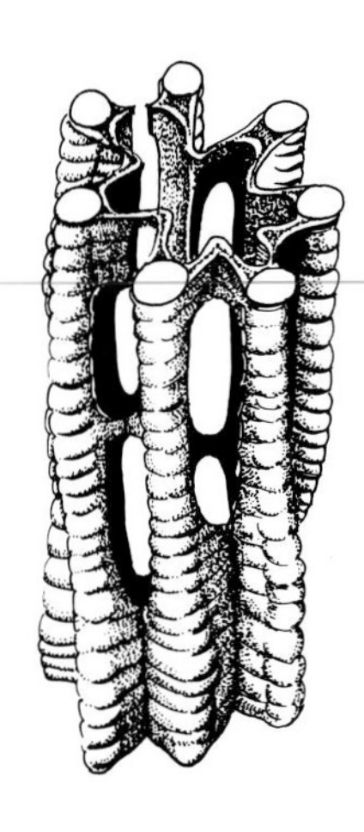

Fig. 61.

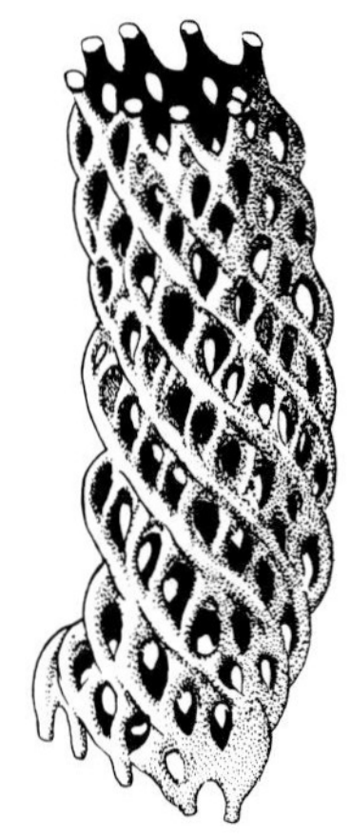

Fig. 62.

Concrete-slab and mushroom-column construction developed over the next thirty years, and as it became more sophisticated, engineers began to design columns that were increasingly efficient—thinner yet able to safely carry the design load. Simultaneously, designers such as Alvar Aalto, pursuing grace as well as structural integrity, used the columns as architectural elements, capable of elucidating a spatial reading or architectural idea.

These two developments reached their apex in the Johnson Wax design. The columns Wright created for the Administration Building are structurally more efficient than their predecessors. The partially hollow column stem and the two- to three-and-a-half inch thick hollow calyx and petal are so thin that they are virtually shell structures—though they were designed before that term was invented. In part, Wright was able to design such thin columnar elements by specifying unusually high-strength concrete: 4,000 psi in the column petal and calyx, and 6,000 psi in the shaft.

Wright achieved this strength by selecting a new early-strength cement manufactured by Marquette Portland Cement; by specifying the internal vibration, and also by using a mixing system known as Pumpcrete in which all the concrete was mixed in one large central hopper and then pumped to where it was needed. This discouraged aggregate from settling out and permitted close monitoring. Peters recalls that slump and water ratio tests were made on each batch of concrete and actual strengths as high as 7,000 psi were reached. The job required unusually stringent standards, and Wright, Tafel, and Peters had high praise for Ben Wiltscheck's careful work.

Wiltscheck asked Wright for detail drawings of the columns in final form on January 14, 1937 so that he could begin manufacturing the steel forms in which they would be poured. A month later he and Peters carefully checked the completed two sheets of structural drawings of the columns at Taliesin. Howe recalls that he drafted the sheets from sketches and calculations that Peters handed to him (fig. 63). As Howe was not a structural engineer, he did not understand what he was drawing, and he relied on Peters to check the sheets thoroughly.

Peters remembers that Wright intuitively drew the profiles of the columns and specified their dimensions. Peters and Glickman slightly adjusted the thickness of the petals so that they could take the required punching shear; but the stems of the columns were built precisely as Wright had intuitively drawn them. The apocryphal story that the columns could not be analyzed by contemporary engineers has been belied by Peters. Although the columns were indeterminate structures, Peters explained that he and Glickman performed calculations necessary to satisfy themselves that the columns would support the required loads—which actually were quite low as most columns were required to support just 400 square feet of roof and snow.[1]

In analyzing the Johnson Wax columns Carl W. Condit writes in *American Building Art: The Twentieth Century*, "All the [circular slabs on the petals] are interconnected at the roof level by short beams, each slab in this way providing partial support for the one adjacent to it. The entire system is in effect a continuous multi-support rigid frame. The resulting absence of bending in the column makes possible the use of an extremely narrow, virtually hinged bearing at the column foot."[2]

The use of point support systems is unusual in Wright's work.[3] Wright used one in the Capital Journal project in which columns were a logical solution to the problem of supporting two-story apartments over the large hall. In its final design the penthouse extended over only a small portion of the Johnson Administration Building's Great Workroom, but the point support system borrowed from the Capital Journal project remained. It was a case of serendipity: the columns, largely freed of their structural raison d'être, became sculptural generators of space.

The columns remain one of the most remarkable structural designs in twentieth-century architecture. In their unprecedented structural and aesthetic success they

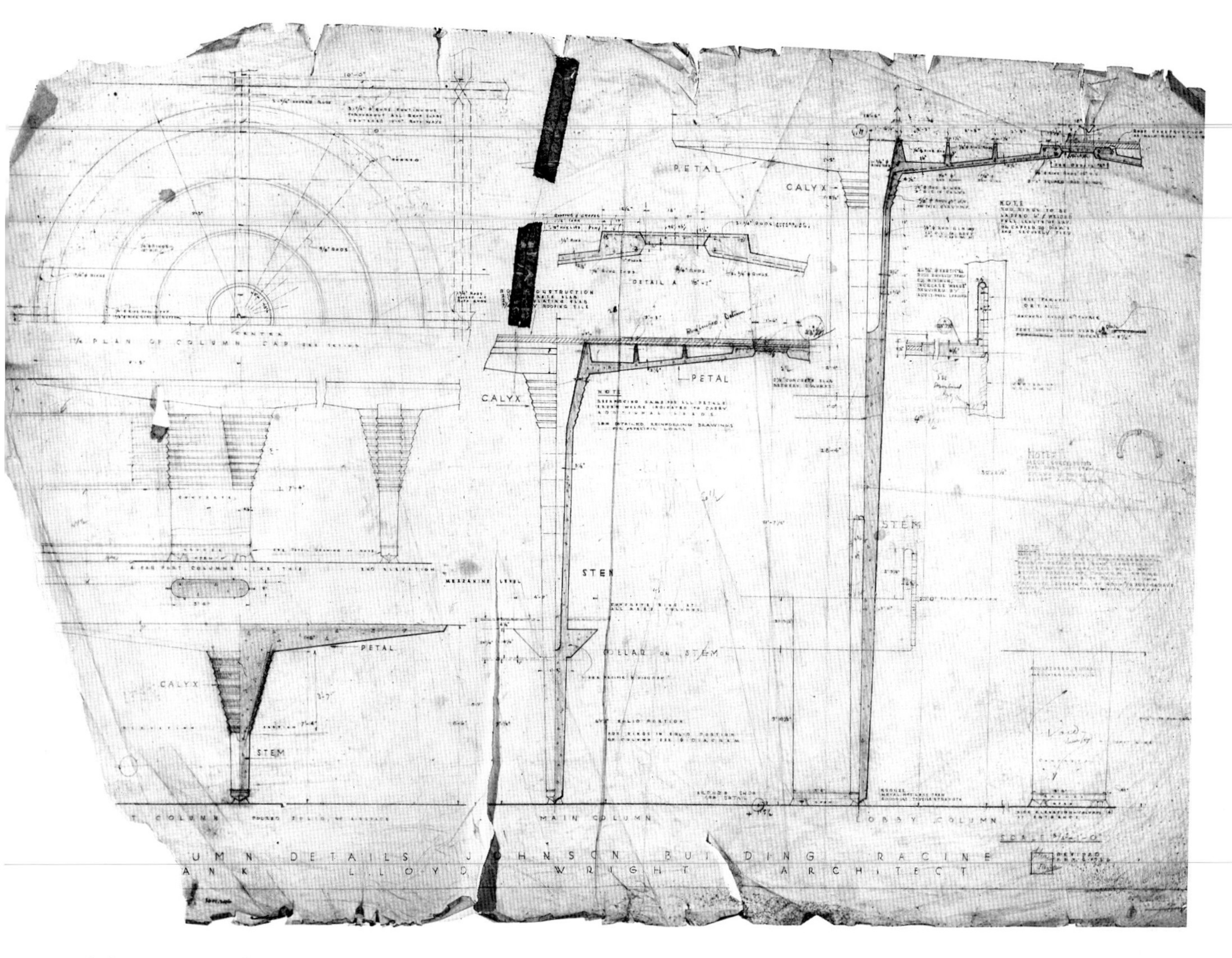

Fig. 61. Skeleton segment of saguaro or barrel cactus. The saguaro and the staghorn are two of the tallest plants in the Arizona desert, however, their trunks are supported by quite different skeletal structures. The saguaro has a thick, fleshy body supported by a ring of vertical wooden ribs, whereas the staghorn cholla is slimmer and has a more efficient skeleton—a perforated wooden cylinder that appears to be woven like a basket. (Drawing by Don Coles)

Fig. 62. Skeleton segment of staghorn cholla. (Drawing by Don Coles)

Fig. 63. Structural details of column. When Wright learned about expanded steel mesh he had a note added to this completed drawing (center, far right) to substitute mesh for rods. Pencil on tracing paper. 42″ × 29″. (Courtesy of the Frank Lloyd Wright Foundation)

Fig. 64. Scaffolding for test column's forms (rear center), 1937. Rows of reusable metal column forms are lined up to the left of the scaffolding, which is located in the center of the future carport. In the foreground, carpenters complete the bottom form for the column's petal. (Courtesy of Johnson Wax)

were the supreme example of Wright's dictum, "Form does not follow function. Rather, form and function are one."

Construction drawings for the columns were complete when a steel manufacturer's representative visiting Taliesin West described to Wright a new process whereby expanded steel mesh was made from cold rolled sheets, substantially increasing its elastic limit and yield point and permitting higher allowable stresses.[4] Peters recalls that Wright enthusiastically embraced the significance of the material. If it were substituted for reinforcing bars in the mushroom columns, it would bond more intimately with concrete, with the tensile strength of sinews, and would withstand stresses in two dimensions, rather than just one. By way of illustration Wright pointed to two cacti nearby the desert, a giant saguaro and a staghorn cholla (figs. 61 and 62). A concrete column reinforced with steel rods might be likened to the giant saguaro, but a column reinforced with a cylindrical basket of steel mesh resembled the staghorn—the natural structure Wright would follow in the Johnson Wax building. On the already completed column construction drawing Howe added the note "Mesh substituted for rods in stem, calyx and petal except [illegible]."

Wiltscheck had trouble getting the metal column bases cast accurately. Peters recalls Wright specified that they be made of bronze, then iron, and finally steel. But even the steel column bases were distorted after being cast and had to be milled six times at great cost before they were shaped precisely.

Although substantial money had been spent on the column bases and forms, the Wisconsin Industrial Commission continued to deny permission to build the columns, refusing to accept Peters and Glickman's calculations. The state code was based on the assumption that a column was situated at right angles to the load it was carrying. The curving profile of Wright's columns carried the stresses in an arc from the horizontal to the vertical plane. An example of the continuity he favored, they were almost perfectly efficient.

In earlier mushroom column design, capitals widening to seven or eight feet in diameter took the shear found at the top of columns. The columns themselves were typically two or three feet thick, reinforced to carry the negative moment of the slabs. But because Wright's columns tapered almost to a point at the bottom, there was virtually no moment at their base. The maximum moment was near the top where the column was thickest. The feet acted almost as joints, which would move the maximum moment high up the shaft. Thus, Peters recalls, Wright felt quite confident in reducing the diameter of the foot. However, according to state codes, twenty-one-foot-high concrete columns with a design load of six tons were required to be thirty inches thick. Wright's columns were to be only nine inches wide at their bases.

A contemporary article in *Business Week* reported that there were several fiery sessions between Wright and the commissioners. Wright attempted to explain anthropomorphically how the columns would hold up the roof by stretching out his arm horizontally and explaining how much more weight it could carry when held vertically. Wright used a similar analogy later when he told artist George McVicker that he got the idea for the columns from seeing a waiter carrying a tray on an upraised arm.[5] Finally, on March 18, Wright wrote to Ramsey, "The commission [sic] being unable to say 'yes' or 'no' have virtually thrown up their hands and allowed us to proceed. I suggested in the first place that we would make any reasonable tests for them at any time during construction. So, so far as we are concerned this is a proper capitulation on their part."

It was agreed that Wright might build one column and test-load it. If it carried twelve tons without failing, construction of the columns might proceed. In mid-May workmen erected scaffolding over a column footing on the construction site. Column stem and calyx were formed by the sectional steel forms, as were the petal rings and ribs, and the hollow core. The column petal slab was formed by sectional plywood gored panels supported by adjustable shores. Steel mesh was dropped into the form

Fig. 65. Wright (right), Johnson (center), and Wiltscheck (far left) watch as crane dumps loose sand on column, 1937. (Courtesy of Johnson Wax)

Fig. 66. Contractor Ben Wiltscheck climbs ladder to top of column to determine how much more sand can be added, 1937. (Courtesy of Johnson Wax)

Fig. 67. Wright, standing almost directly beneath fully loaded column, 1937. (Photo by Frank Scherschel; courtesy of the *Milwaukee Journal*)

of the shaft, and steel rings were placed in the petal. The concrete was poured on May 26. After the concrete had hardened, the scaffolding was removed and the forms stripped. Four cross-braced wooden beams were propped against the column to prevent it from tipping over.

The test was held on June 4, after the concrete had cured for just one week. A wooden platform was built on top of the petal and workmen hoisted by crane began placing sacks of sand in a ring on the platform. A building engineer and a building inspector from the state Industrial Commission, the Racine city building inspector, the city engineer, an engineer from the Marquette Cement Company, and representatives from the steel mesh manufacturer watched closely, and photographers from the local, state, and national press documented the test. Johnson, company employees, Wiltscheck, and Wright gathered, along with two carloads of apprentices Wright brought from Taliesin to view the performance.

As workmen loaded more and more sandbags on the column a crowd gradually gathered. Onlookers recall that Wright confidently explained the principles behind the column's strength to interested spectators, drawing sketches in a notebook to illustrate his points.

At twelve tons the state inspectors were satisfied. Wright, however, was not, and he continued the test. There was a break for lunch in the company recreation building, and the crowd grew so large that police roped off the site. Herbert Jacobs, a journalist covering the event, and himself a client of Wright, recorded some of the dialogue that day. At thirty tons, enjoying the drama, Wright directed the loading crew, "Keep piling."

Next, the crane deposited loose sand in the center of the ring of sandbags. When it became evident that the column might hold all of the sand that would fit on it, Wiltscheck climbed a ladder to the top of the column and examined the load. Deciding that a heavier material was needed, he ordered the crane operator to dump pig iron onto the column. Wright, still confident, stood almost directly beneath the column. Tafel remembers that Wright kicked it and hit it periodically with his cane (figs. 65–67).

By late afternoon there was no more room at the top of the column. Wright scrutinized the concrete shaft through binoculars, searching for cracks. His creation was carrying sixty tons, five times the load required by the state, and was only now displaying slight cracks at the calyx.

"Well, I guess that's enough. Pull the column down," Wright ordered as sunset approached.[6] The crane jerked out one of the timber braces. The column snapped cleanly at the calyx and fell. The impact was so great that a drainpipe ten feet underground was broken. The slender shaft of the column, however, remained intact.

Wright had called the steel mesh he had used the "bones and sinew" in a body of steel and concrete. With that test, Wright noted "new precedents for reinforced concrete construction were established. . . . This marks the end of rod reinforced columns."

Ironically, the test did not begin to duplicate the worst of the column's loading conditions, which would be borne by the six higher columns framing the lobby. Not only did they carry an additional floor, but also were loaded eccentrically. Even without this ultimate test, the representatives of the Industrial Commission were satisfied, if not embarrassed, and allowed construction to proceed.

With permission granted to erect the columns, it was necessary for Wright to choose the treatment of the glass forming the building's clerestories and skylights. The design of the Great Workroom, if not detailed properly, might result in the boxlike room, whose destruction Wright pursued throughout his career. He felt passionately that spaces confined by four walls and a ceiling compress the human spirit. But by supporting the roof of the Great Workroom on columns, the ceiling could be lifted well above the walls. Five-foot-wide clerestories circling the building

Fig. 68. Column petal falling, 1937. (Courtesy of Johnson Wax)

Fig. 69. Inspectors examine fallen shaft of column, surrounded by spectators, 1937. (Courtesy of Johnson Wax)

separated wall from ceiling, while a lower clerestory separated the mezzanine from the wall beneath it. Wright wrote, "[Until now] no one has looked through the box at the sky up there at the upper angle, have they? . . . [But] in the Johnson building you catch no sense of enclosure at any angle, top or sides. You are looking at the sky and feel the freedom of *space*."[7]

Although Wright wanted to flood the Great Workroom with sunlight, he refused to install plate glass in the clerestories because he did not want the users of his building to view the surrounding neighborhood. To accomplish this, he required a configuration of glass that was translucent, rather than transparent. In addition, the glass had to be capable of being angled to produce an irregular profile, and curved to accommodate the corners of the building, and it had to be composed of horizontal layers to reinforce the streamlined horizontality of the building (see fig. 70).

Fig. 70. Exterior view of west parapet of Great Workroom, showing clerestory before tubing is installed, 1938. An aluminum rack designed to support tubes is visible at right. (Courtesy of Johnson Wax)

It took well over a year of experimentation before Wright solved the complex glazing problem. On August 20, 1936 Wright asked Steuben Glass, Libbey-Owens-Ford, and the American Three-Way Luxfer Prism Company to send consultants to Taliesin. One of Wright's first ideas was to form the translucent clerestories with the Luxfer Company's glass blocks. These functioned as prisms, permitting sunlight to be thrown deep into a room. The Luxfer Company's response to his inquiry is not recorded, but there was no more interest in the company.

He also sent a drawing calling for glass blocks to Libbey-Owens-Ford (see fig. 71 for possible example), who forwarded the drawing to the Owens-Illinois Glass Company. Owens-Illinois sent Wright a drawing showing how its standard glass block could be used. Apparently, the company was not willing to produce a new block to Wright's specifications. Wright then requested DuPont's Plastics Department to send him samples of clear Pyralin sheets. At the end of September the samples arrived and Wright's apprentices cut them up and experimented with them, but pursued the Pyralin no further when Wright concluded that he wanted to use a fluted rather than a flat surface.

On September 7, a representative of Corning Glass came to Taliesin to discuss producing some form of extruded glass tubing. After the meeting Corning's engineers explored producing Wright's "special structural glass design" composed of large diameter tubing. On October 14 Corning representative E. J. Winship reported to Wright that the company could not offer any suggestions, and was at a loss to understand how Wright intended to accomplish such an installation. Corning, however, was eager to work further with him, so Wright made plans to visit Corning's plant on his next trip east. Wright's proposal was for a stack of three-inch diameter fluted tubing, sealed at each end, but on March 9, 1937 Winship wrote to Wright that such a device would be too expensive. He asked whether Wright would consider using plain three-inch-diameter tubes, and enclosed a sketch. Apparently, this was the origin of the detail Wright ultimately used in the Johnson building (fig. 73).

Wright continued to experiment with another possible solution, cast-glass panels. In April, however, Libbey-Owens-Ford wrote Wright that the panels would be prohibitively expensive if they were more than two feet long.

Tafel sent Corning a schedule of one- and two-inch-diameter glass tubes in May and the company began to estimate the cost of producing them. At this point Wright apparently ceased pursuing any other glass companies, perhaps because Corning showed itself to be interested in innovation and willing to invest in the experimentation Wright required. Also, Corning could provide him with Pyrex, a patented form of glass it had developed that would not discolor and that would resist extremes of temperature. Until this time Pyrex was used for test tubes and other chemical and industrial applications.

Winship sent a number of tubes to Taliesin and the apprentices constructed a mock-up of a clerestory band in June. Wright was out of the country at the time and Tafel wrote that the mock-up was "beyond description in effect." Wright wrote to Johnson, "[the tubes] are fine and the conclusive figure."

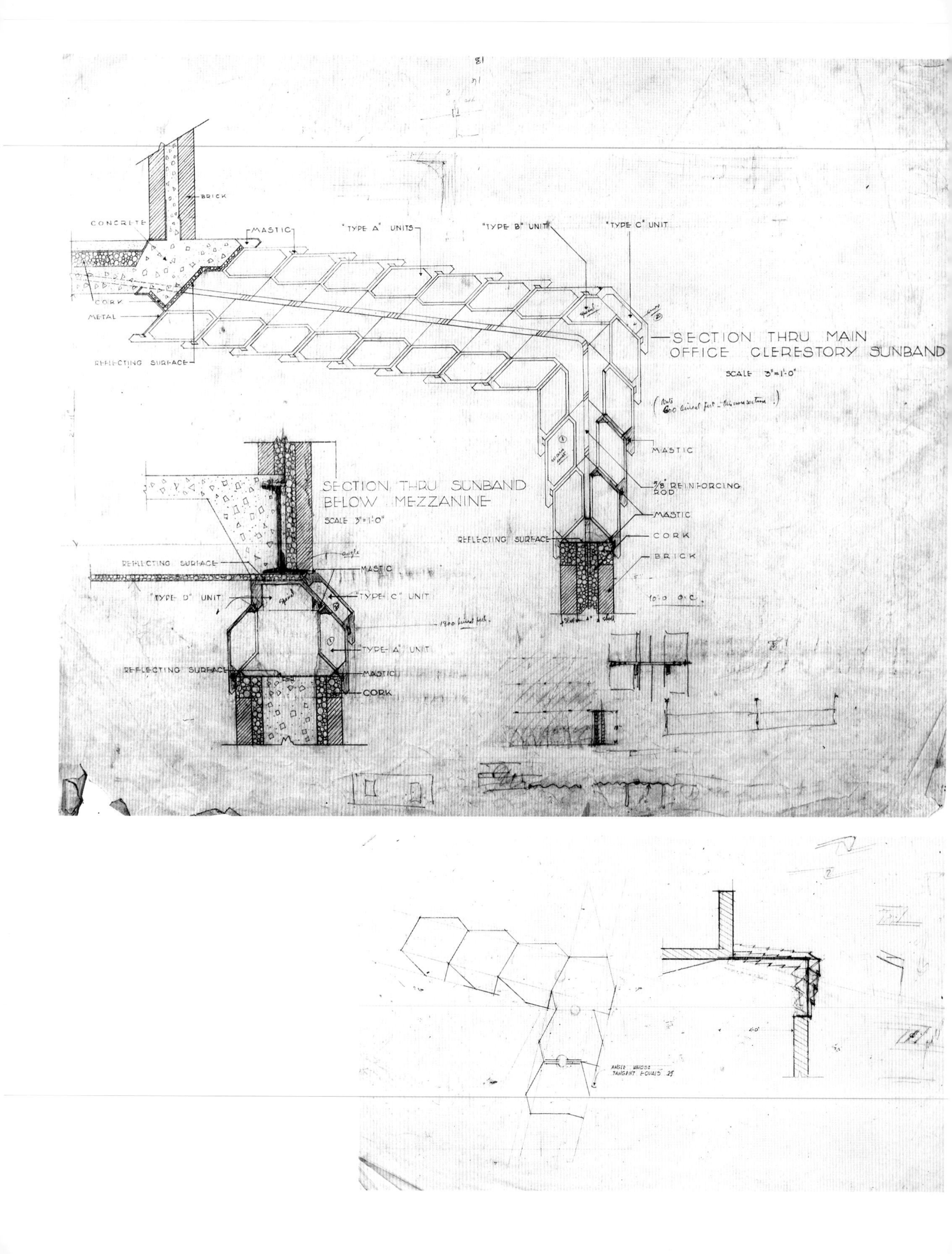
BRICK
CONCRETE
MASTIC
"TYPE A" UNITS
"TYPE B" UNIT
"TYPE C" UNIT
CORK
METAL
REFLECTING SURFACE
SECTION THRU MAIN OFFICE CLERESTORY SUNBAND
SCALE 3"=1'-0"
MASTIC
5/8" REINFORCING ROD
MASTIC
REFLECTING SURFACE
CORK
BRICK
10'-0" O.C.
SECTION THRU SUNBAND BELOW MEZZANINE
SCALE 3"=1'-0"
REFLECTING SURFACE
MASTIC
"TYPE D" UNIT
"TYPE C" UNIT
"TYPE A" UNIT
REFLECTING SURFACE
MASTIC
CORK
ANGLE WHOSE TANGENT EQUALS .25

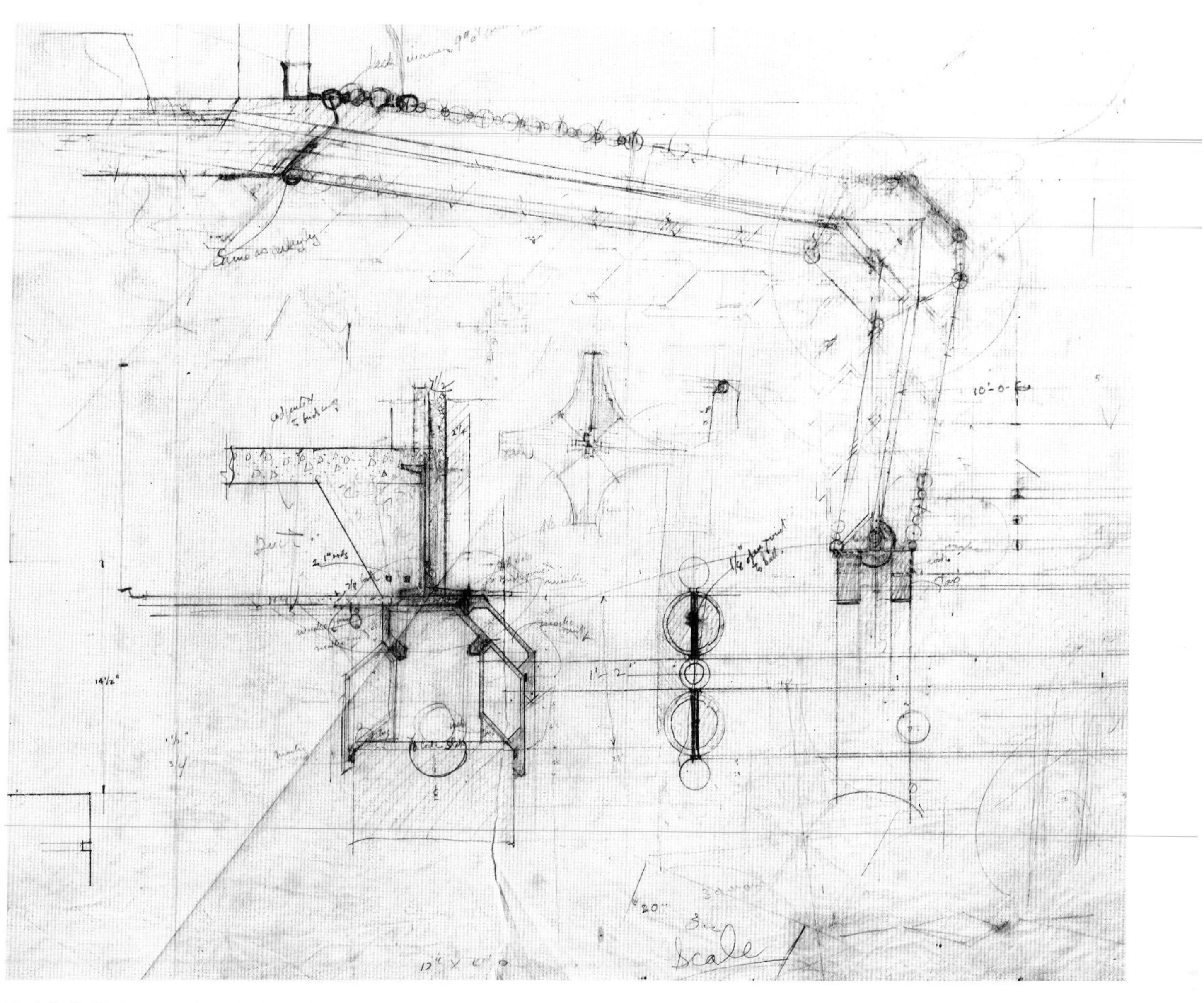

Fig. 71. Preliminary glazing detail sections using custom-shaped glass blocks, apparently anchored on caulked rods. Pencil on tracing paper. 42" × 33". (Courtesy of the Frank Lloyd Wright Foundation)

Fig. 72. Section through upper clerestory with preliminary glazing details composed of two or three rows of interlocking glass strips. Pencil on tracing paper. Detail of larger drawing. (Courtesy of the Frank Lloyd Wright Foundation)

Fig. 73. Sections of glass tubing details in clerestories. On this drawing prisms from an earlier glazing proposal were erased, and two stacks of glass tubes were drawn over them. Pencil on tracing paper. 40" × 34". (Courtesy of the Frank Lloyd Wright Foundation)

Because Corning was able to produce the tubes in curved segments, the clerestories could run smoothly around the curved corners of the building. Wrapping prisms around curves would have been complicated, and may be one reason why Wright settled on using the tubes. The tubes and the shadows in the gaps between them would appear as alternating horizontal light and dark bands. To Wright the horizontal line—parallel to the horizon—emphasized the intimate connection of his buildings with the earth.

Winship submitted an estimate of $36,000 to supply the tubing, and Wright budgeted that amount. However, in late February of 1938 Winship wrote to Wright that Corning was revising its bid to $55,000 due to an error of 20,000 square feet of glass that it had discovered in its calculations. Furious, Wright drove to Corning where he convinced the president of the company to lower his price in recognition of the publicity that the job would bring. Wright was a most persuasive speaker; Corning dropped its bid back to $36,000.

To support the tubes Wright designed aluminum "racks"—braces with scalloped profiles shaped to rest against the tubes. A tight loop of wire would bind each tube a millimeter from the racks, and mastic would seal the horizontal joint between the tubes. Butt joints would be sealed by inserting slightly smaller tubes snugly in the joint. The tubes were to be installed in four-foot lengths.

Wright had not yet decided how to connect the butt joints when Corning sent its first shipment of tubes to Racine in the spring of 1938, and workmen erected a single four-foot long section in the clerestory gap between the wall and roof of the Great Workroom. Ramsey studied the sample section and cabled Wright in Spring Green on April 29: "Section glass tubing set up on upper level throws absolutely intolerable flash into eyes at any position in interior main office. Needs your best thought and immediate attention please."

Under any circumstances the cornice is a dangerous location at which to introduce direct sunlight into a room, as light streams in at an angle that can produce an irritating glare. Perhaps one reason why Wright experimented with glass blocks and tubes was to diffuse the glare. As Ramsey discovered from the sample section, however, occasionally the tubes actually focused the sunlight, producing flashes of bright light in the room. It was a problem that was not apparent until the glass was erected—an unanticipated property of the newly invented detail—and it was a problem that Wright was unable to eliminate.

Early in May the U.S. Patent Office awarded Wright seven patents on the Pyrex details, but tube installation was delayed through June and July when the Aluminum Company of America reported that it was having difficulties casting the tube racks and was discarding one out of every four it made. Also, Corning encountered delays making couplers, the two-inch long narrow tubes that were to hold adjoining tubes together at butt joints. Wright, meanwhile, studied more than a dozen brands of mastic sent to him by Wiltscheck, pondering which one to caulk the tubes with. Eventually, he chose a mastic made by Vulcanite that he had used successfully for decades.

A jurisdiction squabble erupted between the construction unions, further delaying the installation of the tubes. Initially, lower-paid unskilled laborers installed the tubes. Carpenters, glaziers, masons, and even plumbers who argued that the tubes were originally pipes,[8] all claimed that they should perform the job. The dispute was settled when the unions agreed to share the installation of the remaining tubes.

That year Wright lost his battle to avoid installing artificial lighting in the building. When Ramsey had asked him two years earlier how employees would be able to work when the sun was not out, Wright suggested that they rely on desk lamps. Eventually, Ramsey prevailed, and Wright agreed to design an artificial lighting system for the building consisting of Lumiline bulbs placed between the double layers of tubes in the clerestories and skylights, concealing the artificial lights and duplicating the effect of natural lighting.

Fig. 74. Pyrex tubes in upper clerestory, wired to aluminum racks. This 1939 photograph was taken during construction on the Administration Building between the two inner rows of tubes. (Courtesy of Johnson Wax)

Fig. 75. *Overleaf*. Construction photograph of Administration Building, October 1937. The masonry work on the walls enclosing the Great Workroom are complete and three of the columns have been poured, as workmen insert the forms for eleven more. The ceiling of the carport has also been poured. (Courtesy of Johnson Wax)

Fig. 74. Pyrex tubes in upper clerestory, wired to aluminum racks. This 1939 photograph was taken during construction on the Administration Building between the two inner rows of tubes. (Courtesy of Johnson Wax)

Fig. 75. *Overleaf.* Construction photograph of Administration Building, October 1937. The masonry work on the walls enclosing the Great Workroom are complete and three of the columns have been poured, as workmen insert the forms for eleven more. The ceiling of the carport has also been poured. (Courtesy of Johnson Wax)

CHAPTER 6

CONCLUDING CONSTRUCTION

Fig. 76. Construction photograph, published in *Architectural Forum*, January 1938. A collar cast integrally with the column supports the cantilevered mezzanine. Behind the column is one of the exterior screen walls. (Courtesy of Johnson Wax)

Construction on the Administration Building proceeded very slowly in 1937, partly because Wright's lingering case of pneumonia left him unable to personally supervise construction. But another cause of delays was Wright's method of design. If every part of the building were to contribute to the unity of the whole, stock details would not suffice. Consequently, Wright was forced to invent almost every construction detail. He wrote to Ramsey, "I have already voluntarily thrown away more drawings than would build this building in the effort to get everything according to my best thoughts as that thought grows up with the building."

As Wright revised details, Wiltscheck and his men—unable to work without the drawings—frequently stood idle. But many times the drawings that satisfied Wright bewildered Wiltscheck. Continually faced with details that were not fully worked out, the crew's pace often slowed to a crawl. Wiltscheck, under increasing pressure as construction fell ever further behind schedule, complained in self-defense to Ramsey about Wright's drawings. On April 7, expressing his strain, Ramsey wrote to Wright, "I hope some miracles happen in the way of elevators, lighting, heating, etc.... Genius, one bird said, consists mainly in the capacity for taking infinite pains. Because our troubles seem to be due mainly to the lack of attention to infinite details, may I revise quotation to 'you furnish the genius, I get the pains.' " Wright responded, "Your 'crab' received—don't be too hard on the boys, and me! Will you? They do pretty damned well with a pretty difficult task—you would say if you knew all. You see the building grows as it is built and is none too easy, therefore, to keep up with always."[1]

An article on the Administration Building published in the *Engineering News-Record* observed, "Construction has been slow, principally because of the manner in which the architect works; his creative effort is continuous until the structure is complete. Thus the contractor started work with only preliminary plans on hand, and many details are worked out as they are reached. Then, too, many changes are made, all for the better, as the work progresses. The owner is in no hurry for the building, being situated in old but comfortable quarters that have served for many years. The owner's attitude—most unusual—is far from that of impatience, but rather is one of delight in watching a new architectural conception evolve into reality."[2]

After the column test in June, and with eighty columns to pour, the pace of construction picked up. Laying the masonry also went relatively smoothly after Wright approved a trial section erected by masons. In mid-June Johnson cabled Wright, in Moscow, "Building progresses well. Tafel making minor decisions like master and Wiltscheck has no major troubles . . . "

Good news was received on July 17, when the Wisconsin Industrial Commission approved another petition for the Johnson building, allowing the heating and ventilating system to supply three air changes per hour in the Great Workroom instead of the required six. Wright estimated that the waiver would save $30,000. High labor costs, however, were throwing Wright's budget estimates off. Johnson recalled

Fig. 77. Construction photograph, May 1938. In the spring, masons brought the nostrils and walls up to the top of the penthouse, and concrete workers prepared to pour the roof slab above it. Masonry work on the bridge from the penthouse to the squash court (upper left) was complete. (Courtesy of Johnson Wax)

Fig. 78. Construction photograph, May 1938. Completed final formwork for the domed carport ceiling. Steel mesh provides most of the reinforcing; curved steel reinforcing bars form tension rings around the base of each dome. (Courtesy of Johnson Wax)

later that Wright apparently was not aware of current labor and material costs because he had built so few buildings in the preceding decade. In his first letter to Wright Johnson asked him to design a $200,000 office building. Within five months the estimate for Wright's design was $300,000. On December 30, 1937 Wright warned Ramsey that he had revised his estimate to $450,000. By the time the building was complete, sixteen months later, the cost, including furnishings, would be almost double that amount. *Architectural Forum* associate editor George Nelson visited Taliesin in late 1937, helping to prepare the special Wright issue. He remembers a meeting at which Johnson complained about the increased cost of the building. Nelson recalled Wright saying later, "He doesn't appreciate that he asked for a memorial to his grandfather. You don't build a memorial out of the same materials and with the same budget as a plain office building."[3]

In October the plans for the theater, cafeteria, and squash court were revised, forcing Wiltscheck to temporarily lay off most of his masons. A week later drawings of the squash court arrived and Wiltscheck put his masons back to work. He complained to Johnson, "[Mr. Wright] has given me a headache with numerous and complicated last minute changes in the theater ceiling, the area around nostrils at the penthouse level, and penthouse floor."

William Wesley Peters recalls one of the last-minute changes. A day before the columns beneath the conference room were to be poured, Wright chose to place seven shrunken columns in a row sixteen feet eight inches on center on the penthouse floor, sheltering the conference room. The contrasting rhythm of the small columns would create an intimate scale to the room, as if the company's directors' power, concentrated in the conference room, could locally distort the building's twenty-foot column grid. Peters hurried to Racine and stopped the workmen from pouring the lower columns. He worked around the clock for two days to calculate the extra steel reinforcing Wright's change would require. Calculations completed, workmen poured the columns just one day late.

Wright was plagued by debts that he had accumulated over the preceding commissionless years. To pay off creditors he asked Johnson for a series of loans and advances. Wright's commission, however, grew as the cost of the building increased, and late in 1937 Johnson became unhappy over their financial relationship. Wright wrote Johnson from Arizona:

> You seem to feel you've paid your old architect an awful lot and the work costs an awful lot more...
>
> No architect creating anything worth naming as creative work ever made or can make any money on what he does.... At no time (soon after recovering from pneumonia) since I began to build your buildings, were there not plans enough lying around to complete the structure as it then stood should anything happen to me. But, not satisfied with that, I suppose I have already made what would be equal to three ordinary sets of plans and details, assumed the engineering throughout, and, incidentally, put up a fight to keep the commissioners from wasting our substance. I have, as you know, given my personal attention to every little matter of minutest detail in both buildings. [Wright is also referring to Wingspread, the house he designed for Johnson in 1937.] To me, neither structure is just a building. Each one is a life in itself, one for the life that is your business life, and one for your personal life.
>
> Now, a few remarks concerning the fee: First, I fought the commissioners to a standstill for an opportunity to save you $30,000.00 on air conditioning, and about $28,000.00 in senseless weights in building and construction. I won that fight. Then, I rejected artificial lighting and worked out a daylight building, saving many thousands on upkeep, and did this at no greater cost than ordinary window lighting. So, I saved to you your entire architect's fee in these items alone, not to mention floor-heating, which looks like "good business" for you. I need not go into all the advantages of the many original ideas that will make your building the first in the world for its purpose, and that means the best, no fooling. All this looks like not only good business, but good advertising—probably as much good money value as the building costs. This goes for the house, too—except the advertising...
>
> I'll never ask for money "off the cards"; and now, to help get started in the desert,

between you all, you could send me quite a check without too great a shock to good business sense, and no very real tax on friendship either.[4]

Johnson responded with a mild chastisement, revealing his close but now strained relationship with Wright:

As I have told you on many occasions, I am pleased with the work, the buildings are going to be beautiful and practical and true creations, but the cost and time element make things embarrassing for me, to say the least. I know it does no good to complain as you are an artist so in love with your work that nothing will make you change your ideas of what the two buildings ought to be, even though it works a hardship on your client. You would rather tell the client whatever comes into your head as to the cost and the time to construct, at the start, just to sell the job and give satisfaction to your art to create something worthwhile, rather than to be accurate in cost estimates. Why didn't you put me wise long ago as to the true costs and time to construct? Would that be unreasonable to ask? That is water over the dam now and I am going to have to take it, but I will never like it. That is, the way you have handled me; the buildings I am going to love.

. . . I am going to include Wiltscheck in this (only changing the part having to do with love for the art) by saying that he should give over to the client some of the time he puts in toward trying to establish his reputation among others as the big contractor and instead really study architect's plans, costs, working schedules, etc.

Now, Frankie, this reply to your letter is no complaint as it would do no good to complain. You have us hooked and we can't get away. Rather, it is written to show you how I feel and, if possible, spur you on to economize on matters still undecided in the buildings. I like to see you work; I know you have the stuff it takes; your talent and personality will forever be endeared to me; and I know I shall be, in the end, one of your best clients to appreciate what you have done and all that sort of thing. Believe me, I mean it.[5]

Johnson concluded the letter by calculating Wright's commission to date on the office, which had cost $291,000 by January 4, 1938, and his house, which had cost $76,000.

Wright's fee was 10 percent of the cost of construction, divided among preliminary drawings, construction drawings, and site supervision. As the estimated cost of the completed building grew, the amount Wright was due for drawings increased proportionately. Periodically, as in his letter of December 30, Wright requested the unpaid difference. In his letter Johnson suggested that they simplify the arrangement by paying Wright 10 percent of the construction costs each month—just as Wiltscheck received his 5 percent. Johnson enclosed Wright the $3,100 then due on the office and house, telling Wright it was "to help you get started on the desert"—referring to Wright's plans for Taliesin West, on which he had recently taken a mortgage.

Wright responded, "I accept your arrangement. It is eminently fair. You are the young man who sometimes talks like a piker and invariably acts like a prince," but he defended his low budget estimates, writing, "I am finding out that buildings cost a lot more than when I last built one of any note—we then had an eight-hour day—all the labor we wanted at one half the present scale and sure action all down the line—I suppose Rip Van Winkle had something like some of my experiences when he 'came back'." Wright pointed out that nonetheless, much of the cost overrun on the building was accounted for by items added to the programs after he made his first estimates.[6]

The strain between the men eased briefly in January when the special Wright issue of *Architectural Forum* was released. William Connolly's publicity-minded strategy was rewarded by prestigious exposure for the Johnson company as well as for Wright. The January 1938 *Forum* remains the finest publication on Wright's work of the 1930s. The prominent position of the Johnson building design in the issue may have helped to account for a later article on the building in *Life* magazine. *Time* also ran a cover story on Wright in January 1938.

Johnson asked Wiltscheck to calculate a new estimate for the office building on January 10. Wiltscheck's reply sheds light on the gradual way Wright worked out

Fig. 79. *Overleaf.* Workmen installing Pyrex tubes in the Great Workroom skylights, 1939. Stacks of uncut tubes are visible at the lower right. Dangling from the top of the left-hand scaffold are two bunches of several-inch-long wires, which workers used to tie the tubes to the scalloped aluminum racks. Light bulbs are visible around the edge of one column petal (upper left) between the two planned layers of tubes. (Courtesy of Johnson Wax)

details on the building, noting that before he could prepare a detailed estimate he required drawings for elevator enclosures and spiral stairs, revised drawings of glass tubing, toilet rooms, various ceiling, roof, and skylight details, and schedules for room finishes, movable partitions, lighting fixtures, millwork, and hardware. Wiltscheck later observed, "There never was a plumbing nor electrical plan for the office building. This work was laid out at the site as the job progressed."

To speed up the on-site drawings Johnson urged Wiltscheck to hire a draftsman to help Tafel. In mid-January Wiltscheck hired the former chief layout artist for Holabird and Root. Two weeks later Johnson cabled Wright in Arizona, "Building progress slowed up on account of cold weather. Tafel, Wiltscheck, draftsmen working on plans, bids, quantities and schedules so as to have things lined up when the weather breaks. Think unnecessary for you to come here for another two months."

Wright's accommodations that first year in the Arizona desert were primitive. Apprentices lived in tents as they built Taliesin West. The original roof of the drafting room was a sheet of stretched linen canvas and there was no glass in the large openings between walls and roof. Consequently, the Johnson Wax drawings were not well protected from the elements, and Peters recalls that after a strong storm, one was missing. Apprentices found the wet drawing in the desert and redrew it.

Plumbers installed the radiant floor heating on the sand bed of the Great Workroom in April. Wright altered his original plan to force steam through hollow tiles, choosing copper pipes instead. Unable to obtain enough copper tubing, he used iron, which years later corroded. Johnson and Ramsey were no longer worried whether the heating scheme would work because that winter one had been successfully installed in a house that Wright had designed for Herbert Jacobs, the Madison journalist who had covered the testing of the first Johnson column in 1937. Plumbers forced water through the pipes at a high pressure and sealed any leaks that were discovered. Near the beginning of June workmen poured the floor slab of the Great Workroom over the pipes.

In late June and July workers poured the carport floor and completed the carport and penthouse roof slabs. Brick and stonework were essentially finished by the end of June. Four masons began pointing and washing the completed brick walls.

On June 28 Herbert Johnson set October first as the completion date for the building. To meet that date Wiltscheck sent Wright a list of nine final details to design. Four of them involved clerestory or skylight glass tubing. Detailing the glass tubing constituted probably Wright's greatest challenge of the entire project.

Wright decided to construct the skylights from the same Pyrex tubing used in the clerestories. However, glass, even Pyrex, expands and contracts with changes in temperature. This movement was not problematic in the vertically stacked clerestory tubes, but in the skylights ponding water managed to work its way between the tubes—in spite of the liberal use of any caulking material then known. Tafel recalls Peters saying that what Wright needed was not mastic, but magic!

Wiltscheck, Peters, and Tafel feared that the skylights would leak, and Tafel and Peters approached Wright several times, asking whether he would change the skylight design. Wright, however, insisted that if the tubing was valid in one place it was valid in another. Finally, Tafel discussed his fears with Wiltscheck. The two men decided to ask a Chicago skylight company to prepare a plate-glass design and a price—with a guarantee that its installation would not leak. The company obligingly made shop drawings. Tafel showed them to Wright, who exploded, "I don't want to see them. I don't want to have anything to do with them."

Back in Racine, Tafel related Wright's response to Wiltscheck and desperately asked his advice. Wiltscheck called Johnson into the construction office and presented the problem. Johnson told him to order the plate-glass skylights. When Johnson left the room, Wiltscheck turned to Tafel and declared formally that he had been told by the owner of the building to use plate-glass skylights, and therefore he was obligated to order them. Tafel replied, "I am the architect's representative. I have

to tell him," and immediately called Wright. Shortly afterward, Johnson came into the room and stormed, "You snitched! Get off the premises. You're fired!" Tafel packed his belongings in his car, drove to a nearby telephone, and called Taliesin. Wright told him to go back. "If he fires you he's fired me."[7]

Wiltscheck sent Wright a memo requesting minor information on Johnson's office, the directors' room, the theater, and basement rest rooms. In a cover letter to Johnson, he peevishly noted, "I am going to drive to Taliesin next Sunday to find out whether they are working on drawings for us or whether they are all out in the fields making hay."[8] Wright responded to the memo just as sharply, sarcastically referring to it as "your obstruction list". After answering the questions he wrote, "I am coming down Monday myself to clean up the clean ups again. I hope we make them stay clean. I am myself puzzled to know why things decided months ago... still keep coming up for settlement."

Olgivanna Wright remembered how frustrated her husband was near the end of the job. She recalled that he returned from visits to the site and said, "I wish the construction... would go faster, but I can't demand it because the workmen are doing their best. They have to be taught everything. They have never built anything like this and it is tough. I feel sorry for them and sorry for myself."[9]

Fig. 80. Iron pipes for radiant heating under floor of Great Workroom, May 1938. The floor slab is to be poured over them. (Courtesy of Johnson Wax)

Fig. 81. Workman caulking Pyrex tubing skylight on roof of Great Workroom, 1939. (Photo by Torkel Korling; courtesy of David Phillips).

Fig. 82. Completed skylight, viewed from below, 1939. (Courtesy of Johnson Wax)

In late August, Wright wrote to Ramsey:

> I think it will be to the best interest of all concerned if you abandon the idea (for the moment) that we are holding up the building and concentrate on getting an adequate working force to execute what is already to execute... [Wiltscheck's] little crowd of workmen is all right but has become a little close corporation hard for him to budge and now stale.
>
> This is not to find fault with Ben but try to help him where he really needs it the most and doesn't seem aware of it, anymore than you do. We never had more than half a working force on this job, if being eye witness to building operations all my life is any basis for judgment.

In the same letter Wright reminded Ramsey that the company owed him a monthly payment, sorely needed because Taliesin had just been sold to the county for $2,285 in back taxes. He closed the letter, "I would like for you not to lose faith in your building and not to lose confidence in your architect. I've tried my best and will continue my best—to try."[10]

The following day Ramsey responded:

> I am enclosing Mr. Johnson's check for everything to date and $3,000 additional on the company account. That ought to pay back taxes a couple of times and leave Taliesin in good shape.
>
> With reference to the building and shifting blame for delay from architect down to contractor down to individual workmen now—I suppose there is something in the possibility of their having gone stale after so long a time and so many changes and so many delays. But as far as the one great delay right now is concerned, namely the glass, . . . the situation simply is that they received that one sample shipment of couplers and those have all been used up and we will probably have no more for a week and additional workmen would simply be useless for the time...
>
> What have you done about lighting? Will that be put off until the day before light is needed and then a month's wait while special gadgets are being ordered?...
>
> No—faith in the building and confidence in the architect's creative ability are not lost. But confidence in his ability to carry out those creations to a sound and workable finish is certainly at a low ebb.... If we must get on the personal side and use such words as faith and confidence, how about giving me a break by coming down and really staying here long enough to follow absolutely everything yourself, and leaving one of the boys here all the time to take care of those details that you do not need to bother with?... Hib will be home Monday, so suppose you come down then and stay until the job is finished.[11]

Tafel estimates that Wright came to the job site about once a month and usually returned to Spring Green the same evening. A frequent visitor to the site recalled that Ramsey once wrote on a large mounted paper tablet, "Frank Lloyd Wright will be here at 11:00 on Monday and will be here through the day to discuss details."

Wright entered the room, noticed the message, tore it off, and announced, "Frank Lloyd Wright is never scheduled."[12]

Though the building was now largely complete, Ramsey and Johnson may have wondered whether they would ever move into it. Successive complications in the design and installation of the glass tubing absorbed the entire summer of 1938. Johnson's daughter Karen Boyd notes, "It was a real trial for my father. He didn't swear a lot but there were a few 'goddamns' in those days. [People] began to think of him as an eccentric too, along with Mr. Wright."[13] Tafel recalls Johnson complaining, "At first, Mr. Wright was working for me. Then we were working together. From now on I'm working for him."[14]

On September 14 the Board of Directors passed a resolution to withhold all payments to Wright and Wiltscheck, and to resume them only if the building was completed by October 22. Charitably, Johnson and Ramsey took steps to assure that the cessation of payments would not be unbearably damaging to Wright or Wiltscheck. Two weeks earlier the company advanced Wright $3,000, and one week earlier Ramsey and Johnson examined Wiltscheck's profit and loss statement and satisfied themselves that he had made a reasonable profit on the building. Johnson noted to Ramsey, "I can't see where Ben could crab about [his income.]"

Although it was clear that all the tubing would not be installed until months after the October deadline, Wiltscheck and Wright kept working, without pay. In October, masons completed minor work on the interior, laborers installed the revolving doors—the first of their kind, and others finished cleaning and patching concrete work. Wiltscheck noted on October 27, "The glass tubing is still the pace setter. We have all the tubing for the skylights but are short of curved tubing for the wall bands."

On December 15, Wiltscheck wrote to Johnson that the building would be substantially complete on February 10. Johnson considered the date optimistic and predicted that he would not miss the building's opening, although he would be out of town until the middle of March. That week he suggested that Ramsey speak to Louis and Connolly about publicizing the opening. He did not seem to suspect the flood of publicity that his office building would receive.

In a final memorandum before leaving, Johnson wrote to Ramsey, ". . . the question of fees to Wright and Wiltscheck on the office building will probably arise during my absence, in view of the memorandum sent them by the Board of Directors of our company. I am opposed to paying them full commission on the building because of their delays, bad estimates, etc., but I suppose some compromise will have to be made. I would suggest you wait until they bring the matter up, and then take it up before the Directors."

Wright had come down with another severe case of pneumonia in December. He refused to go to the hospital, and Mrs. Wright and the apprentices nursed him in his bedroom between visits by a country doctor. When he was well enough to travel he took a train to Arizona to recuperate, but on January 9, before leaving, he visited the Johnson building, which he had left in Tafel's care.

En route to Arizona he wrote to Ramsey:

> This building is not the building I first saw when we began it. That might have been a crude unfinished sketch of this one.
>
> . . . I realize fully the strain the growth of this great landmark in new-world architecture has thrown upon you—and do not resent the breakdown of good feeling and consequently of good sense. These breaks have been only few however . . .
>
> Had I realized what would be demanded of me—the refusal of other work for eighteen months—the cross country driving in all weathers (pneumonia a little incident) the ceaseless vexations and chafing at delays—all this for two years—I would not have had the courage at this time in my life (I am 69) to take it on—Jack.[15]

Ramsey replied:

> I appreciate the letter you wrote me on the train. And I am sure that Hib too would have

appreciated it, because it does show some understanding of the terrific strain that we have been under.

I don't mean that I agree with you in every detail. For instance, I can't subscribe to the statement that we ever lost "good sense"; but I freely admit that "good nature" took an awful long vacation . . .

You will either laugh or get mad, but there is something almost paternally protective in all our crabbing about costs and details. Harken to your worst enemies in the profession: "Wright is the great designer but he will have a bit of your plumbing in the wrong place and end up with a leak in the roof."

Granting a wax salesman's architectural incompetence to do anything about it, still the subconscious motive in our criticizing is "That's idiotic; our Wright is going to finish this job as perfectly in the final set of a toilet partition as it is in the grand sweep of the building's exterior."[16]

Ramsey's ire at the end of the letter was over the laminated wood toilet partitions in the basement washrooms, then being installed, as the first ones were warped. Fortunately, all the following ones were suitably flat. On January 30, Tafel wrote to Wright, "We have again had trouble with the glass tubing men. The masons and the bricklayers were fighting it out for three days while the building stood idle. It all ended up with the glaziers continuing the work, and there is nothing to be done about it. The workmanship is not as good and they are much slower, but they have got it."[17]

Wright wrote Ramsey:

I should have thrown up my hands (or committed suicide) when the union insisted on taking over the tubes as masonry, carpentry and glazing—none of which they are—but just unclassified common labor. And how could anyone gauge the interminable slow pace of the union on everything on the job—costs of renting equipment and of insurance, etc., etc.; the time lag of the back-drag, the lack of forceful organization on the work itself—oh well, why hold post-mortems? There are plenty, fore and aft. It seems incredible that neither Ben nor myself could have foreseen the financial outcome of it all any closer than we did.

And perhaps I took the whole thing too seriously by putting the best of everything, including myself, into it. A peculiar optimism has characterized the whole effort and on the part of everyone concerned, I should say. There was never anything quite like it, I believe, and I only hope the results will be equally remarkable.[18]

In January 1939 workmen began painting the columns with an off-white pigment. As the paint began to dry they blew sand into it, giving the surface of the columns the slight texture Wright desired. As the columns were completed, the Cherokee-red rubber floor tiles were glued down. Carpenters began installing the movable partitions above and beneath the Great Workroom mezzanine, and the Pyrex tubing installations neared completion.

The next month Tafel flew to Arizona to update Wright, and Ramsey wrote to Wright, "By now Edgar will have reported to you and you know how things are going with the building. Warping millwork is still my personal bête noire, but I still have hope. Ben's, I think, is the nine leaks in the tubing that developed after a severe rain storm last week. Otherwise things are shaping up slowly (as always) but beautifully and it would probably cure your bronchitis to step in the building this bright and sunshiny morning . . . "

As it neared completion, the Administration Building had a dramatic effect on its viewers. In February, the construction workers rallied Ramsey into allowing them to take friends and family through the building one weekend. Apprentice John Lautner recalls that when he took his mother to see it just before it was completed, she found it so beautiful that she wept.[19] Critic Alexander Woolcott was more vocal when brought to the site. According to Tafel, when Woolcott saw the partially finished building he waved his hands and exclaimed to Wright, "Frank, I want to dance, I want to dance!"[20]

COLUMN
GLASS VASE
SET OVER METAL
TEMPORARY FILES
LIGHTING TUBE
TILL
TO PIVOT
APRON
LIGHT AND TELEPHONE BOXES
ELEVATION OF DESK
BALL BEARINGS
ELEVATION OF DESK AND CHAIR
END OF DESK
UPPER DESK LEVEL
REMOVABLE
WASTE BOX
FILING
TILL
MAIN DESK LEVEL
TYPEWRITER
DESK LEVEL
TILL OPEN
PLAN OF DESK
UPPER DESK LEVEL
LIGHTING TUBE
CENTER DROP LEAF
MAIN DESK LEVEL
TYPEWRITER DESK LEVEL
DESK SECTION
CHAIR
LEATHER SEAT AND BACK
DESK AND CHAIR FOR THE S C JOHNSON AND SON OFFICE BUILDING
CAST ALUMINUM FRAMES OIL POLISHED WOOD TOPS
PATENT APPLIED FOR NOV.

CHAPTER 7

FURNISHING THE ADMINISTRATION BUILDING

And it is quite impossible to consider the building as one thing and its furnishings another.
FRANK LLOYD WRIGHT

Fig. 83. Plan and elevation of desk and chair, published in *Architectural Forum*, 1938. The desk is supported by an aluminum frame, whose components are cruciform in section. Attached to the frame are rounded pivoting metal tills that serve as trays, file drawer, and trash container. The desk has three wooden surfaces, each with rounded edges. The main surface is much larger than the standard 1930s desk, and two inches lower than normal, at twenty-eight and one-half inches. A semicircular segment of this surface can be removed so that a typewriter can be placed on a smaller, lower surface beneath it. Cantilevered from the rear of the desk is a small, higher fixture that holds temporary files. A tubular light fixture is attached to its underside. The chairs shown in the elevations have three legs, however, the chairs in the plans have four. Black ink on tracing paper. 36″ × 24″. (Courtesy of the Frank Lloyd Wright Foundation)

Throughout Wright's career, furniture design was an integral part of his architectural projects, including his earlier office commission, the Larkin Building. Wright offered to design furniture for the Johnson building at one of his first meetings with the company in 1936. Ramsey responded cautiously, "We should like to see what you would suggest. . . . " but warned that the furnishings must meet the company's requirements "both as to practicality and expense."

Ramsey mentioned to Wright his family's contacts with several furniture companies, in Grand Rapids, Michigan, in particular, Edgar Hunting, secretary of the Stow-Davis Furniture Company, and Hunting's son, David, secretary and part-owner of Steelcase Inc., then the Metal Office Furniture Company.

Wright obligingly summoned representatives of Stow-Davis to Spring Green for a preliminary discussion in November 1936. In need of the extra income, Wright hoped the furniture project would proceed quickly. On December 10 he wrote to Ramsey, ". . . to get the maximum benefit out of the building, the furniture should go with it." He noted that he charged the Larkin Company and other clients 20 percent for furniture designs, but offered to design a complete layout for Johnson at his 10 percent architectural rate if Ramsey would advance him the full $3,000 (assuming a furniture cost of $30,000) for designs he had not yet seen.[1]

The building work was already running over its earliest estimates, causing Ramsey to respond, "As to furniture, therefore, how can we get anything new? Money is an irritating part of this world, but we've got to take it into account—not for piling up gold for its own sake, but just so that this business continues to run properly and serve the very human destiny that it has for fifty years. And—this is difficult to express, because I do have the greatest belief in the architect—even if we could splurge on some new furnishings, to accept blindly in advance whatever you might give us in the way of such pragmatic items as office furniture. . . . We'd still like to 'see' but cannot commit ourselves until we do."[2] Six weeks later he wrote, "You might send (a set of drawings) to Bennett of the Stow-Davis people in Grand Rapids if you are making any progress on furniture proposals."[3]

Wright responded, "I've been thinking a lot about furniture—and have been scribbling around the matter. Am I going to be able to sell you my devoted heart and soul in this meticulous matter in connection with our great building? It would mean a lot of patience on your part as on mine, but I think less so, ultimately, than to try to adapt or accommodate stock-stuff. I am for it if you are."[4]

Ramsey did not want to assume the extra cost of new furnishings, and he went to Johnson for advice. Johnson took Ramsey's suggestion to "tell him to forget furniture for a while." Wright brought up the furniture question again late that summer and this time Johnson and Ramsey convinced him to submit designs without an advance.

His first known version of a desk and chair are intimately wedded to the building in conception. Composed of straight and rounded forms, they reflect the orthogonal

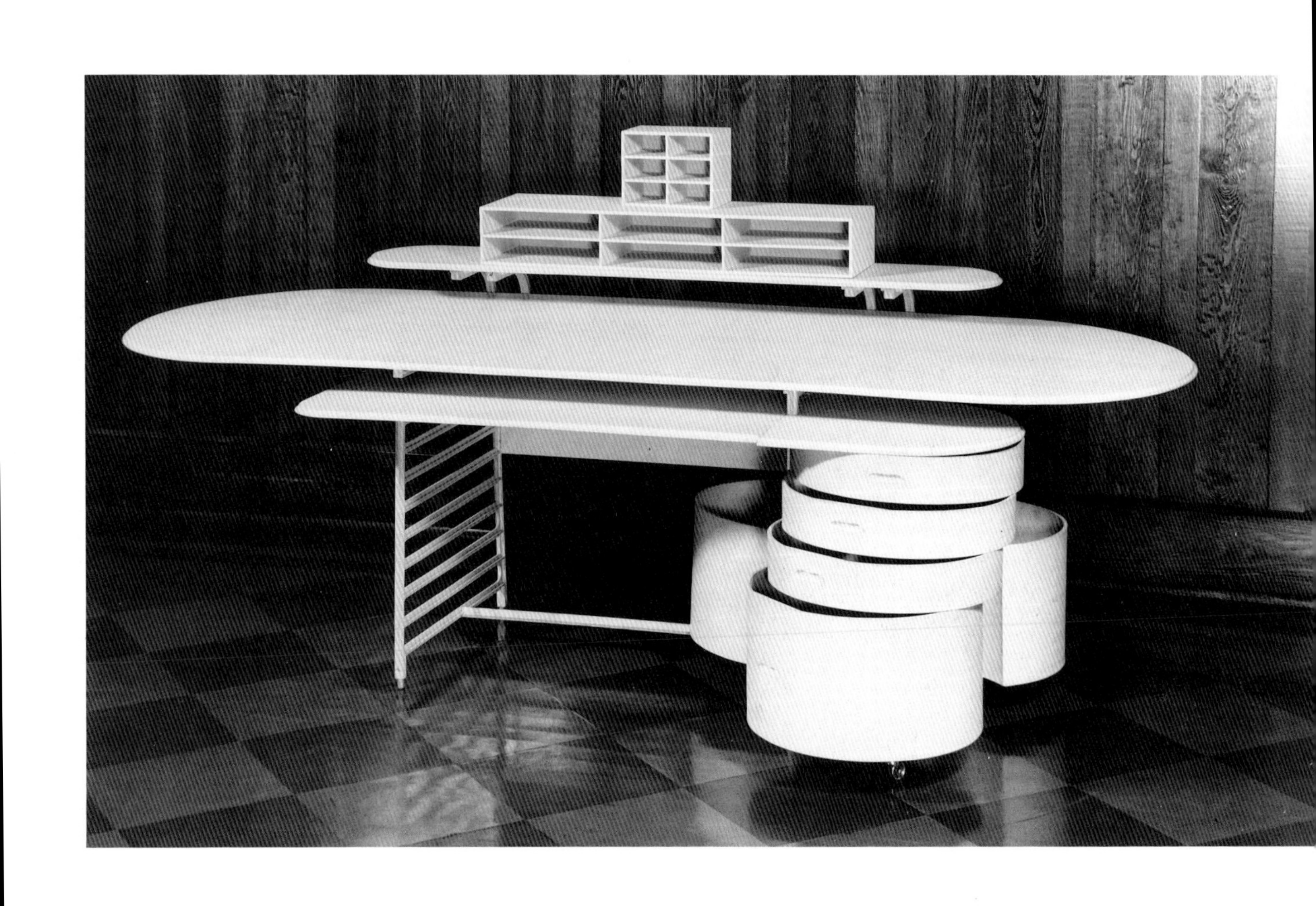

Fig. 84. Prototype of desk, 1938, built by Gillen Woodworking, Milwaukee of laminated wood. Apparently destroyed. Gillen did the cabinetry work for Wingspread and Fallingwater. (Courtesy of Johnson Wax)

Fig. 85. Prototype of Johnson Company desk, 1938, built by Warren McArthur. (Courtesy of Johnson Wax)

and circular geometries of the building. The desk's three work surfaces extend well beyond the aluminum frame, displaying the cantilever principle used in the building. The stretchers in the frames align with the building's brick courses, and the main work surface actually engages a mushroom column[5] (figs. 83 and 84).

Elements of the Johnson chair can be seen in earlier furniture designs by Wright. His original design for the Darwin Martin house (1904) dining room chairs does not have conventional legs. Rather it features a base composed of a T-like strut that approximates the effect of two rear legs and a single central front leg. His three-legged chair designed and built for the Larkin Building had a single leg in back, an odd configuration that created a particularly unstable chair. Another precedent is Wright's unbuilt Midway Gardens (1914) outdoor furniture, of which Wright placed a rendering opposite his drawing of the Johnson furniture in the January 1938 issue of *Architectural Forum* (see fig. 87).

Stow-Davis, a manufacturer of wood furniture, withdrew from the Johnson commission, undoubtedly because it was not equipped to make furnishings that were primarily metal. Two other furniture makers who had made their reputation building metal furniture were enlisted: Steelcase Inc. and Warren McArthur, the son of a client of Wright's.[6]

For the Johnson building, both Steelcase and Warren McArthur produced furniture composed of metal tubes. There is no record to indicate whether the use of tubes was suggested by one of them or by Wright. Tubes were far cheaper than the milled, welded heavy sheet-aluminum indicated in Wright's drawing, and were often used in avant-garde furniture of the time. Tubular steel furniture was first designed by Marcel Breuer in 1925, and Ludwig Mies van der Rohe and Le Corbusier designed famous tubular steel pieces shortly after Breuer. While it is tempting to propose that Wright meant the Johnson furniture to be a demonstration of his mastery of the fashionable material, it is just as likely that costs forced him to use tubing.

McArthur made several trips to Racine and produced a prototype of a desk, a secretary's chair, and a low, half-round table. The work surfaces resemble those on Wright's drawing, but the tubular aluminum frames are different, containing enlarged joints, giving them a less refined appearance (fig. 85).

Ramsey called David Hunting at Steelcase to say that his company had an architect who wanted furniture unlike anything on the market. Hunting met with Ramsey and Wright in Racine and later said, "[Wright] was quite definite about his ideas. He had made no drawings of his desks, but he took an envelope or a paper out of his pocket, made some rough sketches on it, and said, 'This is about what I'd like.' And that was the information we received. I never saw a detailed sketch from Frank Lloyd Wright's office about the furniture." Hunting recalls that Wright wanted the furniture to reflect the columns' treatment of cantilevers, round surfaces, and light base supports. Desks of the 1930s had large bases to protect the floor, but Wright wanted the desk legs to narrow at the base. At Ramsey's suggestion Hunting had Steelcase's engineering department make some preliminary sketches. Wright repeatedly corrected their drawings until he was satisfied.[7] Wright accepted their version and the Johnson company awarded the contract to Steelcase in June 1938, paying Warren McArthur $2,000 for his work.

Hunting tried to talk Wright out of the three-legged chairs he had proposed, but Wright was firm. He argued that the front legs of standard chairs were in the way of the user's feet; and that his chair would impose correct posture because it would tip only if users sat incorrectly. He gave the seats and backs foam-rubber padding and made them easily adjustable. He also had the seat back pivoted, with fabric on both sides, increasing comfort and decreasing wear on the fabric. Wright specified four fabric colors: red for the credit department, blue for the branch house records department, green for the billing department, and beige for the sales promotion department. The chair cushions acted as accents of color in the otherwise

Fig. 86. Tub desk, 1939. This eight-foot-seven-inch-wide desk was designed for clerks in the branch house records department and best shows Wright's thorough analysis of the needs of office workers. Heavy ledger trays could be moved from the master filing cabinet in a small rolling stand (lower center) and placed in the hanging bins in the desk for temporary use. (Courtesy of Johnson Wax)

Fig. 87. Unbuilt dining table and chairs for Midway Gardens, 1914. The frames were to be made of twisted wire. A modified version of the chair was built at Taliesen in 1961. Original drawing lost.

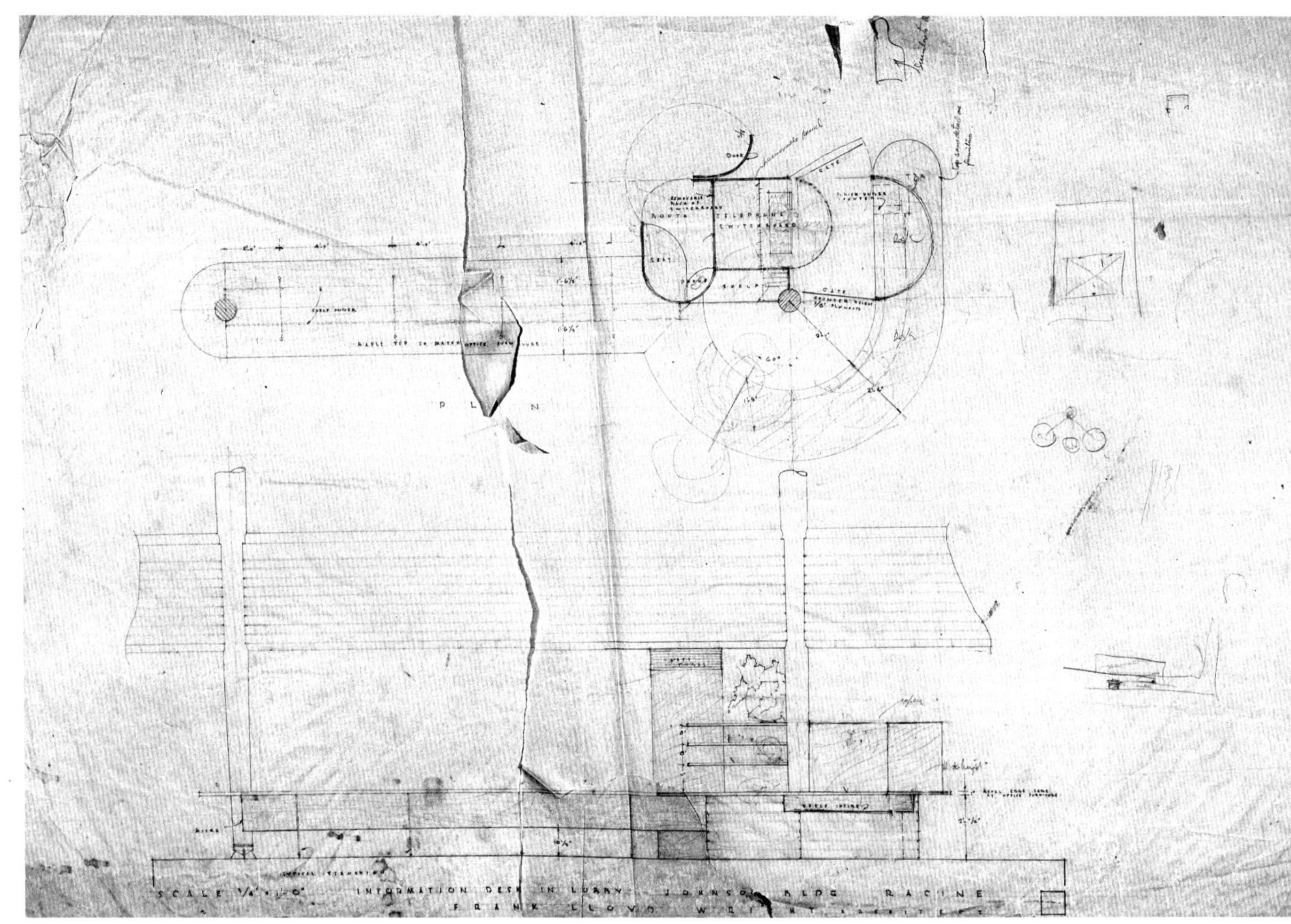

Fig. 88. Information desk. The desk's twenty-eight-foot-long maple surface is divided into two parts. The straight surface (left) is supported by a tubular frame and serves as a display stand; behind it are mail pigeonholes for employees. The semicircular surface (right) is a work station for a receptionist and telephone operator. Shelving conceals the switchboard. Pencil on tracing paper. 36″ × 25″. (Courtesy of the Frank Lloyd Wright Foundation)

almost monochromatic Great Workroom. The metal frames of the furniture were painted Cherokee red.

The Johnson company's employees were pleased with the desks, and most found the three-legged chairs comfortable after they learned how to sit in them. The chairs were unstable if one leaned back at an angle, and a number of employees fell off them in the first few days. Samuel Johnson recalls his father told him that even Wright fell out of one, but still insisted that everyone would soon grow used to them. Just before the building opened Wright designed a large four-legged lounge chair, which he called an officer's chair[8] (see fig. 99). He may have designed it to allay Johnson's concern for visitors sitting for the first time in the unstable three-legged chairs. The company later installed two front legs on most of the remaining chairs, according to a design Wright approved.

Wright modified the desk design slightly for executives in the penthouse. Their work surfaces were made in American walnut, rather than the maple specified for the Great Workroom furniture, and some had a square end positioned against a wall. He also designed a larger version of the three-legged chair with armrests for the executives (see fig. 112).

According to Hunting, no manufacturer was capable of producing Wright's furniture in its own plant. Steelcase hired Stow-Davis to manufacture the wooden work surfaces, and another Grand Rapids firm, American Seating Company (then making tubular seats for its own chairs), to produce the frames. The fabric covering on the chairs was created by the Chase Furniture Company, and Steelcase produced the sheet metalwork and finished and assembled the components.

Nine variations on the basic desk were designed for clerical employees, to accommodate different tasks. Most were 84 inches by 32 inches, approximately two feet longer than a standard desk (fig. 86). There were also square, rectangular, and round tables for use in the mail room and other departments, as well as one-of-a-kind pieces, such as Johnson's desk and the conference room table (see figs. 111 and 113). A total of over forty different pieces of furniture were designed. According to Hunting they were the forerunner of contemporary open office furniture design, with equally sophisticated paper-handling systems.

Wright also designed one major piece of built-in furniture for the Johnson building: the information desk (fig. 88; see also fig. 109, lower left). Located at the most dynamic point in the building, the junction between the lobby and the Great Workroom, the desk runs directly beneath the mezzanine bridge. The two forms reinforce one another and create a precise degree of transparency between the two rooms. One end of the desk wraps around a mushroom column, representing the most complete integration of furniture and structure in the building.

CHAPTER 8

WORKING IN THE ADMINISTRATION BUILDING

This great building is as inspiring a place to work in as any cathedral ever was in which to worship.
FRANK LLOYD WRIGHT

Fig. 89. West carport exit of Administration Building, 1939. (Courtesy of Johnson Wax)

On the opening of the Administration Building long illustrated articles appeared in the local press, and a wire service carried the story to other newspapers. The new building was also featured in national business magazines, and the articles gave Johnson Wax an association with innovation and quality. Reporters were overwhelmed by the Great Workroom and wrote unusually lyrical stories. The financial editor of the *Milwaukee Journal* wrote, "A silly urge comes over you to lie flat upon the bottom of this pool of liquid light and stare up at the lily pads—of concrete—that float upon its glassy surface."[1] The Johnson company produced an eight-page press release to assist reporters, but the most widely read article came from an unexpected source. Chicago botanist and nature photographer Torkel Korling, intrigued by articles on the building, photographed it and sold his photos to *Life* magazine. *Life* ran them as the lead article in its May 8, 1939 issue. Comparing the building to the recently opened New York World's Fair, *Life* wrote:

> [The] $155,000,000 World's Fair, sprawling its gigantic mass of freak and futuristic buildings, is undeniably a great show. But future historians may well decide that a truer glimpse of the shape of things to come was given last week by a single structure, built strictly for business, which opened in a drab section of Racine, Wis.

The completed building was opened for a tour by employees on Friday, April 21, and the company issued an invitation to the entire city to tour the building that weekend. Twenty-six thousand people, over one third of Racine's population, passed through its doors on Saturday and Sunday after waiting for two hours in lines that extended for two city blocks. Beaming, Herbert Johnson greeted many of the visitors, who were directed through the building by uniformed Boy Scouts. Employees began working in the new building the following Monday.

Concern had been voiced that the Great Workroom would be noisy, but employees found it quiet by the standards of the day, and one business magazine reported, "There is no noise to be heard."[2] Cork on the underside of the mezzanine absorbed some sound, and the irregularly angled ceiling muffled distinct sounds so that a satisfactory, low "white noise" pervaded the room. Employees' reactions to the innovative natural lighting varied. Retired payroll clerk Elsie Dostal remembers having very good light coming over her shoulder, but other employees complained of glare at certain times of the day. On Wright's recommendation the company installed Aeroshades—hanging blinds composed of thin wooden strips—on the clerestories to lessen the glare.

Wright's decision to put all the clerical workers in a single room had several implications. He considered work to have a spiritual value, in that it promoted self-development, noting that the Administration Building "is simply and sincerely an interpretation of modern business conditions, and of business too, itself designed to be as inspiring to live and work in as any cathedral ever was to worship in."[3] To employees, too, the great sunlit space, reached after passing through a carefully staged sequence of darkness and light, evoked a feeling of unity similar to that experienced in Gothic cathedrals and the hypostylic halls of ecclesiastic buildings and reinforced the already present familylike spirit of the Johnson company (see fig. 115).[4]

Herbert Johnson's son Samuel C. Johnson, today Chief Executive Officer of the company, recalls that the original idea of the Great Workroom was in part the result of Wright and Herbert Johnson's feeling that in addition to creating a greater sense of cooperation, it would be more efficient if the clerical employees had direct access to one another. When the employees moved into the new building in 1939 they enthusiastically accepted being together in the large room. One retiree recalled that every employee he knew was very happy with the building.[5]

Gathering all the company's clerical workers into a single room succeeded on functional grounds as well. Wright laid out the departments to promote the most efficient flow of information through the room. Paperwork followed a linear route, related departments were near one another, and departments used by all employees were centrally located. A study concluded that as a result of moving into the new building the efficiency of the company's office operations improved by 15 percent, with some departments improving over 25 percent.[6]

Each department had its own filing area, but the company's general files were centered under the south mezzanine near the middle of the Great Workroom. The ledger files were immediately to the north, beneath a ninety-foot-long wooden counter, and to their north, occupying the center of the room, was the branch house records department, which used the ledger files (see fig. 102). To the west were the billing and credit departments; sales promotion and records were to the east. Glass-enclosed rooms beneath the east mezzanine contained the noisy multigraph, multilith, addressograph, and graphotype machines (see rear of fig. 99). The outgoing mail department was located next to them, with the loading dock near it, concealed in the carport outside the northeast corner of the Great Workroom.

The cost and traffic departments were located in the east and west wings of the mezzanine. The assistant treasurer had a glazed private office in the southwest corner of the mezzanine next to the accounting department, which occupied the south wing (see fig. 102, center background).

Within a few years the expanding company filled the Great Workroom and began to contemplate additional office space. Wright would provide this space in his subsequent design for the Johnson company.

Fig. 90. Visitors in lobby, viewing the newly opened Administration Building, 1939. (Courtesy of Johnson Wax)

Plate 1.
Aerial view of Administration Building, 1939.
(Courtesy of Johnson Wax)

Plate 2.
Administration Building passerelle, 1952.
(Courtesy of the Museum of Modern Art,
New York City)

Plate 3.
Great Workroom of Administration Building, 1939. (Courtesy of Johnson Wax)

Plate 4.
Administration Building lobby, 1952.
(Courtesy of the Museum of Modern Art,
New York City)

Plate 5.
Research Tower and Administration Building, 1955. (Courtesy of Johnson Wax)

Plate 6.
Research Tower, 1952. (Courtesy of the Museum of Modern Art, New York City)

Plate 7.
Laboratory in Research Tower, 1952. (Courtesy of the Museum of Modern Art, New York City)

Plate 8.
Advertising department, located over Research Tower carport, 1952. (Courtesy of the Museum of Modern Art, New York City)

Fig. 91. Aerial view of Administration Building from the west. Clerestories glow at sunset from interior lighting. (Courtesy of Johnson Wax)

Fig. 92. Aerial view of Administration Building at night from the west. (Courtesy of Johnson Wax)

Fig. 93. West side of Administration Building. (Photo by Torkel Korling; courtesy of David Phillips).

Fig. 94. Porte cochere, viewed from the east. The loading dock is visible at the lower left. The glazed bridge from the penthouse to the squash court is located top center. (Courtesy of Johnson Wax)

Fig. 95. Exterior detail of Administration Building, 1939. The loading dock is hidden behind the low wall in the foreground. (Courtesy of Johnson Wax)

Fig. 96. Lobby, with carport visible in background, 1939. (Courtesy of Johnson Wax)

Fig. 97. Lobby viewed from west end. Built-in information desk can be seen in the right foreground. The bulge in the mezzanine-level wall conceals a loudspeaker. (Courtesy of Johnson Wax)

Fig. 98. Lobby detail, 1950. (Courtesy of Johnson Wax)

Fig. 99. Lobby (left) and Great Workroom (right) viewed from mezzanine, circa 1958. The chairs on the lobby floor are four-legged lounge (officers') chairs designed by Wright in 1939. The chairs on the mezzanine (lower left) are four-legged modifications of the original three-legged chair. (Courtesy of Johnson Wax)

Fig. 100. *Overleaf.* Great Workroom viewed from south mezzanine, 1939. The lobby and carport are visible at the center rear.

Fig. 101. Great Workroom viewed from northwest mezzanine, 1950. Wright wrote, "The penthouse . . . is open to the big room below in order to preserve intimate connection between work and officials: the unity of the whole." (Photo by Ezra Stoller; © Esto)

Fig. 102. Detail of Great Workroom, 1939. (Courtesy of Johnson Wax)

Fig. 103. Elevator cage, 1939. Horizontal brass strips align with alternating brick courses. Wright wanted to omit the vertical strips but the state Industrial Commission insisted on them. The elevators are the plunger-type, without cables. A spiral staircase leading to the basement is visible at lower right. (Courtesy of Johnson Wax)

Fig. 104. Detail of mezzanine above lobby, 1939. The theater is located behind the planters. (Courtesy of Johnson Wax)

Fig. 105. Recreation deck over carport with the company's name is on the rear wall (1939). The squash court and bridge are at the far right. (Courtesy of Johnson Wax)

Fig. 106. Lobby between theater and carport roof deck, 1939. The walls are composed entirely of Pyrex tubes. (Courtesy of Johnson Wax)

Fig. 107. Detail of theater wall, 1939. The Pyrex tubing walls engage the column. (Photo by Torkel Korling; courtesy of David Phillips)

Fig. 108. Theater, mezzanine level, 1939. The ceiling is composed of stepped semicircles. A projection booth can be seen at right. Not visible in photograph are sliding panels located behind rostrum that separate the theater from the lobby and provide a projection screen. (Courtesy of Johnson Wax)

Fig. 109. Lobby and Great Workroom viewed from penthouse, 1939. The curved ornamental wall at the upper left is made of Pyrex tubes. A conference room is located behind the wall. (Photo by Torkel Korling; courtesy of David Phillips).

Fig. 110. Penthouse, showing Herbert Johnson's office (left), 1939. (Courtesy of Chicago Architectural Photographers)

Fig. 111. Herbert Johnson's office, 1939. The desk doubles as a small conference table. The exterior wall is made entirely of Pyrex tubing. (Courtesy of Johnson Wax)

Fig. 112. Private penthouse office, 1939. The desk engages the built-in cabinet. (Courtesy of Johnson Wax)

Fig. 113. Conference room in penthouse, 1939. The conference table is a variation of Wright's desks. The right wall also serves as a display rack and conceals storage. Above the rack is a wall mural composed of curved tubes. Air-conditioning vents can be seen in the column calyx. Through the plate-glass window (left) the skyline is visible above the roof of the Great Workroom (Courtesy of Johnson Wax)

Fig. 114. Glazed bridge leading from penthouse to squash court, 1939. (Courtesy of Johnson Wax)

Fig. 115. *Overleaf.* Herbert Johnson addressing employees in Great Workroom during Christmas profit-sharing meeting, 1939. The ecclesiastic nature of the hypostylic hall is amplified in this photo. To Johnson's left is the company choir, to his right is the company band. Wright's earliest version of the design had an organ located on the bridge that can be seen above Johnson's head. (Courtesy of Johnson Wax)

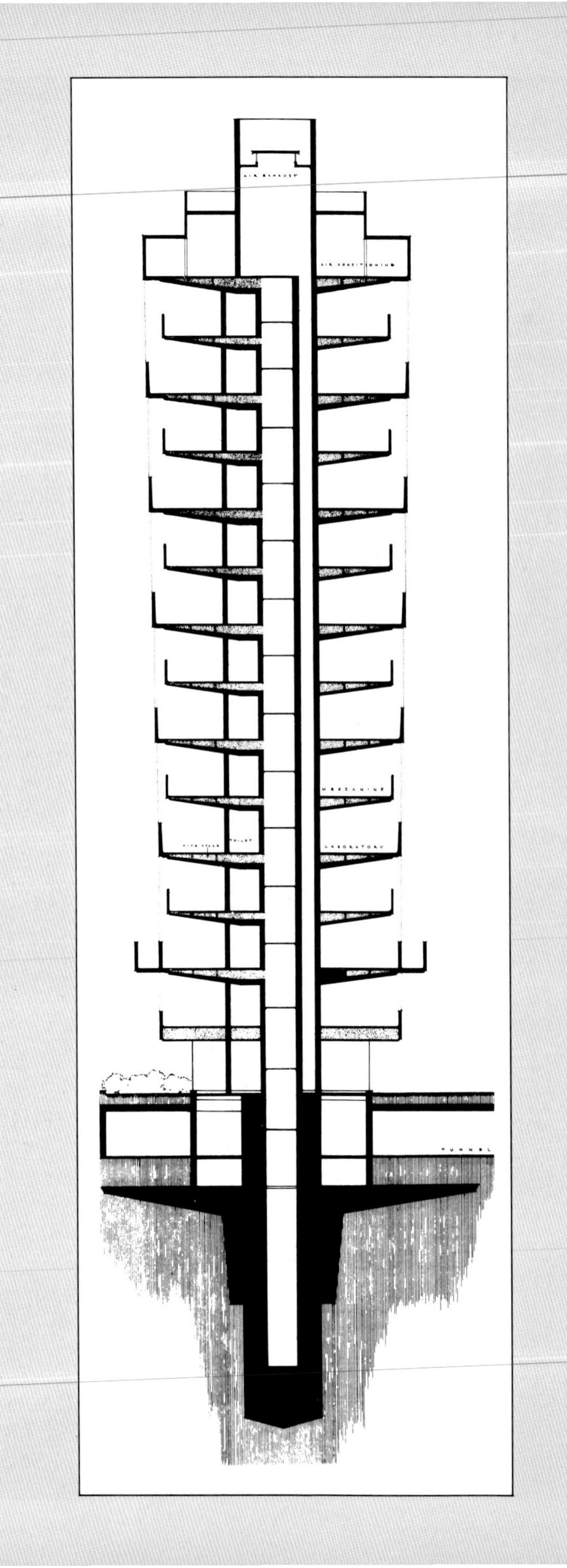
AIR EXHAUST
AIR CONDITIONING
MEZZANINE
PIPE SPACE
TOILET
LABORATORY
TUNNEL

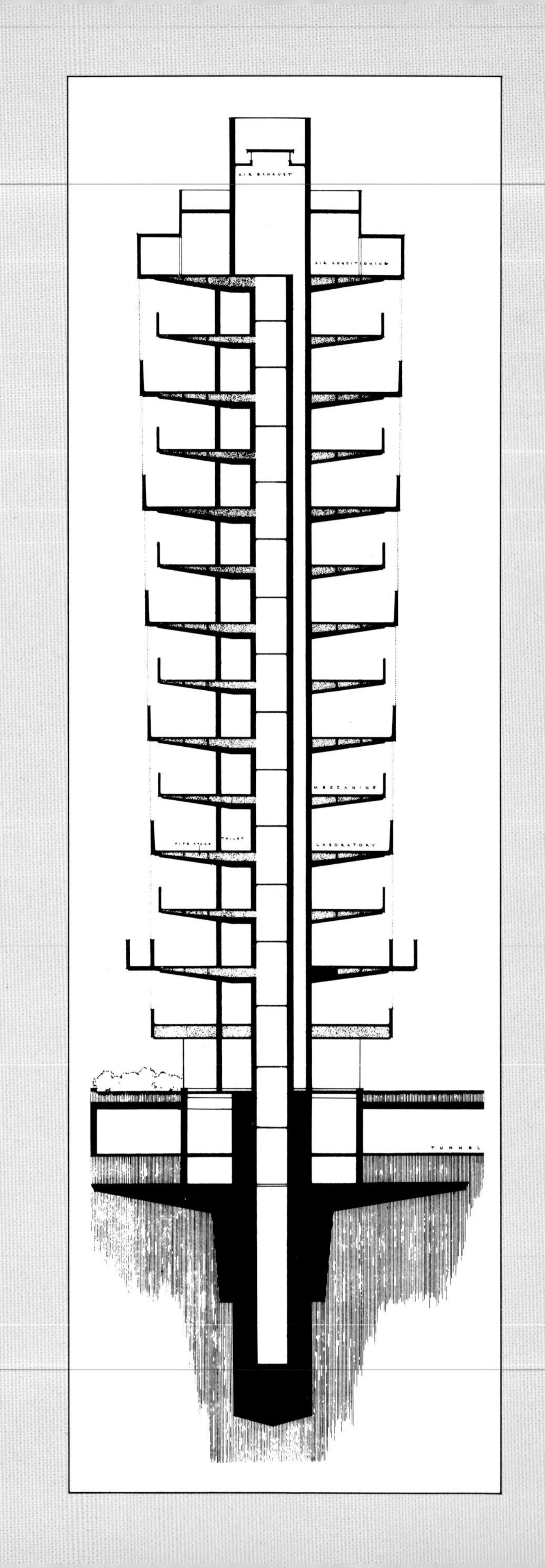
AIR EXHAUST
AIR CONDITIONING
MEZZANINE
PIPE SPACE
TOILET
LABORATORY
TUNNEL

CHAPTER 9

GENESIS OF THE RESEARCH TOWER

We'll put up a stack, that's the prime essential in laboratory design, and then hang all the space needed from it.

FRANK LLOYD WRIGHT

Fig. 116. Presentation section of Research Tower. The Johnson tower reinterprets the Administration Building's mushroom columns. The tower's novel foundation, which Wright dubbed a "taproot," is even more clearly the offspring of the mushroom column. Splayed in three sections, it is suggestive of the hollow shaft, calyx, and petal of the column. Black ink on tracing paper. 30″ × 68″. (Courtesy of the Frank Lloyd Wright Foundation)

The Johnson Research Tower, built ten years after the Administration Building, was shaped by the interplay of two ideals: the company's desire for a model working laboratory building, and Wright's desire to build his first cantilever-core tower. The give and take between client and architect resulted in a building that was less flexible than the Administration Building, but nevertheless a brilliant rethinking of function and form.

Originally, the Johnson company had emphasized merchandising, and the growth of its scientific research lagged behind the growth of business. The company's Research and Development Division began modestly in 1919 when Herbert Johnson, Sr., hired a chemist to support the company's foray into the production of paints and varnishes. In the 1930s the company entered the more specialized industrial wax field, and moved into further industrial production during World War II to aid the war effort. By 1943 the Johnson laboratories employed twenty-five people, directed by J. Vernon Steinle. According to Steinle, in the mid-1920s the company maintained the only wax laboratory in the world. Although others were established in the next twenty years, Steinle believes that the 1943 laboratory and its library were the largest in the world devoted to wax.[1] The company became known as the world's largest manufacturer of consumer and industrial wax products, and product research conducted in its laboratories helped keep it ahead of its competitors.

Like the company's office facilities in the mid-1930s, by the early 1940s the company's research quarters were inefficiently housed in portions of two different buildings. Steinle and Johnson toured laboratories in universities and other companies and periodically discussed building a new laboratory. In July 1943 Steinle wrote a nineteen-page memo to Johnson detailing what he called his dream of postwar expansion for the Johnson laboratories. The memo outlined facilities suitable for research in the areas of synthetic and natural wax, emulsions, paint, varnish, organic and physical chemistry, and biology, and Steinle proposed more than doubling his department, to fifty-two persons. He developed a program, breaking the department into eight divisions: product research; fundamental research; control, analysis and testing; experimental engineering, sales research, home economics; patents; and the library. In the memo Steinle sketched a possible layout for a new 42,000-square-foot laboratory building: a U-shaped two-story structure with a double-loaded corridor and a full basement. As heavily trafficked streets bounded the company to the west and south and a railroad spur formed an edge to the north, the best location for the new laboratory building was to the east of the existing factory complex—immediately north of Wright's Administration Building.

Johnson accepted the general terms of the expansion proposal. At William Connolly's urging, Johnson forwarded a copy of Steinle's memo to Wright on October 4, 1943. In his cover letter to Wright, Johnson wrote:

In our Company's plan for the Post-War Period we are thinking about new Research and Control Laboratories. The proposition is like this:

We insist the building should be built on competitive bids, so final plans and specifications will have to be submitted in detail in advance. . . . The site to be adjacent to our existing office building and plant, with underground connections. . . .

There will be a large amount of piping and wiring because of the nature of the work being done in the laboratories. The building should be air-conditioned. All industrial commission rulings of course will have to be complied with. Second and first floor escapes will be important. All now owned laboratory tables, benches, and sinks to be used. Any new laboratory equipment to be purchased by us, and not to be considered a part of the building. A minimum of ornament and architectural detail is our idea, as the building and work to be done in it only complement the main office.

To be frank, Frank, we simply will not consider a financial and construction nightmare like the office building. It is a plain factory kind of job that should be built by an engineer or contractor like our other factory buildings. Yet because of its proximity to your masterpiece, it should have a relationship thereto and we feel it would be unfair to you and a mistake on our part if we didn't ask how you think you would want to fit into such a picture.

Wright responded vigorously on October 8:

You aren't losing your good hunches, are you Hib? The ones that made you what you are today? I hope the laboratory is better at research than it is at planning because what you show me sets up a competition with our masterpiece very much to the competitor's shame and the detriment of the masterpiece. . . .

I think what we do now should be quite easy. It should be planned in shape for competitive bids—needs no more experiments and should be no headache to any of us at any point. . . .

But the plan your department made is like all plans made by departmental minds—just a little hole for the little cat and a big hole for the big cat. I understand why you want to keep me out of the "fixtures" and I agree. If you say so, then scat!

But let us, for God's sake, honor our labor-pains and protect the baby from the assault-and-battery of a mere department by sensibly proceeding from generals to particulars. Every building is a great opportunity to do the right thing in every direction. Let's aim at doing it? At least.

In considering having Wright design the new building Johnson was concerned that the trials he had experienced during construction of the Administration Building not be repeated, and he put off Wright's repeated attempts to arrange a meeting.[2] Perhaps he thought that Wright's powers of genius and persuasion were sufficient to secure the commission in a face-to-face meeting, and he wanted to avoid a visit with Wright until he had received his design and studied it independently. During the next month Johnson declined three invitations to Taliesin, and asked Wright to simply mail him a proposal. When Wright cabled Johnson that he would come to Racine to meet him and obtain more detailed information, Johnson telephoned him instead. In their conversation Johnson asked Wright to develop several alternate schemes, and to minimize the amount of land needed, Johnson suggested that the building "go up in the air." This may have come from their conversations in 1936 in which Wright had proposed that if the complex were ever expanded it should include a tower. Wright seized Johnson's suggestion, and Wes Peters remembers that Wright worked out the initial form of a tower in just a few days. Johnson's suggestion gave him the opportunity to apply a tower concept that he had been trying to use for the previous fourteen years.

Just one month after the telephone call Wright cabled Johnson, "Am ready with scheme one whenever you are." When Johnson replied, "Why don't you mail the plan so I can get some idea of it before our discussion,"[3] Wright immediately responded:

I would be glad to send the scheme on to you without me but it is a pretty sweeping execution of your suggestion to "go up in the air." I've been unusually successful. The scheme makes the present building-investment a lot better and the present building-investment makes the extension more valuable than it ever could be otherwise. In short the whole is so much greater than the part that the advantages of the whole add up to a superb thing of great value to you. An ideal "Laboratory" if ever one was.

No experimental technicalities are involved but we use what we have already worked out and know all about.

I should like to be in the presentation ceremony not only because I've never let "the opus" travel unintroduced but also because I really want to see you and talk with you.[4]

Johnson still refused to see him, responding, "I note you want to bring the plans in but it is so very difficult travelling nowadays [a reference to war-time gasoline and tire rationing] that I think it would be better if you would just mail it in, and we could make arrangements to discuss it somewhere after the first of the year."[5]

Apparently convinced that Johnson would not meet with him soon, Wright described and supported his design in a series of three letters written over five days. The first letter described new glass tubing details he had created for the Guggenheim Museum project he was then designing, which he predicted would be more watertight than the Administration Building's skylights and clerestories (although ultimately the museum was built without the tubing). The letter continued:

6. And, Hib, there are lots of things I think you would need in your new building—for instance—an Art Department. And certainly exhibition-galleries for your products, demonstrations, and experiments—top lighted, for one thing. There are others of course.

7. Parking is increasingly important as you say. ⅔rds of the entire new ground-area wouldn't be too much for that—affording free and easy parking for about 60 or more cars.

8. There is no use incurring the great expense of going down into the sand-and-water underneath you for space which can only be artificially lit. Especially as most of the ground level itself should go for parking. And the building begins above that.

The present car-port should only be a portico for the whole business both ways, etc., etc., etc. . . .

Note. A daylight research-laboratory would be great if hung to a tall central stack—say eighteen floors with direct access to the stack for retorts and heaters and vapor,—dead air-spaces between floors, overhead to avoid the expense and ugliness of the miles of ducts you would incur in the departmental layout you sent on, etc. etc.

The departmental plan has great outside wall-surface areas—poor horizontal circulation, much "time and space" waste to and fro, bad light, etc. It is a great big expensive building at that. . . .

N.B. "THE WHOLE IS GREATER THAN THE PART." And don't you forget it![6]

The following day Wright continued in a more colorful vein:

O And thou sayest, and then be not sleepy, tell us more of thy pleasant tales? Whereupon Shaharazad [sic] replied "With Love and good will. It hath reached me, O King of the Age that Aladdin said to the Sultan . . .

Dear Hibbard:

11. Why build a heavy building sodden upon the ground—facing awkwardly upon unsightly streets when by creating a charming interior court-space for parking the lighting would come from above or from the court. A gallery would follow above and around that court space, O master. And bridge-tunnels would be seen connecting this space and the administration building itself to the research laboratory which as a tall-shaft would rise from the center of the court. Etc., my lord! Etc.

Thy subjects would like to traverse the bridge-tunnels even similar to the one thou now hast, etc., etc., from which to look down upon a goodly garden in the center of the spacious "parking" with adequate garage-shelter bordering the court on three sides instead of space open to the street. Or descending into a blind basement?

12. And, O Caliph, why not broadcast, the year around, your good tidings (and amusing too) from the top of the eighteen stories—from an inexpensive but beautiful radio-mast rising out of the upmost height?

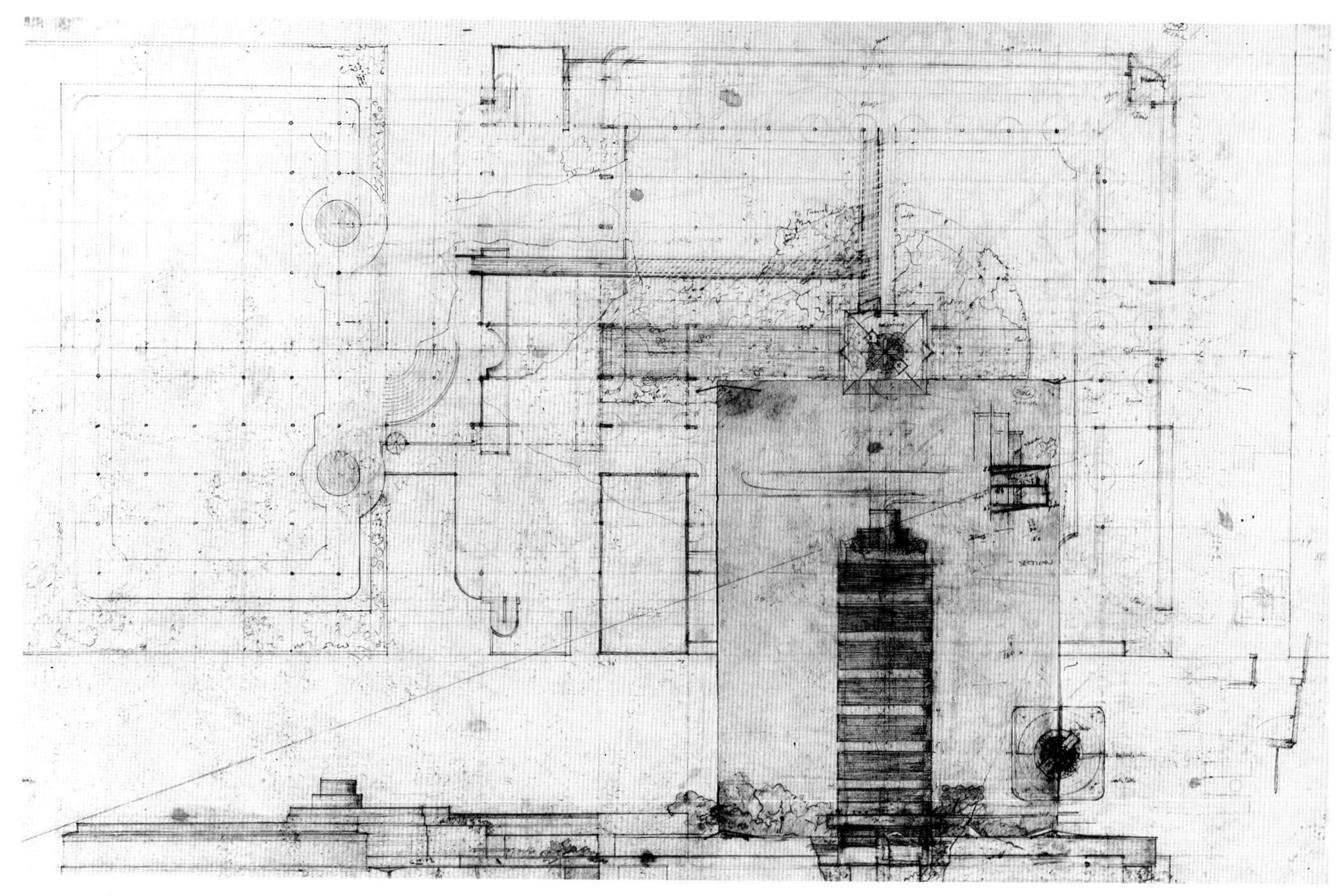

Fig. 117. Conceptual split plan and elevation of Administration Building and Research Tower. Probably Wright's first drawing of the tower. The elevation of the tower itself is on a separate sheet, laid over the drawing. The tower and north entrance to the courtyard are located on the main axis of the Administration Building. This, along with the same geometric language, materials, and detailing convincingly wed the new building to the existing one. 33″ × 24″. Pencil on tracing paper. (Courtesy of the Frank Lloyd Wright Foundation)

13. And should not thy research extend to packaging—to containers—to labels, etc., etc., etc., and find a complete little printing-plant with the offset process for color reproduction where the researchers of the Art-department could find immediate execution? And the Jonwax Journal [the Johnson Company's employee publication] issue forth a good and worthy job? And brochures by thyself such as thou hast sent me to read? Also,

14. The photograph-studios and such work-rooms should adjoin. And all this be well set forth and provided for in the space above the garage-shelter surrounding the great open interior-court from which the great laboratory-shaft would nobly rise in the light connected to this surrounding space above the parking-level of the interior-court by bridge-tunnels. And also lead direct to and from the Administration building itself, my Lord?

What a miracle of beautiful planning will be there to instruct thy foes, delight thy friends and convince thy subjects of the illustrious character of thy reign, O my Caliph?

And end all arguments as to thy power, excellence and Majesty?

15. And what of Brazil and the wax-gatherers there under thy direction and aegis? Should not the Carnauba palm [from which wax was obtained] be set forth in the court-garden above a pool of water—in spring, summer and fall?—And in winter be seen in a panorama in the galleries? Thy activities which extend so far to the South should find exposition at hand?

Shaharazad [sic] was surprised by the dawn of day and ceased to say her permitted say . . . [7]

Two days later Wright resumed:

And to build it satisfactorily why not make Ben Wiltscheck superintendent over the successful bidder on the complete plans according to A.I.A. rules; his salary paid, half by the owner and half by the Architect, and the Architect's duties be thus restricted to plan-making, detailing, specification writing and general supervision? And the owner's worries be confined to getting what he wants properly drawn and specified.

"The Devil you do know is always better than the Devil you don't know?"

The contractor could then get away with very little. And the ideas and plans of the Owner and his Architect who is more Hib than he is himself or vice versa (when it comes to actual building) would be sure of faithful execution and no great worries for you or me.

. . . We want a building so good for its purpose and so much better adapted to it in every way that no business man could ever understand how in hell we arrived at it!

. . . What is the end and aim of Research? Bigger profits? Right. But what kind of profits and for whom and how? More sales? Or more Light to live by, more fun, and live happier—gratified by the fine things of the Mind? Why not both? . . . [8]

At Johnson's request Wright followed up his lyrical letters with a detailed written comparison of the square footage to surface-area ratios of his scheme versus Steinle's, concluding that his own design contained exactly twice as much office, storage, and covered parking space per square foot of outside wall and roof. [9]

Sometime that week Wright gave Johnson his drawings of the tower (figs. 118 and 119). The drawings portray very much what Wright described in his letters: an eighteen-story laboratory tower with floors cantilevered from a central shaft, and the tower placed in the center of a courtyard used for automobile parking. Wright proposed that the tower be connected to the rest of the complex by three glass-tubing bridges, similar to the existing bridge connecting the squash court to the penthouse. The bridges highlight the fragile, objectlike role of the tower in the composition, at once a part of the complex, and yet withdrawn from it. [10]

At this early stage Wright's design for the tower was the sort of abstract form appropriate to an edifice less functional than symbolic, such as a campanile or church steeple. It was one of the most symmetrical, ideal forms that Wright ever designed, and it is significant that he created it for one of the most mundane commissions of his career, "a plain factory kind of job," in Johnson's words. Clearly, Wright was designing an icon that expresses what product research represents to a manufacturing

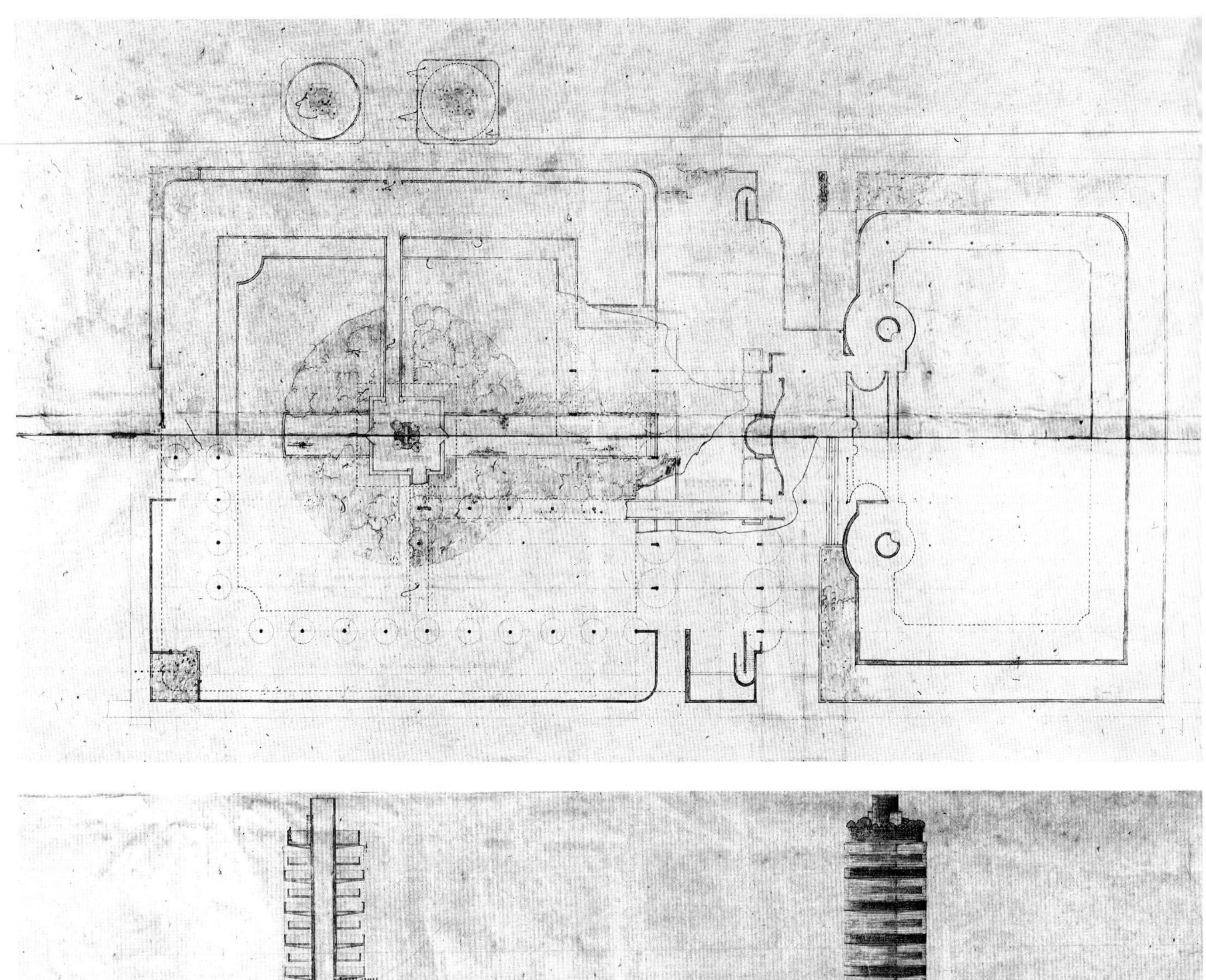

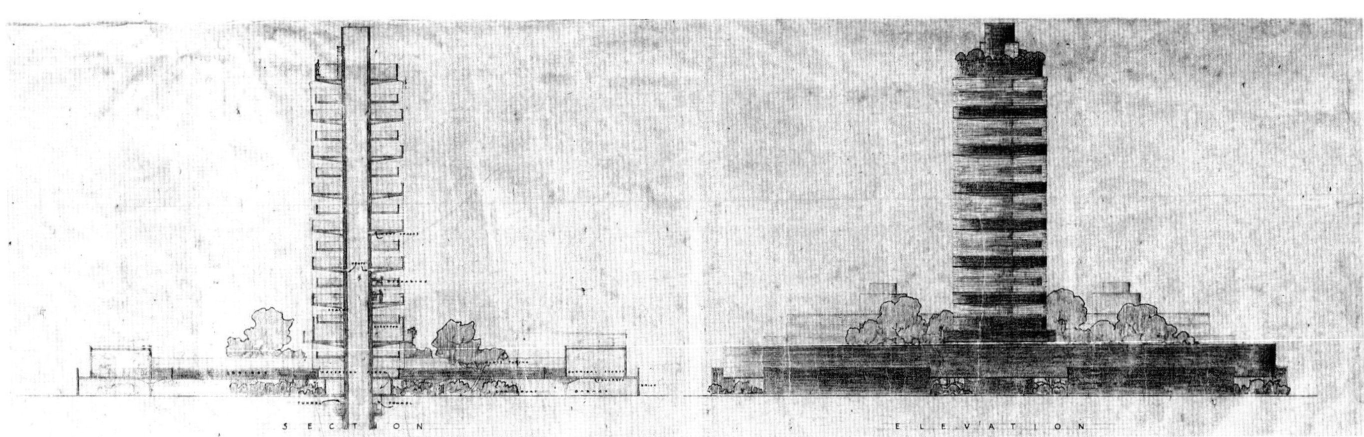

Fig. 118. Split ground-floor and mezzanine plan. In some ways this plan is still an unfinished, schematic design: above the outer carport building, surrounding the tower, is a large, undeveloped, U-shaped second story, which is simply labeled "chemical stores, etc." 19″ × 16″. Pencil on tracing paper (Courtesy of the Frank Lloyd Wright Foundation)

Fig. 119. Section and north elevation of Research Tower. The tower consists of alternating square and round floors cantilevered from a reinforced concrete shaft, which contains two spiral staircases and elevators, and of the supply and return ducts for the laboratories. Wright called the central shaft the corridor of the tower. 37″ × 13″. Pencil and colored pencil on tracing paper. (Courtesy of the Frank Lloyd Wright Foundation)

corporation. The protected yet highly visible tower celebrates the secret but essential functions of research and development that are the life's blood of the company.

Wright first developed the tower's structural system in 1929 for three unbuilt apartment towers he proposed for the grounds of Saint Mark's Church in the Bowery, in Manhattan (figs. 120 and 121), and he continued to use it in towers throughout his career. Wright added new layers of metaphoric meaning to the system, however, when he applied it in the Johnson complex: the tower can be considered a reinterpretation of the Administration Building's mushroom columns (fig. 115). In the Administration Building a forest of columns fills the great central room; but in the second building the central space—a courtyard—is occupied by a single, large "column." Its hollow, central, structural shaft carries not only heating and cooling ducts, but also the chemical supplies and vents that constitute the special technical needs of a laboratory. Wright's mechanistic conception of the tower was revealed when he told Johnson in 1943 that they could build a stack and hang their laboratories from it.[11]

This conception is suggestive of Buckminster Fuller's 1927 4-D Apartment Tower (compare figs. 122 and 123), which, along with Fuller's 1928 Dymaxion House model, highly publicized when they were displayed in Chicago, may have been catalysts for Wright's 1929 Saint Mark's Towers. Somewhat different structurally, the Dymaxion House was to consist of transparent glass walls and inflated rubber flooring suspended by metal cables from a central aluminum mast. It was designed totally for efficient, industrial production, and it celebrated modern technology. Wright, however, disliked overt mechanistic imagery in residential design. Although he wrote that the Saint Mark's Towers were completely standardized for prefabrication, he softened their machine-cut facades with ornamental copper panels and a profusion of hanging plants. The later Johnson Research Tower was an industrial, rather than a residential, building, and Wright gave it a more austere facade and a central shaft that approximated Fuller's round, hollow aluminum mast more closely than did the four piers of the Saint Mark's Towers.[12]

Both Fuller and Wright's towers not only took new technology to its structural limits, but included components that were designed for technologies not yet invented. In spite of this similarity and their uncanny resemblance, the two innovative buildings express very different attitudes toward architectural design. Fuller hoped to create a generic type, the one "final best design," that could be inexpensively mass-produced. Wright, on the other hand, was using a real project as an opportunity to manifest one of an infinite number of possible forms. To build his tower, new technology would be combined with a highly labor-intensive installation: technology was neither more nor less important than craft. Both were merely tools to be used to produce an efficient, graceful structure.

Another difference between the two approaches is revealed by differing attitudes toward context. Fuller proposed millions of Dymaxion towers to be dropped by zeppelins on sites around the world. Technology was to dominate Fuller's utopian visual environment. Wright, however, repeatedly tried to integrate his towers into their contexts. In his mixed-use Crystal Heights project of 1940, for example, twenty-four towers were incorporated into a large, sophisticated composition. The Johnson Research Tower, as Wright designed it, was part of a careful one-city-block composition, and its dark red brick nearly matched the brick of other nearby industrial buildings.

It is also significant that the main elements of Wright's Johnson complex, a great columnar hall and a narrow tower, are two of the most commonly recurring forms in ecclesiastic architecture. The usual precedents for an office building and a research laboratory suggested no such forms; it required distinct intention on Wright's part to create them. Herbert Johnson later said, "In life, as in business, the deep spiritual values truly must never be lost sight of—but, at the same time, we cannot be prone to disregard the material values in life. The two must be molded together to form a dynamic whole."[13] In the Johnson buildings Wright intended to uplift the employees

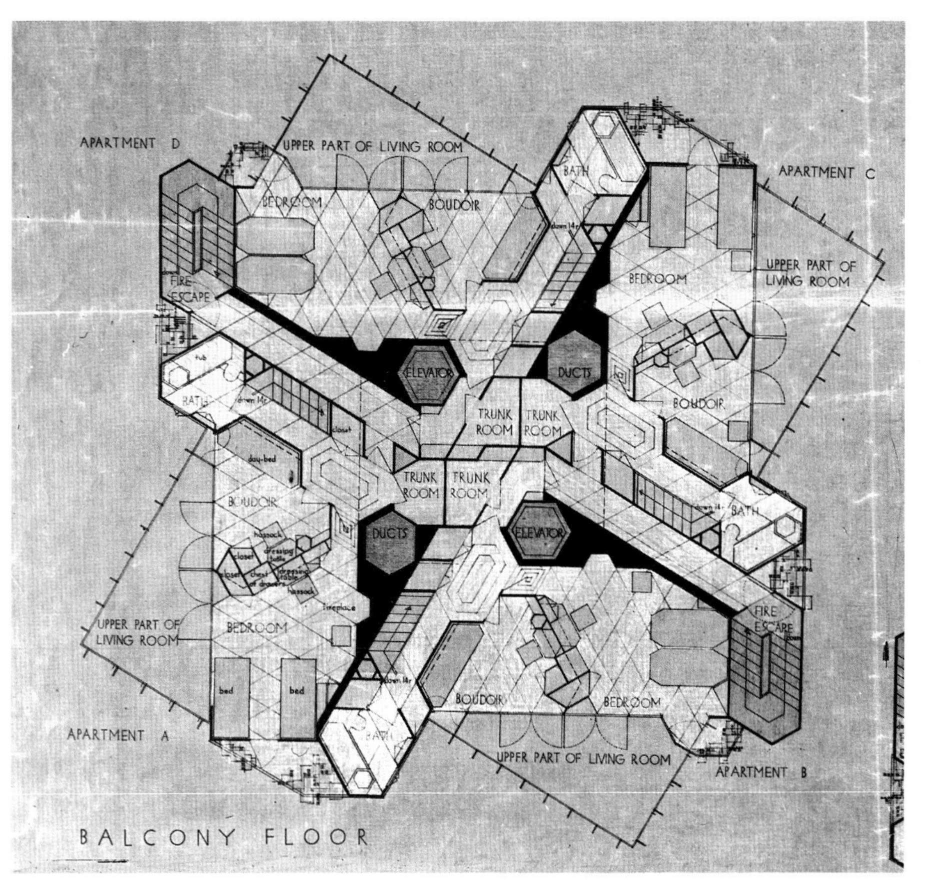

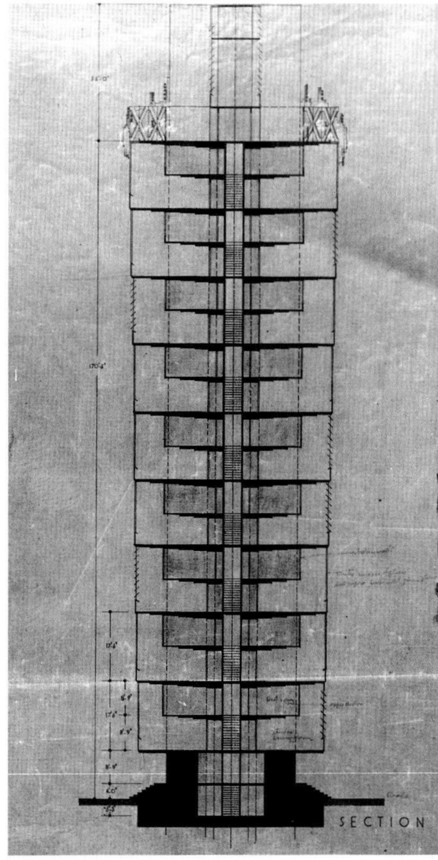

Fig. 120. Saint Mark's Towers, New York City, 1929. Plan of typical alternating mezzanine floor. Although these towers are almost identical to the Research Tower in section, in plan they are very different. In the typical Saint Mark's tower the floors are hung from four great structural piers that divide the plan into quadrangles, each containing stacked duplex apartments, with each unit oriented toward the view outside. In the Johnson tower each pair of floors constitutes a single two-story laboratory space, and the structural piers have been consolidated into a single central cylinder—a substantive transformation of the treelike structure of the tower, producing a very different building. (Courtesy of the Frank Lloyd Wright Foundation)

Fig. 121. Saint Mark's Towers, New York City, 1929. Section. (Courtesy of the Frank Lloyd Wright Foundation)

Fig. 122. "Zeppelin Delivery of 4-D Houses." Cartoon by Buckminster Fuller, 1927. Although it appears to have been drawn humorously, Fuller, as well as the public, took his apartment building seriously. (Courtesy of the Buckminster Fuller Institute, Los Angeles)

Fig. 123. Forming ninth floor of the Research Tower, April 1949. (Courtesy of Johnson Wax)

by inspiring them. Ecclesiastic architects throughout history have attempted to do the same, and it is not surprising that they have generated similar forms.

The strongest comparisons with the Johnson buildings are to Japanese religious complexes.[14] For example, in the Horyu-ji Temple in Nara (fig. 125) a columniated one-story structure encloses a rectangular courtyard, oriented to the cardinal points. Within the courtyard is a serene world in miniature with two buildings centered on its long axis: the shrine, which consists of one large room, and the pagoda, or prayer tower. All of the structures emphasize horizontality, and the permeable pagoda, with broadly cantilevered roofs extending above each floor, brings the Johnson tower to mind, particularly as it looked before the translucent tube walls were installed.

There are also similarities between the Johnson complex and the form of a mosque. They share a hall filled with outward-flaring columns, a tower *cum* minaret, complexly used domes and the exuberant play of curves. The Administration Building also makes various references to the Egyptian unidirectional hypostylic hall. Wright's unusual name for his mushroom columns, dendriform, in fact refers to the Egyptian column, and the aqueous quality of the Administration Building's interior, so often described as giving the sense of being in a pond beneath lily pads, suggests the Egyptian re-creation of the underworld.[15] The horizontal streamlined detailing of the building reinforces this reading.

In making these cross-cultural comparisons it is important to remember that Wright began his career as an eclectic architect, designing in the Shingle, Queen Anne, Tudor, Colonial Revival and other styles between 1887 and 1895. While he was young he displayed a rare mastery of the diverse styles prevailing in the Victorian era. The Johnson buildings exemplify the skill he displayed throughout his career at absorbing elements of architecture from various cultures, and selectively transforming and incorporating aspects of them into original, personal forms, his own profound vision of the architecture of twentieth-century America.

Fig. 124. Administration Building and Research Tower, 1956. Wright called the tower a "heliolab" and a "sun worshipper." The globe in the foreground was installed in 1954, fulfilling Wright's 1936 intention. Built-up skylights over the Great Workroom were added in the mid-1950s to prevent leaks. (Courtesy of Johnson Wax)

Fig. 125. Horyu-ji Temple, Nara, Japan, circa A.D. 607. Shrine and pagoda. A hall and a tower occupy a courtyard, which is entered at the center of its long axis. (Photo courtesy of Photri/Orion; drawing courtesy of Horizon Press)

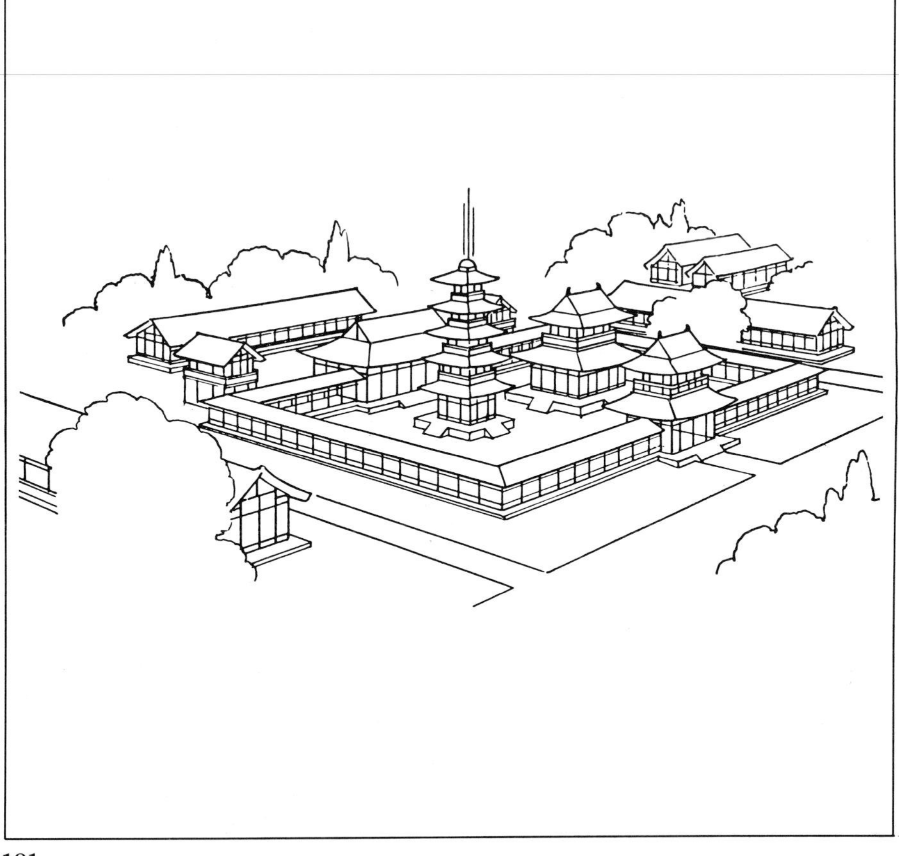

CHAPTER 10

DEVELOPMENT OF THE TOWER

Fig. 126. Perspective view of Research Tower from courtyard interior. Preliminary proposal in which each floor of the tower is slightly wider than the one below. 27″ × 23″. Sepia ink on tracing paper. (Courtesy of the Frank Lloyd Wright Foundation)

Both Herbert Johnson and J. Vernon Steinle received Wright's proposal enthusiastically. Steinle wrote a thoughtful critique of the plans for Johnson that began:

> Let me preface my remarks by stating that . . . I consider the plans to be extremely beautiful and that they probably can be worked out practically. I am, particularly, enthused about the possibilities of working out the tower idea with the services taken care of in the central shaft.[1]

Steinle went on to point out various difficulties he foresaw in the scheme and Jack Ramsey also wrote Johnson a critique. Over the next four years Wright modified the design, solving most of their problems.

Foremost was the difficulty of circulation. Both Ramsey and Steinle suggested eliminating one of the three bridges to the tower and adding a tunnel to connect it to the Administration Building. In Wright's design the only interior route from the Administration Building to the U-shaped second story of the courtyard building was through a series of two bridges. Steinle needled Wright for doing just what Wright had criticized in Steinle's earlier floor plans, noting that "... long and rather wasteful corridors must be provided" in the twenty-five-foot-wide U-shaped wing.[2] Ramsey cogently suggested converting the squash court and the adjacent carport deck into office space, a suggestion Wright later adopted. The original scheme would have produced a more hermetic complex, with closed two-story facades on all sides. By doing away with the second floor on the three street facades of the courtyard, Wright opened up the complex to its surroundings.

Steinle was also concerned about circulation within the tower. Wright had proposed two tiny elevators and two equally small spiral staircases. Steinle noted that one of the elevators should be large enough to transport freight, and Ramsey suggested that one elevator might do the job. Accordingly, Wright later substituted one larger elevator for the two small ones. Similarly, Steinle wryly commented on the practicality of five-foot-diameter spiral staircases in an eighteen-story building: "Although one [staircase] should be sufficient, I can readily see why two have been provided, since one must be for going up and the other for going down."[3] Indeed, Wright later designed one larger bullnose staircase to replace them. Also, Steinle was concerned about headroom in the tower, which varied from seven feet to five-and-a-half feet next to the central shaft.

Steinle invited Wright to go through the company's laboratories, as well as others in Milwaukee, with Ramsey, Johnson, and himself in order to come to a better mutual understanding about the facilities they would need. Wright arrived on February 2. During that day Wright argued in favor of retaining maximum simplicity throughout the building. He urged a minimum number of outlets and pipe runs beyond the perimeter of the central core and suggested that to minimize pipe runs, the outlets on the shaft at each floor feed gasoline and distilled water tanks, which the technicians would wheel to their workbenches. Steinle, who was skeptical as to whether Wright had the specialized technical knowledge needed to lay out a laboratory, teased him for proposing "something like a blowtorch" as a heat source for experiments.[4] Wright referred to the "vital organs" and "vital fluids" in the building, leading Steinle to challenge, "I will be looking for those anatomical drawings showing the flow of the life blood and nervous system of our building."[5]

Wright presented Steinle with slightly revised plans later that month. After seeing them Johnson requested that Wright draw up another scheme, complaining, "They have become more complicated and more expensive . . . I do not like the additional office space; and I am beginning to think that the housing around the central shaft is too far away from our operations, expensive, and not suited to our needs.[6] Steinle was more positive, writing, "I am satisfied that together we can make a laboratory out of your proposed tower."[7]

The next month Wright prepared a revised scheme partially developing the U-shaped building surrounding the tower. The scheme earmarked part of the first floor of the courtyard wings for storage, with a two-story light well that would allow people in offices above to see into it. Wright was attempting to open up spaces as he did throughout the complex, but Johnson understandably questioned the appropriateness of a laboratory whose supplies and equipment would be so visible. Johnson also suggested moving some nonlaboratory space from the tower to the surrounding building, in order to trim the tower by two pairs of floors. He wrote, "This no doubt will cut down the cost considerably, and can you give me any reason why it would not be practical architecturally?" At the same time he proposed moving the advertising department into the new building from the Administration Building, which was already beginning to become crowded. Finally, he suggested that the first and second floors of the tower, which Wright was enclosing with brick walls, be opened up with glass, as were the higher floors.

Wright responded in a letter from Arizona on May 22, "I've gone over your tentative suggestions hastily—without the drawings (which are at Taliesin) and should say that all you want to do can be done. But the two upper floors of the tall-laboratory are the cheapest space you can get—merely a duplicate of existing structure—elevators same, etc. The exuberance of a tall building is in its tallness."[8]

Johnson visited Wright at Taliesin on September 11 as Wright was developing a new design responding to most of the points Johnson, Connolly, Steinle, and Ramsey had made during the preceding months. Johnson suggested that as an alternative Wright develop a design in which the tower would be located across Howe Street, to the west of the Administration Building. Presumably, Johnson's intention was to bring the laboratories closer to the manufacturing buildings. Accordingly, Wright prepared a set of drawings in which the carport was unchanged, but in which the courtyard stood empty, with the tower across the street, west of the entrance to the Administration Building. The scheme was not pursued further, and apparently was not even shown to the other executives (figs. 127 and 128).

In September, when Connolly prepared a program for a 2,500-square-foot advertising department, he urged that the tower design be made less abstract and symmetrical. Most of the changes in the next, nearly final, version of Wright's scheme seem to be responses to his points. He wrote referring to Wright's early version of the design:

> It is, I believe, Wright's philosophy that the functions which are to be carried on in a building should pretty much determine its size and contour. I have a little feeling that in the new building . . . he is attempting to force [the advertising and several other departments] into a preconceived setting.
>
> . . . I know Wright likes to keep things open and I am in sympathy with that, but in the section of the new building where we shall be located, nearly half of the space on the second floor . . . is represented by a hole in the floor and a walkway around it.
>
> . . . I should like to see [Wright] approach the design of . . . [our] . . . floor <u>from a fresh viewpoint</u> . . . [and] it would be desirable for us to have an open area for visitors and possibly a receptionist.

He proposed that the advertising department be located near the squash court, at the north end of the existing bridge.[9]

On September 30 Wright presented another new design, responding to most of the points of the past few months. In a compromise with Johnson, Wright lowered the tower by one pair of floors from the original design. The bridges to the tower and the U-shaped second story over the carport deck were removed and replaced by a fluid second- and third-story wing surrounding and incorporating the former squash court. The wing would contain an advertising department, lecture room, and a model apartment. In his original memo to Johnson, which served as a program for the project, Steinle had proposed a model apartment in which the Johnson company and its competitors' products would be tested under actual home-use conditions. In response Wright designed an exhibition dwelling over the east end of the carport roof, directly beneath the advertising department (figs. 129–131).

Johnson was pleased with the new design for the complex. After Wright presented it to him, Ben Wiltscheck, and Steinle, Johnson wrote:

> Wright to my way of thinking now has a workable plan suited to our needs. It is new in several respects and, generally speaking, all of the new ideas are improvements. Of course many details are to be worked out.[10]

During October 1944 company executives gave Wright a list of desired alterations, which Wright entered directly on the drawings. The most significant changes consisted of turning the exhibition dwelling bedroom into a field research office, eliminating a bridge across Howe Street (replaced with a less expensive tunnel), and moving the proposed salesmen's lecture room out of the existing squash court, replacing it with a darkroom. Later in the month they decided to eliminate the salesmen's lecture room entirely and use the Administration Building theater for a lecture room when one was needed. On November 2 Herbert Johnson signed the drawings to indicate his approval.

As "client" for the tower, Steinle had the primary responsibility to see that he ended up with satisfactory laboratories, and he and Wright engaged in somewhat heated debates over the tower ceiling heights, floor area, and central shaft and elevator sizes. In particular, he pressed Wright to enlarge the tower to forty-two feet in width and to substitute seven foot six inch ceilings for the proposed six foot six inch ones, which he felt were too low for the laboratory apparatus needed. His changes, however, would have disturbed the delicate composition of the complex. The first would have weakened the relationship of the courtyard to the tower, while the second would have attenuated the dynamic compression and expansion of space within the laboratories and also cause the Administration Building to appear somewhat diminutive when viewed with the tower behind it. Wright testily proposed a compromise of forty feet in width with ceilings at seven feet three inches, cabling to Johnson, "[Steinle] wants to add substantially to building costs and hurt the relationship of lab to administration."[11]

Steinle was irked by the telegram, and felt that Johnson was letting Wright go over his head. Steinle wrote to Johnson that if he was to " 'fight out' with Mr. Wright the details which are necessary for the proper functioning of the building," he had to be able to speak with Johnson's full authority. Although happy with the general form of the building, Steinle nonetheless continued:

> I do not mean that the architectural scheme should be disrupted in order to obtain 100% efficiency in the laboratory functions, but on the other hand I do not believe that Frank Lloyd Wright's ideas are so static that they are impossible [sic] of being changed. I have faith that he can . . . alter his basic tower principle . . . in a manner to make it functional as a laboratory without losing its beauty of form and design . . . but I am certain he will not do it unless he is wheedled into it by continued insistence that it must not be a tower of Bable erected as a monument to his folly, but a tower of light and knowledge which will function as a modern laboratory building.[12]

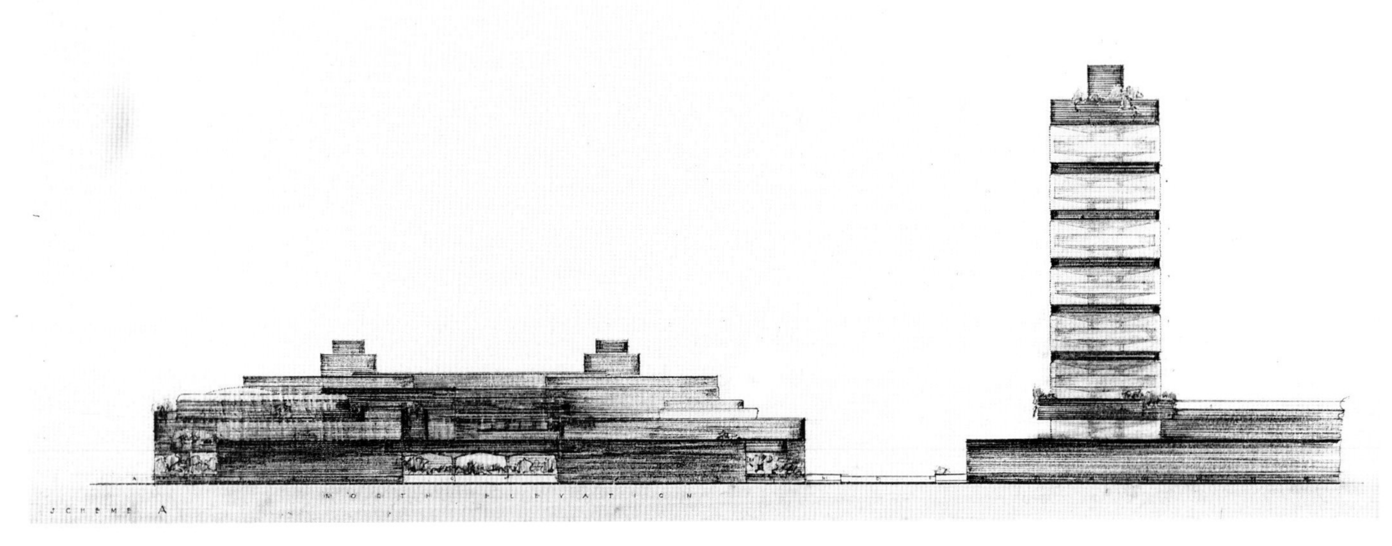

Fig. 127. North elevation of Alternate Scheme "A". In this design the courtyard is empty and the tower is located on the opposite side of Howe Street. 36" × 31". Pencil and colored pencil on tracing paper. (Courtesy of the Frank Lloyd Wright Foundation)

Fig. 128. Ground-floor plan of Alternate Scheme "A". This design, drawn up at Herbert Johnson's suggestion, was abandoned immediately. 36" × 31". Pencil and colored pencil on tracing paper. (Courtesy of the Frank Lloyd Wright Foundation)

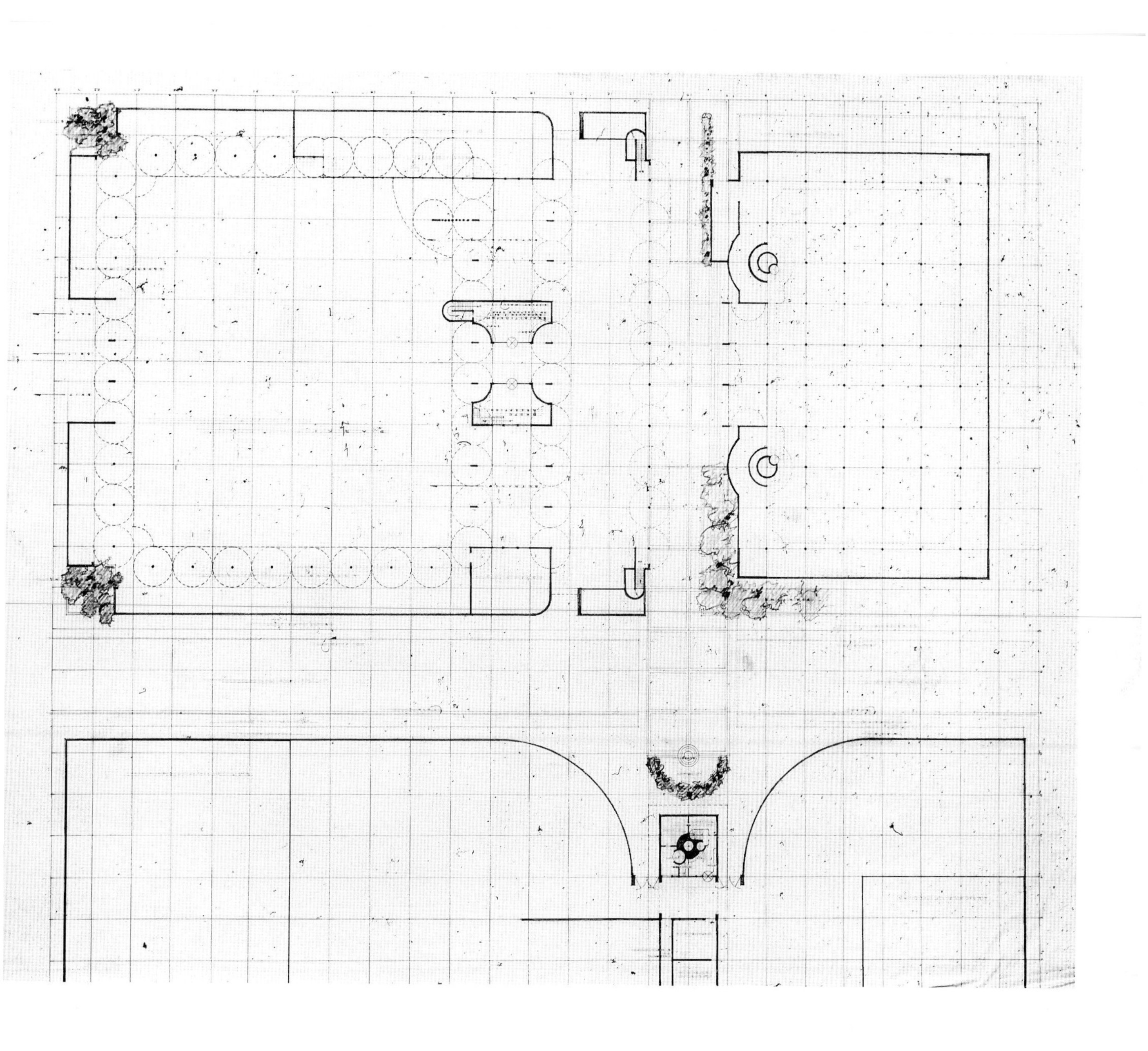

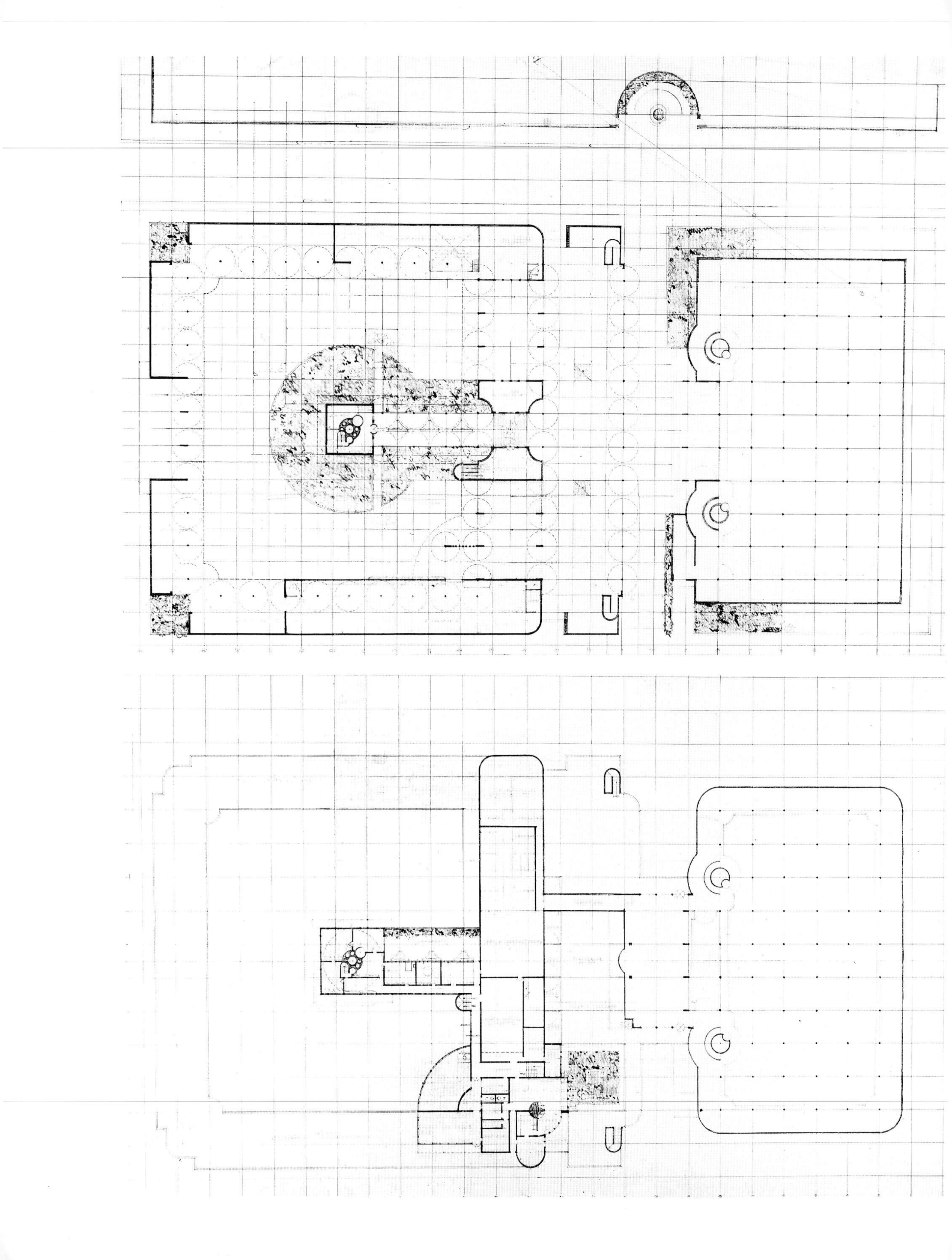

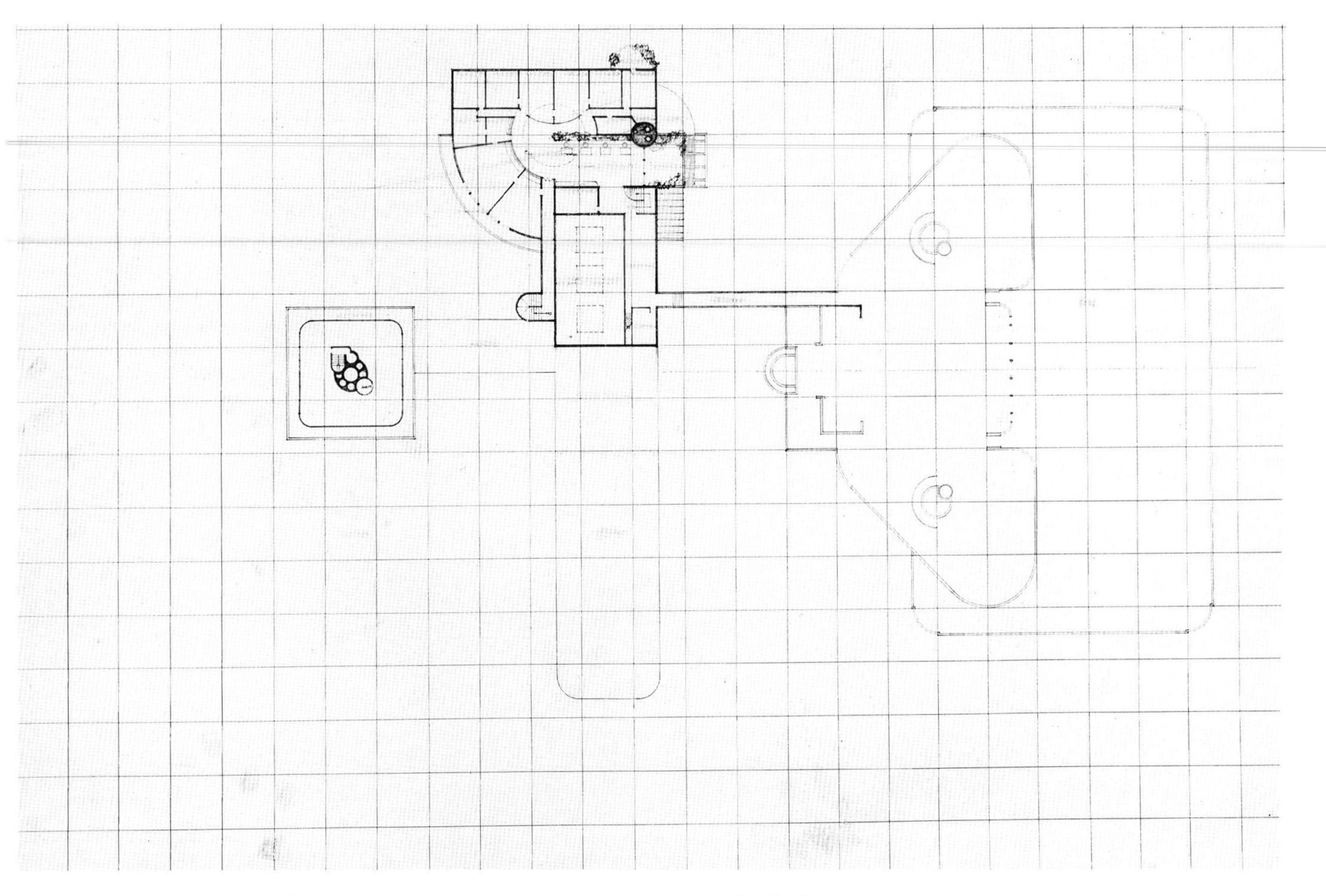

Fig. 129. Ground-floor plan of Administration Building and Research Tower. 36″ × 22″. Pencil and colored pencil on tracing paper. November 1944. Signed and approved by Herbert Johnson. (Courtesy of the Frank Lloyd Wright Foundation)

Fig. 130. Second-floor (mezzanine-level) plan of Administration Building and Research Tower. The squash court has been transformed into a two-story photography studio with darkrooms, and so on to be laid out to the west of the court. A second bridge (later eliminated) connects this area to the mezzanine of the Great Workroom. The most intriguing element of the new composition is the widened link to the tower. Formerly, the tower floated in isolation in the center of the courtyard, linked to the rest of the complex by fragile bridges. In the present scheme, it is connected along the main axis of the complex by a gallery (containing a conference room and office for Steinle) as wide as the tower itself, integrating the tower dynamically and fluidly into the composition. 36″ × 22″. Pencil and colored pencil on tracing paper. November 1944. Signed and approved by Herbert Johnson. (Courtesy of the Frank Lloyd Wright Foundation)

Fig. 131. Third-floor (penthouse-level) plan of Administration Building and Research Tower. Above the exhibition dwelling is the advertising department. Wright organized the department around a central area into which a semicircular wall of glass tubing protrudes, with a large glass dome hovering above. 36″ × 22″. Pencil and colored pencil on tracing paper. November 1944. Signed and approved by Herbert Johnson. (Courtesy of the Frank Lloyd Wright Foundation)

The layout of the laboratories was placed in Steinle's hands rather than Wright's. Whether this was Johnson's desire or the result of a lack of interest on Wright's part is unclear. To assess possible equipment layouts, and thus determine whether the compromise dimensions would be workable, Steinle proposed having made a scale model of two main floors and one mezzanine of the tower, but it was never built. Instead, the following year Steinle went to the extraordinary length of having carpenters build a full-scale mock-up of a complete tower floor and mezzanine. A representative of the Hamilton Manufacturing Company (suppliers of the tower's laboratory furniture) came to Racine, and in mid-November of 1945, Steinle had each of his department heads lay out his department's furnishings at full scale in the mock-up. The Hamilton representative took notes, from which he prepared shop drawings of each floor's furniture.

Steinle lobbied again for a larger elevator in the tower in 1948, complaining that the proposed elevator was too small to lift large equipment and that in case of chemical explosion too few persons could fit in the elevator for quick evacuation. Wright dispensed with Steinle's objections, writing to Johnson that there was a way to lift equipment somewhat larger than the cab he had designed by hanging it from the elevator; that the elevator was not meant to be used as an emergency escape—that the stairwell was the only protected, fire-proof channel; and finally, that the amount of concrete in the shaft had already been reduced to a minimum—if it were trimmed any further Wright would absolve himself of all responsibility for the matter. Johnson arranged a meeting at which Steinle agreed to accept Wright's elevator dimensions.

In December 1943 Wright suggested to Johnson that they jointly hire Ben Wiltscheck to supervise the contractor for the project. Accordingly, the company contacted Wiltscheck, and he agreed to take on the job. In his detailed proposal he noted:

I will give general direction to the work. I will spend a lot of time with Mr. Wright to get the information which I will need to make the work go smoothly and rapidly . . . instead of writing letters, telephoning or waiting for Mr. Wright to come to Racine, I will go to Taliesin for my information. I will make my own working drawings and take them to him for approval or corrections.[13]

The remainder of Wiltscheck's proposal makes it clear that he saw himself in the role of general contractor, although he had recently retired and although Johnson had asked him to get involved in the process earlier than was typical for a contractor. Two weeks later he proposed to work with Wright on the development of plans, furnish them to the mechanical engineers and coordinate the engineer's drawings, and prepare a cost estimate.

Johnson put Wiltscheck on the company payroll on June 26 to ensure that a complete, biddable set of drawings was on hand for contractors when the company was ready to begin construction. Wiltscheck met with Wright at Taliesin several times that week to discuss his plan of operation and reported to Johnson:

[Wright] was pleased with the program and feels that it will work much better than that followed in the construction of the administration building. He liked the suggestion that I bring my draftsman to Taliesin to start working drawings just as soon as the general plans are developed sufficiently for this purpose.[14]

Wright drew one-eighth-inch scale plans and elevations of the project in November, and asked Wiltscheck to have a deep test boring and soil analysis done, in preparation for designing footings for the tower. Wes Peters enlisted the aid of Mendel Glickman, the engineer who had worked with him on the structural calculations for the Administration Building, to assist him with the calculations for the Research Tower. Glickman was no longer residing at Taliesin but in Milwaukee. Peters, however, ended up doing all of the structural work on the tower alone, a formidable task because while the engineering calculations for such a structure were complex, no applicable handbooks or tables existed for him to consult, and no similar building had ever been built.

Progress on the building plans slowed down during the course of 1945. Wright failed to complete the detailed plans of the building that year, and consequently Wes Peters could not complete the structural drawings. Wiltscheck, with John Halama, a young architect whom he hired in May, hoped to do working and shop drawings, but with Wright and Peters's drawings incomplete, their work was minimal. Similarly, a mechanical engineer who worked out in theory the mechanical systems in the tower with Wright in the summer of 1945 was also unable to prepare his drawings. The Hamilton Manufacturing Company promised to deliver preliminary furniture layouts of the laboratories by late January 1945 but did not complete them until the end of the year. Although Wiltscheck pressed Wright to complete his work, there was not a great sense of urgency to his requests, as it appeared that the project would be unable to obtain either materials or Federal government approval to build until the war was over.

Wright had selected the Carrier Air Conditioning Company over Westerlin & Campbell Company to lay out and supply the air-conditioning system in the building. The Carrier Company's manpower, however, was restricted by the war effort and when it finally submitted to Wright a partial plan for heating the tower, he rejected the proposal as insufficiently imaginative. In March 1945, citing the pressure of war work, Carrier declined to do additional planning and recommended that Wright hire Chicago mechanical engineer Samuel Lewis instead. Lewis came to Spring Green near the end of April and satisfied Wright, who in a subsequent letter to Johnson called Lewis "a tops engineer." Wright decided to employ him to draw up plumbing and electrical plans for the building as well as plans for heating and air-conditioning.

Nevertheless, when Wiltscheck asked Wright's permission to bring Lewis to Racine for a meeting without Wright, Wright responded:

> Conferences between my experts and my clients, when I am not present, could only result in confusion and undesirable division of Authority. Which would only demoralize the building, not help build it. And not just maybe either.[15]

Wiltscheck forwarded Wright's letter to Johnson and noted,

> I do not think that he is altogether wrong in what he says. He is afraid that we will steer Sam Lewis into some scheme which he can not approve and will then have to do a lot of arguing to undo it. In spite of much public opinion to the contrary, Mr. Wright does not like to be unpleasant.[16]

On August 1 Lewis, Wiltscheck, Johnson, and Steinle met with Wright in Spring Green and reached agreement on the heating, air-conditioning, and mechanical systems for the tower. According to the plan, service pipes, rising up the central shaft of the core supplied the laboratories with hot, cold, and distilled water; illuminating gas; compressed air; carbon dioxide or nitrogen; steam; and D.C. and A.C. (both 110 and 120) electricity. To provide safe access a door to the pipe shaft was provided at each stair platform level. A safety working platform in the shaft was located just below each door. For temperature isolation, steam supply and return pipes ran through a separate recess in the side of the stair alcove. At each floor services passed from the central shaft through the floor, to the exterior wall, and around to the laboratory desks.

Two air-handling units for hot and cooled air supply and exhaust were at the top of the central core, projecting above the tower. Supply ducts passing down the central shaft fed through the hollow floors and vented through grilles in the ceilings of the main floors. Exhaust grilles in the ceiling above the mezzanine floors conducted air through a duct in the floor above, and into the central pipe shaft. Supplemental fin radiators were placed behind the brick around the circumference of each floor, and a small supplemental air intake grille was located on each floor. The offices over the carport were cooled by a separate forced air system and heated by radiant hot water ceiling panels.

Wright and Peters's work was near enough to completion by early 1946 for Lewis to make a preliminary layout of the heating and air-conditioning system, which Wright approved. When Lewis started to size ducts and equipment, however, he found that several areas in the building were too narrow, so at a series of meetings in Lewis's Chicago office, he and Wiltscheck worked out minor dimensional alterations to the building. Wiltscheck proposed them in September to Wright at Taliesin, who accepted them. Halama drew them up, as he did almost every revision that was made from then on. Lewis then proceeded with detailed planning of the system, with Wiltscheck acting as his liaison. Until Lewis finally worked out the system, Steinle's worry over fitting the many services into the narrow central shaft was so great that he recalled finding himself waking up at night with nightmares of pipes wrapping around his throat.[17]

In May 1944, as a model for a contract between them, Wright had sent Johnson a copy of a contract he had prepared for the Solomon R. Guggenheim Foundation to build its museum. The contract specified a fee of 10 percent of construction costs: 3 percent payable upon acceptance of preliminary studies, 5 percent payable for plans and specifications when contracts were let and there was a reasonable assurance that costs would not exceed $750,000, and 2 percent upon completion and acceptance of the building, with architect and client to share equally the cost of a superintendent. These terms were comparable to common architectural fees for house design but were higher than the usual architectural fee for industrial buildings. The terms were rather more favorable to Wright than his original terms for design of the Administration Building had been: 2½ percent upon submission of plans plus 7½ percent paid only if the plans were used under Wright's supervision. A contract for the design of the Research Tower was not forthcoming, but on May 22, 1944 Wright requested his preliminary payment, which, based on his estimate that the tower might cost $750,000, came to $22,500. Johnson paid him only $15,000, arguing that the building might end up costing well under the estimated amount.

In November Wright asked for another $10,000, writing:

> May I say that I think it a great mistake to estimate the cost for our present project at less than $750,000.00? . . . We haven't stinted you, Hib, and won't. You won't stint us either, if I know you . . .
>
> Always faithfully broke—
>
> Frank Lloyd Wright[18]

Johnson sent him a check for the amount, replying, "If it is a question of need with you, and I assume it is or you would not have written, I will go along with you."[19]

Johnson's two payments to Wright in 1944, totaling $25,000, more than covered the 3 percent of the building's estimated cost of $750,000, which Wright was due for preliminary drawings. In May of 1945 Johnson agreed to pay Wright another $5,000 per month for seven months—payment in full of the 5 percent he agreed to pay for construction drawings. Johnson was not obligated to pay any of the $35,000 until the drawings were done, but agreed to pay in installments as work progressed, at Wright's request.

In October 1946 Wright proposed to Johnson that the building would cost $1.2 million, entitling him to an additional $31,000 for plans. Failing to get an answer to his letter, Wright sent Johnson a brief note ten days later saying, "We are strictly up against it—Like the good client and true friend you really are—won't you come across—"[20]

Unknown to Wright, Johnson had turned the matter over to Wiltscheck, who, accepting the revised estimate, suggested paying Wright $4,000 per month for the next three months, withholding the remaining $15,000 until the Wisconsin Industrial Commission approved the design. Johnson accepted Wiltscheck's proposal and forwarded the first $4,000 check to Wright.

The estimate stood for a year and a half, but in May 1948 the company accepted a revised estimate of $2 million, and Johnson agreed to pay Wright the additional amount outstanding to him on a commission of $200,000, to be paid monthly over a two-year period. At the same time Johnson insisted that Wright agree that he would be entitled to no further commission should costs exceed $2 million.

Apparently Johnson was enormously satisfied with Wright's work and not overly concerned with the higher estimated cost of the Research Tower, because that summer he attempted to undertake a far larger project with Wright—a building program for his employees in which he would aid them in obtaining mortgages to build homes on a large parcel of land he owned. He hoped to build as many as 200 to 400 houses and wanted Wright to design them. It may be that he was attempting to follow through on Wright's suggestion to him twelve years earlier to build an entire Johnson development, according to the principles of Broadacre City. Had this project materialized it would have been the largest of Wright's career. However, when Johnson failed to raise the funds needed for the mortgages from real estate equity firms, he relinquished the venture.[21]

The wave of publicity that had accompanied the opening of the Administration Building seven years earlier alerted William Connolly of the promotional value of a major new Wright building. In March 1946 the company sent a press release announcing the new design to newspapers and news, business, and trade magazines. An artist prepared an accompanying rendering of the Research Tower with the Administration Building, and the cover letter billed the press release as "The story of Frank Lloyd Wright's latest creation—a 15-story test tube to be built in Racine, Wisconsin, for Johnson's Wax—a laboratory the like of which the world has never seen."

The release also included a quote by Wright describing the tower:

> This . . . tall free-standing experiment-station on behalf of the American housewife is to be a thing of great beauty in itself. It will stand free in a spacious court, adjacent to the present Administration Building, completing an entire free-standing block. This tall shaft of brick, glass and reinforced concrete will house in proper and natural relationship flowing downward, the Wax Research Laboratories, Development Laboratories, Control Laboratories, and library. . . . A complete modern house-unit, designed to exemplify various finishes and treatments to be applied by the American housewife to her home, is one of the many units, complete in itself, making up this harmonious group which together will constitute one of the truly great examples of architecture in the business of modern times.

Earlier that year, as *Life* magazine photographed Wingspread (the house Wright designed for Johnson in 1937) for an article on Wright, Johnson wrote to him, "How can anyone at your age carry on the amazing amount of social activity, and still maintain the preeminence of the world's leading architect—you do it, and it will always remain with me an amazing and fine example of what man can do."[22]

CHAPTER 11

CONSTRUCTION

Fig. 132. Research Tower under construction, June 1949. (Courtesy of Johnson Wax)

The architectural, structural, and mechanical drawings for the Research Tower were largely complete by the end of 1946,[1] and on January 3, 1947 the Johnson company filed an application for construction approval with the Federal government's Civilian Production Administration office in Milwaukee. One week later the C.P.A.'s Office of Temporary Controls (regulating industrial production during the years after the war) denied the application. The company immediately appealed the decision, but the O.T.C.'s board denied the appeal.

A lobbying firm, Management Planning of Washington, was hired to attempt to win approval for the project, and in late June, with the aid of Wisconsin congressman Lawrence Smith, secured a partial approval, sufficient to begin construction. Apparently, construction approval was then received from the Wisconsin Industrial Commission, and at last the company looked forward to beginning construction.

Wiltscheck was expected to leave the company's payroll to become the project's general contractor, but having dissolved his firm in the early 1940s when he retired, he had no foreman, no crew, and no equipment. Another Racine construction company, Nelson, Incorporated, had done recent work for the Johnson company, and its owner agreed to enter into a one-time partnership with Wiltscheck to build the Research Tower. The new company was named Wiltscheck and Nelson, and it signed a construction contract for the job on August 29, 1947.

Six years earlier Herbert Johnson had insisted to Wright that the company learn the construction costs ahead of time by letting the job out for bid. However, although Wright's office finished the fairly complete thirty-page set of construction drawings in 1946, Wiltscheck and Nelson refused to submit a fixed bid on the unconventional building. They insisted on using the same arrangement Wiltscheck had required when he built the Administration Building: although they would provide periodic estimates, they would be paid monthly for real expenses, plus 6 percent for overhead and profit. It may be that they knew that costs would far exceed their estimate of $1.2 million. Indeed, if Johnson and his board of directors had known the final cost of the building before construction began they might well have abandoned the project.

Ground was broken on November 6, 1947, and excavators raced against impending frost and snow. In January of 1948, with excavation largely complete, concrete workers began pouring the foundations of the west wing of the carport. The fifty-four-foot-deep tap root tower foundation was excavated that same month. Set into hard blue clay soil, the inverted cone shape of the foundation was dug partly by hand. Three workmen used clay spades to excavate and trim the perimeter of the hole manually. A crane with a clamshell removed loose earth and clay. They did not reach bedrock in their excavation, but the upper petal of the foundation acted as a spread footing. Peters recalled that at the time the foundation was put in much of the detailing for the tower had not yet been resolved, although all the structural work was complete. Detailing was worked out in 1948 during construction in what today would be called fast-tracking.

Workers formed and poured many of the subgrade walls in February and also poured the massive foundation of the tower early that month. Peters specified that they were to pour it without forms to ensure a bond with the surrounding soil. The bottom nineteen-foot shaft of the foundation, held in place by the spread petal above, was entirely in compression and completely unreinforced. The upper section of the foundation, containing 300 cubic yards of concrete, was poured in a single nonstop twenty-four-hour operation. A contemporary magazine reported that this was the largest continuous pour ever made in Wisconsin. The concrete was delivered both by trucks and the Pumpcrete mixer used in the construction of the Administration Building.

Wiltscheck and Nelson's concrete workers poured foundations, basements, and floors throughout the site during the summer of 1948. The work was fairly straightforward, except at the core of the tower, which required precise, curved forms and unusually thorough agitating to allow the concrete to penetrate the densely placed steel rods and Steelcrete mesh. Wes Peters specified pea gravel, far smaller than standard aggregate, and small enough to pass through the steel mesh. Unusually large amounts of steel were required to carry the load of the cantilevered tower. Research chemist Edward Wilder, watching construction, noted that it seemed as if more steel than concrete was being used.

It is unlikely that a building had ever been built that was as completely cantilevered as the Johnson company Research Tower. Wiltscheck and Nelson's foreman, Jacob [Jake] Stocker, recalled that when the first floor was poured, one of the heads of Nelson Construction who could not understand how the small core, with seven- to ten-inch thick walls, would support a twenty-one-and-a-half-foot cantilever told him, "If that thing comes down, think nothing of it"[2] (fig. 136). The day the form was stripped Stocker drew a horizontal line across the side of the floor to measure its deflection (common in cantilevers) and was surprised to see that the line remained horizontal: there was virtually no deflection. John Halama remembers that Stocker was so pleased that he said, "I wouldn't be afraid to build this thing sky high!"[3]

Halama, Stocker and others associated with the project had high praise for Wes Peters's innovative structural design and thorough structural drawings. Peters conceived of the tower floors very much as he had conceived of the petals in the mushroom columns ten years before, and his structural design used the same principles: the radial stresses in the tower floors were confined with radial rings—reinforcing bars encircling the floor—while the shear was contained by ribs radiating from the core.

The first cantilevered floor took seven weeks to frame and pour. Stocker recalls that the concrete work on the following floors went well, though slowly. With practice, the workers were able to complete one floor every three weeks, excluding finishing and glazing. The eighty-two cubic yards of high-strength 5,000 psi concrete in each floor and its segment of the central core had to be poured in a single operation. On top of each new floor, to support forms for the next one, workmen erected closely spaced lolly jacks—adjustable steel pipe jacks which are normally used to support sagging floor beams. Workers built two complete sets of forms for the main floors and the mezzanines to allow work to proceed as the concrete cured.

The hollow floor slabs were poured in two stages. After the lower slab and ribs were poured, plumbers and electricians set their pipes and conduit in place on the slab. Next, steel sheets and a framework of reinforcing bars were placed on top of the ribs, and finally the top slab was poured directly on the steel sheets.[4]

The tower was to be clad in the same Cherokee-red brick used on the Administration Building, and Wright intended it to be built in the same unusual manner, with workmen laying several courses of the inner and outer walls of brick and then pouring concrete between them, using the brick as forms. The technique had proved to be slow in the previous building, but had resulted in a monolithic edifice in which the brick was more than a finishing material. It was clear to Wiltscheck and Nelson,

. 133. Scooping earth from Research
wer excavation, February 1948. An eight-
eight-inch mirror has been set up to
ow the clamshell operator to see into the
-four-foot-deep hole. The partially
troyed north wall of the Administration
ding carport is visible in the background.
urtesy of the Nelson Construction
npany)

Fig. 134. Graceful tower core forms rise from basement- to grade-level, June 1948. (Courtesy of Johnson Wax)

Fig. 135. Welded steel mesh and reinforcing bars in first cantilevered floor of tower, August 1948. Although Wright had used the cold-drawn steel mesh in the Administration Building, it was still an unusual construction material in 1948 and the crew of the Nelson Construction Company had never used it before. The photograph was taken before the concrete was poured. (Courtesy of Johnson Wax)

Fig. 136. Two floors of the tower have been poured and stripped, and the first round mezzanine has been formed, December 1948. (Courtesy of Johnson Wax)

however, that such a system would be far slower yet when applied to the Research Tower. Laying perfectly straight circles of brick 100 feet in the air would be much more difficult than it had been near the ground, and it would be an inefficient use of masons' and concrete workers' time to alternate work every few courses. They began construction in the conventional manner, forming the concrete floors and shafts in reusable plywood forms, shooting ties in, and then laying slim bricks as a veneer against the concrete. In May 1948 Wiltscheck wrote Johnson a memo estimating the comparative costs in time and wages. He calculated that using the conventional system for the tower shaft would save $8,500 and fifteen weeks—one week per floor. Doing so on the outside walls of the tower would save $2,500 and another fifteen weeks. Using the same method on the surrounding building would save five weeks and $11,000. Johnson forwarded Wiltscheck's figures to Wright. Several days later Johnson discussed the matter by telephone with Wright, who agreed to the veneer method for the tower shaft, but not for the other parts of the building. Both client and builder decided to disregard Wright's decision and use the veneer method throughout. Naturally, they had to tell Peters, but they hoped Wright would not find out.

Fig. 137. Topping off the tower, October 1949. The top nostril of the tower has been formed, but not yet poured. The roof of the Administration Building is visible on the left. (Courtesy of Johnson Wax)

Peters oversaw the job for Wright, driving to Racine weekly. Wright, who was based in Arizona for the winter, rarely came. Halama, promoted to Johnson Company architect when Wiltscheck left the payroll, was on the site every day, and made many necessary clarifying drawings. When Peters was sent to San Francisco in the summer of 1949 for a lengthy trip to supervise construction of the V. C. Morris Gift Shop, Wright's confidence in Halama and Wiltscheck was high enough that he sent no one to replace Peters. The work by that time was largely repetitious, consisting of forming the upper floors of the tower.

The crew attempted to use the Pumpcrete mixer to supply concrete for the tower, but they had problems with it, and had to clean the concrete out of its pipes each time they shut it down. As they were installing a temporary crane on the building to lift up men and materials, they switched to using conventional concrete mixers on the ground, hoisting concrete buggies with the crane. When they reached the third floor they erected a scaffolding around the building. To allow them to continue pouring in the winter of 1949 they covered each top floor's scaffolding with temporary sheeting.

In October 1949, two years after ground was broken, the concrete work for the tower was completed. The slow pace of the job was partly caused by the need for extremely accurate work. The crew's work was indeed unusually precise: when engineers from the Otis Elevator Company came to check the completed elevator shaft for clearance, they tested it with a plumb bob and found that it was no more than one-fourth inch off.[5] In Wiltscheck's opinion the concrete formwork was more like cabinetwork than common formwork, and his carpenters went to the unusual length of using planes to finish concrete forms.[6] The troweled concrete floors of the tower had to be brought precisely to vertical unit lines so that a half-inch mortar joint would show between the finished floor and the first course of interior bricks. The masonry work had to be as exact as the concrete work; as in the Administration Building, the doors Wright designed were mere light, pintled panels, with none of the jambs, trim, or scribed moldings in the masonry openings routinely used to conceal imprecise work.

From the outset, Wright planned to clad the Research Tower in Pyrex tubes. To the Johnson company's displeasure, however, in the mid-1940s the Pyrex clere-stories in the Administration Building were still leaking. Any application of tubes in the new building would have to be watertight. In Wright's earliest surviving detailed section of the tower, the highest tube wall projects about one and one half feet wider than the parapet above, and the tube wall curves up and in for closure (fig. 138). In other early drawings all the tube walls project slightly beyond their parapets; each glass wall curving out at the bottom and in at the top (see fig. 126). This detail would have taken Wright's destruction of the box further by emphasizing the nonstructural nature of the facade. Also, the gentle curves would have highlighted the ethereal quality of the tubes. Unfortunately, the detail would also have been especially prone to leakage, and Wright abandoned it. In all of his later drawings of the tower the tubes are stacked vertically, the easiest configuration to make watertight.

Seventy percent of the tower's facade was to be glass; but in late 1949, with the concrete and masonry work almost complete, Wright and the glass manufacturers had not yet established a practical, watertight tubing detail for the new building, although not for want of ideas. In one of Wright's first letters to Johnson concerning the tower, dated December 8, 1943, he described four different possible glass tubing systems with which he was experimenting for use in the Guggenheim Museum. In the first system a single row of Pyrex tubes would be wired into a scalloped metal rack, as before. The tubes were to be separated from each other by the one-fourth-inch-wide projecting tip of the scallop. Caulking would be applied in the gap between tubes, adhering to a sandblasted strip on the top and bottom edge of each tube. The second system required having Pyrex tubes drawn with two one-eighth-inch grooves on opposite sides. Mastic was to be applied into the grooves and then a metal strip wedged into the grooves of adjacent tubes and screwed into the rack. Wright wrote that this system would be somewhat more expensive, but impregnable. The third system was a single wall of abutting tubes, without mastic. A second wall of plate-glass sash would be hung inside, hinged for cleaning. Wright wrote, "This is an extremely brilliant wall—and of course tight—but much more expensive." His final idea was to substitute solid tubes for some of the hollow tubes, ". . . to give a marvelous irridescence—using these in places where we want a particularly rich effect." At the end of the letter he noted, "No experimental technicalities are involved but we use what we have already worked out and know all about." That note, however, was unduly optimistic.

Fig. 138. Preliminary section through Research Tower, with detail sections. In this very early section, the top parapet is narrower than the lower floors, and the top wall of glass tubing curves into the parapet, as shown in detail W. 20″ × 35″. Ink on tracing paper. (Courtesy of the Frank Lloyd Wright Foundation)

In the first tower scheme Wright submitted, in December 1943, Wright used the third of the tubing alternatives. On December 30, after seeing Wright's drawings, Steinle cautioned Johnson, "All the walls of the tower are constructed of glass tubing. As we know, this is not very easy to clean. As we also know, laboratories, even though air and dust conditioned, produce fumes which condense on wall surfaces and fog glass in a short time. It would be very difficult to keep these glass tubes clean and presentable, and translucent enough to give proper lighting." Steinle's objections were overstated, and Wright proceeded with his plan.

In the set of construction drawings that Wright completed in 1946, the glazing, as in his third 1943 alternative, was composed of a single stack of two-inch tubes resting against scalloped metal racks. To the inside of the rack was a sheet of plate glass, pivoted for cleaning. The drawings left several questions unanswered. They did not specify how the tubes were to be attached to the metal racks, nor did they show the butt joint detail at the ends of tubes. Most important, the drawings did not explain how the horizontal joints between tubes would be sealed. It is possible that he still contemplated leaving them unsealed, with the inner plate-glass alone providing watertight closure.

Blueprints from 1949 of Wright's construction drawings show no further development of the detail. However, Wright, the Johnson company, and Corning Glass Works were pursuing solutions. Corning reported to Wright in October 1948 that, "our best people are now working on the problem of recommending a perfect method of sealing glass tubing on the job as a building material."[7] Although an adequate seal had not yet been found, Wright was confident enough that he had Wiltscheck send a tubing schedule to Corning for bidding in January of 1949. The Johnson company signed a contract with Corning four months later, advancing Corning $14,000 for tools and molds the next month. That autumn Corning shipped enough tubes and couplers to Racine for Wiltscheck and Nelson to erect a test panel on the roof of the old research building. They tested dozens of caulks and cements unsuccessfully.

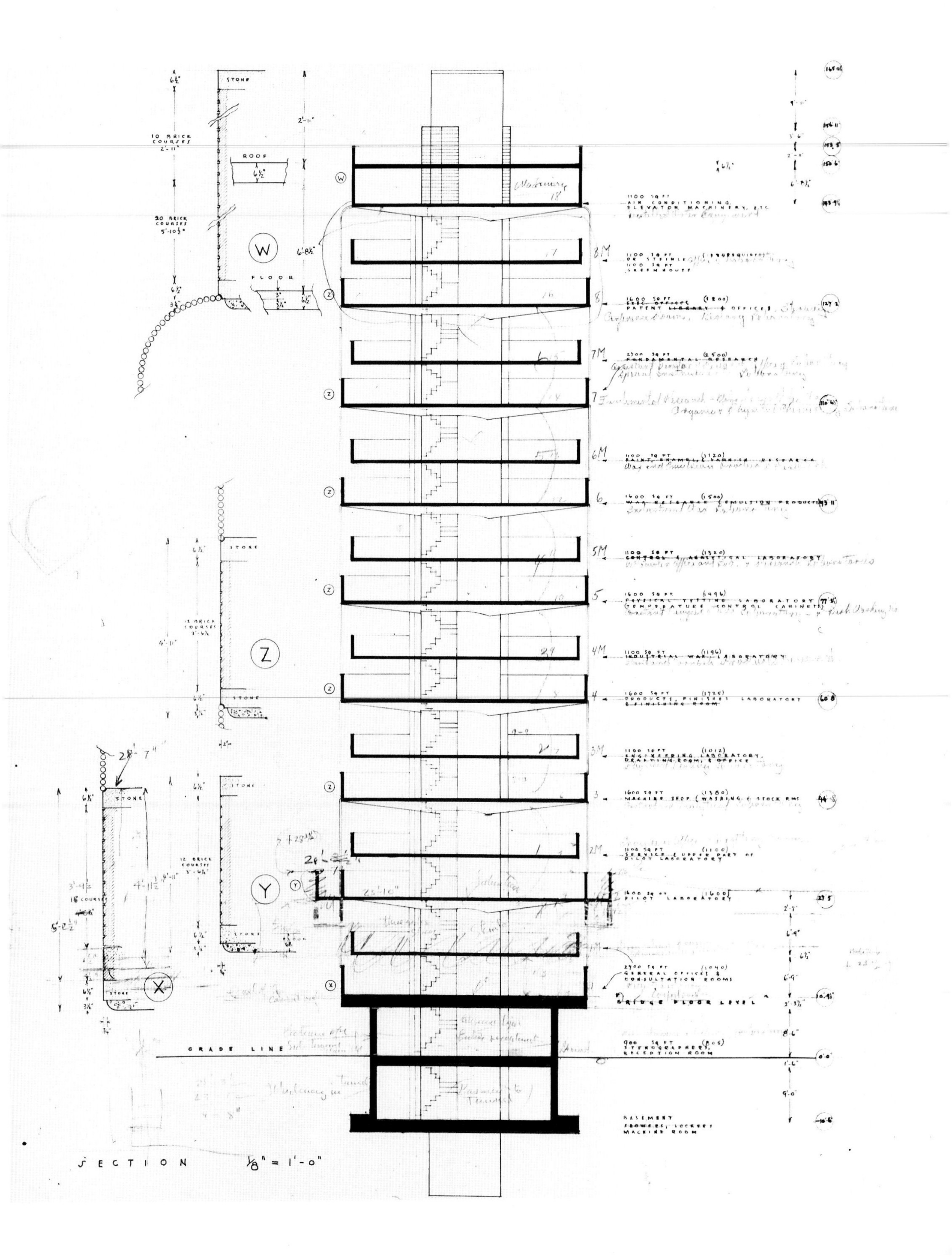

STONE
ROOF
FLOOR
10 BRICK COURSES 2'-11"
20 BRICK COURSES 5'-10½"
12 BRICK COURSES 3'-6½"
W
Z
Y
X
1100 SQ FT
AIR CONDITIONING,
ELEVATOR MACHINERY, ETC.
8M
1100 SQ FT
DR STEINLE
1100 SQ FT
GREEN HOUSE
8
1600 SQ FT (1200)
EXEC. OFFICES
PATENT LIBRARY + OFFICES
7M
2700 SQ FT (2500)
FUNDAMENTAL RESEARCH
7
6M
1100 SQ FT (1120)
PAINT, ENAMEL, & VARNISH RESEARCH
6
1600 SQ FT (1500)
WAX RESEARCH (EMULSION PRODUCTS)
5M
1100 SQ FT (1320)
CONTROL & ANALYTICAL LABORATORY
5
1600 SQ FT (1496)
PHYSICAL TESTING LABORATORY
(TEMPERATURE CONTROL CABINETS)
4M
1100 SQ FT (1196)
INDUSTRIAL WAX LABORATORY
4
1600 SQ FT (1725)
PRODUCTS, FINISHES LABORATORY
& FINISHING ROOM
3M
1100 SQ FT (1012)
ENGINEERING LABORATORY,
DRAFTING ROOM, & OFFICE
3
1600 SQ FT (1380)
MACHINE SHOP (WASHING & STOCK RMS
2M
1100 SQ FT (1100)
SERVICE & UPPER PART OF
PILOT LABORATORY
1600 SQ FT (1600)
PILOT LABORATORY
1M
2700 SQ FT (1040)
GENERAL OFFICES &
CONSULTATION ROOMS
BRIDGE FLOOR LEVEL
GRADE LINE
900 SQ FT (805)
STENOGRAPHERS,
RECEPTION ROOM
BASEMENT
SHOWERS, LOCKERS
MACHINE ROOM
SECTION 1/8" = 1'-0"

Fig. 139. Workman installs Koroseal weatherproofing gasket in Pyrex tubing wall of Research Tower, 1950. The sun-resistant vinyl gasket has two air cells separated by a web. Pyrex couplers with Koroseal seals are also visible, held to aluminum racks with wire. After the tubes have been put in place a sheet of plate glass will be installed in front of them. (Courtesy of Johnson Wax)

Fig. 140. Worker welding steel rings, reinforcing the shallow concrete floor slab of the advertising department, April 1949. Hidden within the floor, this ten-and-one-half-inch-thick slab, spanning forty feet, is almost as remarkable as the Pyrex dome above it. (Courtesy of Johnson Wax)

Fig. 141. Lower half of Research Tower viewed from courtyard, showing base of core unenclosed, 1950. (Courtesy of Johnson Wax)

Corning engineers attempted to design a gasket that could seal the joints, while Wright began pursuing another alternative, this time with Owens-Illinois Glass (Kimble Glass division). He asked them to devise a method of producing a tube with two deep grooves in it. This corresponded to the second of the systems Wright described in 1943, in which a caulked metal strip would be wedged into grooves in adjacent tubes and screwed into the rack. The glass company hoped to draw tubes with walls heavy enough that the tubes could be reheated and grooves then pressed into them. However, Wright concluded that too much time would be lost at the factory installing special machinery needed to make the grooved tubes.

At the same time Corning product engineers designed a continuous weatherproofing gasket out of Koroseal (a polyvinyl chloride produced by the B. F. Goodrich Company), which was molded to fit against the tubes snugly. They also designed a Koroseal ring to weatherseal the butt joints where tubes were to be joined by Pyrex couplers (fig. 139).

Wright approved the Koroseal gasket and ring, and Wiltscheck and Nelson ordered the tubes from Corning in November 1949. They hoped to open the building in ten months. By enclosing the tower with board sheeting mounted on the scaffolding and installing temporary heaters, the building was sufficiently protected from the cold to allow workmen to install tubes on all but the coldest days of the winter. Corning began shipping tubes in January, but glazing was held up until the end of March because of problems with the Koroseal gaskets, which had to be redesigned twice in an attempt to create a gasket thin enough to compress into the already determined space between tubes, but thick enough to accommodate the inevitable variations in tube diameters.

Such precision was extraordinary for building construction. When a B. F. Goodrich engineer was on the site examining the test panel of Pyrex tubes for slight variations in their diameter, pondering how to modify the Koroseal gasket, Stocker humorously told Wiltscheck, "This is the first job I have ever been on where they take measurements on the building with a micrometer."[8]

The workmen began installing tubes in earnest in April, but two more problems emerged. When a corner tube wall of the full height of twelve feet seven inches was installed, they discovered that the weight of all the tubes distorted the lowest gaskets so much that tiny leaks developed around them. Stocker solved the problem with small pieces of plastic he bought in a hardware store, which were wedged into each gasket, one directly beneath another. The pieces of plastic acted as columns and took the weight of the tubes off the gaskets.

The other problem was also solved cleverly: Wiltscheck and Nelson had masons begin installing the glass tubes, but the glaziers objected, and called a jurisdictional strike. After several meetings they agreed to divide the work, and the contractor had them install the tubes on alternate floors. The trades felt that they were in competition, and consequently worked as fast as they could to prove that each was better than the other. They completed installation of the tower's seventeen-and-a-half miles of glass tubes early in June.

The laboratory equipment began arriving in early April, so to save time workers installed equipment and glass simultaneously. When the equipment was in place on each floor glaziers installed the large sheets of plate glass.

In Wright's plans the first floor of the tower, a reception area, was enclosed by plate glass. This would allow anyone in the courtyard to observe that the entire tower was cantilevered from the slender core. In April 1950, with construction almost complete, Wright decided to make the view even more dramatic by relocating the reception area and eliminating the plate glass, leaving the base of the tower exposed (fig. 141).

While the construction tower had been fraught with delays, one job had been completed months earlier than necessary: running the many ducts and fixture lines through the building, a task that is normally enormous in a laboratory building. Its speed in this building was a tribute to Wright's argument that a research tower hung from a central stack would allow a more efficient layout of ducts and pipes.

The only large task remaining in the summer of 1950 was to hook up the huge number of plumbing and electrical fittings. In spite of working nine-hour, six-day weeks, the construction crew missed Johnson's September 1 goal for completion, and just missed his November 1 goal as well.

The entire project, including laboratory equipment, tunnels, and architectural fees, cost $3,500,000. The cost of the tower and connecting bridge alone was $1,500,000 or $74.00 per square foot. The cost per cubic foot was $6.80, almost exactly ten times Wright's early estimate of 69 cents. The main factor in the increase, however, was beyond Wright's control—the dramatic inflation in salaries in the U.S. construction industry through the late 1940s, fed by the postwar building boom. As the Johnson project was unusually labor-intensive, and involved extensive overtime, it was triply affected by the inflation of wages.[9]

Fig. 142. Research Tower, 1950. Round mezzanines are visible through glass tubing. (Courtesy of Johnson Wax)

CHAPTER 12

USING THE COMPLEX

The Johnson company mounted a vigorous campaign to publicize the tower, and spent months planning a day-long opening ceremony, held on November 17, 1950. Hundreds of figures in industry, education, politics, and the media were invited, and the company made available a special press room in which reporters could digest press packets containing photos, renderings, and a press release prepared by a New York advertising agency. The glowing release was used almost word for word in articles in *Architect and Engineer, Buildings*, and other periodicals. Additional articles ran in *Architecture d'Aujourd'hui*, and *Architect's Journal*. The nation's architectural press had been publicizing the building's radical structural system since before construction began, and the story in *Architectural Record* on the opening called the building "already long-famous," and noted that "Its significance in architecture and engineering is already demonstrated in the frequency with which sections of its core-type structure and renderings have appeared in the literature."[1] The Museum of Modern Art mounted an exhibit in 1952 focusing exclusively on the two Johnson buildings and also featured the tower prominently in its 1953 exhibit "Built in U.S.A.: Postwar Architecture."

The popular press also covered the building: *Fortune*, newspapers and publications throughout Europe, as well as in Brazil and Japan published articles on it. *Life* magazine ran a three-page feature on the tower and compared it to ". . . an outstretched electrical coil, standing on end and lighted from within."[2]

Over time, employees were able to evaluate how well the Research Tower functioned. Chemists J. Vernon Steinle and Edward Wilder, interviewed by the author after having worked in it for two decades, were pleased, but largely because the chemists had carefully designed each floor's layout in the full-size mock-up first. They felt that they would have been equally satisfied with a conventional laboratory building, and that almost every way in which the building varied from conventionality imposed some compromise on them.

The most serious problem was the most subtle: a tower limits casual communication, and industries favor horizontal laboratories for that reason. According to Wilder, chemists often refine ideas by casually discussing them with one another, making it important that they be able to stroll to other laboratories unhindered. In the Research Tower, however, the chemists would often decide to talk to colleagues later because they did not want to take the time to wait for the elevator, and, often by that time the moment of inspiration had passed. On the positive side, another scientist recalled that because all the workers shared a single, slow elevator, other spontaneous, productive conversations occurred as they met going up and down.

To Wright's credit in this matter, Wes Peters claims that Wright created the two-story laboratories to counter the isolation of small laboratories. A square floor and a round mezzanine together contained almost as much space as five of the small laboratories in Steinle's 1943 proposal. Although many of the technicians were not particularly conscious of it, it is clear that the large, two-story spaces were a great

Fig. 143. Administration Building and Research Tower viewed from southeast, 1950. (Courtesy of Johnson Wax)

Fig. 144. Courtyard of Research Tower in the evening, 1950. Round mezzanines cast crescent-shaped shadows on translucent walls of the tower. The glowing advertising dome is visible to the immediate right of the tower. A semicircle of twelve illuminated, tiny domelike skylights over the photographic department can be seen at the lower right. (Courtesy of Johnson Wax)

Fig. 145. *Overleaf.* Aerial view of the Johnson company from the southeast, with the Administration Building and completed Research Tower at the right, circa 1961. The company's property is highlighted. (Courtesy of Johnson Wax)

psychological amenity. Eugene Kitzke, who as a company microbiologist moved into the top mezzanine in 1950, said he felt as if he was in heaven in his spacious laboratory and he appreciated working near six other scientists rather than one or two.[3] In designing the two-story laboratories Wright successfully created a minor recapitulation of the large two-story space enjoyed by the clerical workers in the Administration Building. The laboratory also boosted morale, and hence productivity in an intangible way, since many of the workers felt a special camaraderie by virtue of sharing the remarkable new building.

Steinle indicated the people in his department did surmount the tower's inherent deficiencies. One problem was caused by the low ceiling near the core of the tower. To support the cantilevers, each ceiling tapered down to a low six feet five inches at the core—precisely where all the laboratories' chemical hoods had to be located to vent their fumes (see fig. 147). Some of the equipment that required venting was too tall to fit under the low hoods; Steinle cleverly had a ratchet installed on some of the work surfaces so that they could be lowered until the equipment on them fit under the hoods.[4]

The tower's temperature was quite comfortable during the first few years it was used, but as the number of people working in the tower increased sharply and new laboratory equipment that produced a large amount of heat was installed, the tower became difficult to heat and cool. Glazed on all four sides, it absorbed an enormous amount of solar radiation all day, and lost a large amount every night. In addition, heat rose to the top of the small two-story spaces. The company installed partially effective shades in the building, but disgruntled workers often hung sheets of aluminum foil behind the west-facing facades to deflect the setting sun's rays.

In spite of all experiments the tube walls leaked: water seeped around the vinyl gaskets and into the building. Charles Folwell, hired as plant engineering manager in 1950, had the 100,000 linear feet of gaskets caulked with a new noncuring synthetic rubber compound. The caulk began cracking from three years from being compressed by the tubes in the summer and flexed in the winter. In 1955 Folwell and Halama enlisted the Dow Corning Company's help. For three years they tested a variety of new materials, until in 1958 Dow Corning devised a one-part silicone rubber compound that Folwell decided to use. The silicone caulking successfully sealed the building and today is used widely around the world.

The first fifteen years of the Research and Development Department's occupancy of the tower were extraordinarily productive. The number of successful new products that the company introduced was the highest in its history to the present day, but the department outgrew the tower almost as soon as it moved in, and the unexpandable building gradually became the victim of its own success.

In 1957, with Wright's approval, John Halama enclosed the ground-floor wings of the carport to turn them into additional laboratories. To preserve the openness of the courtyard the new walls were made of simple sheets of plate glass. The physical chemistry and analytical divisions were moved out of the tower into the new laboratories, but as the organic chemistry division, which produced toxic and explosive fumes, grew, it was deemed safest to move it out of the tower from which evacuation was problematic. The safer analytic division was invited back into the tower and the organic chemistry division moved into the carport.[5]

During construction Johnson Wax's insurance company announced that it would refuse to insure the tower if it were built without a sprinkler system. Wright strenuously objected to the appearance of sprinkler heads hanging from the ceilings and insisted that they were unnecessary because the building was completely fireproof. Herbert Johnson was eager to save the $25,000 cost of the sprinklers, and convinced the insurance company to permit him to eliminate sprinklers in exchange for a slightly higher premium. However, later fears over evacuation in case of an explosion (exacerbated because the tower had only one stairwell) were great enough that eventually the company banned all combustible material from the tower. This incon-

Fig. 146. Typical square tower floor, 1950, showing mezzanine. (Courtesy of Johnson Wax)

Fig. 147. Technician in front of one of the chemical hoods that vent directly into the central core, at a work surface that cannot be lowered, 1950. (Courtesy of Johnson Wax)

Fig. 148. Advertising department reception area. The space provides a minor recapitulation of the theme of relating individual work stations to a central area. The ornate dome of glass tubing is a reworking of the design for the dome Wright intended to cover the Guggenheim Museum. The dome, in combination with a bulging, streamlined reception desk and protruding glass tubing wall as a backdrop, produce a highly mannered, almost Baroque space, which may be Wright's response to Connolly's emphatic request for an advertising department designed "from a fresh viewpoint." (Photo by Ezra Stoller; © Esto)

Fig. 149. Exhibition dwelling, or Causerie, 1950. When the Research Tower opened the model home was used as the executive dining room. Johnson dubbed it the Causerie, and later made it his private office. This is surely one of Wright's more unexpected interiors, juxtaposing his familiar residential compressed pinwheel plan and central fireplace with the high-tech, futuristic detailing of curved Pyrex tubing windows and exposed aluminum racks. (Courtesy of Johnson Wax)

Fig. 150. Formal garden on Research Tower carport deck, 1950. On the deck outside the Causerie (center) Wright designed this small formal garden with a stone surface and a shallow pool. A greenhouse is at the left, and the advertising department is located above the exhibition dwelling. (Courtesy of Johnson Wax)

Fig. 151. Pilot laboratory, 1950. Wright's Johnson buildings are occasionally referred to as factory buildings. The term is misleading, but it does apply to this extraordinary space, the intermediate step between an applied research laboratory and a factory assembly line. Wright located the two-story space half below grade, as Steinle proposed, beneath the west wing of the courtyard. It is a spectacular industrial space, with a ceiling-mounted hoist and a maze of pipes and industrial equipment surrounding twenty-foot-high mushroom columns that engage a mezzanine. The curves of the mushroom columns, walls, and parapets echo the curves of the labyrinth of pipes, highlighted by Wright's dramatic lighting. True to his vision of a monolithic building, Wright built the laboratory of the same materials he used throughout the rest of the complex. His detailing and sense of proportion give drama to what could have been the most mundane room in the complex. (Courtesy of Johnson Wax)

venience forced chemists to go to another part of the factory complex whenever they wanted to perform experiments involving combustibles.

The largest alteration to the complex was carried out in 1961, roughly according to a proposal Wright had introduced long before. In 1947 Herbert Johnson asked Wright how the complex should be expanded when more offices were needed. Wright suggested a two-story addition over the east wing of the tower carport, extending north from the model home and the advertising department. John Halama drew up a version of Wright's suggestion, which Wright enlivened by running a two-story light well through the center and terminating the wing with a round, semidetached conference room (figs. 152 and 153).[6] In 1957 the company seriously began to contemplate building the addition. To obtain slightly more office space Halama redrew Wright's plans, widening the wing by approximately five feet, to the full width of the carport. The next time Wright came to the plant, Halama showed him the plans, and Wright gave his approval. In 1960, the year after Wright's death the Johnson Company decided to proceed with the addition. The company was growing rapidly, and to obtain still more office space it decided to eliminate the lightwell. Taliesin Associated Architects (successor to Wright's practice) was engaged to draw up the revisions. Wes Peters designed the addition, completed the following year (fig. 154).

Over the years that the company occupied Wright's buildings, it was perhaps inevitable that the Pyrex tubes would need to be replaced. The skylights in the Administration Building were the most problematic of the tubing installations for several reasons. Because they were flat rooftop installations they were highly prone to leakage. For many years employees in the Great Workroom kept empty five-gallon buckets near their desks to catch the drips, and they humorously rated the intensity of storms according to how many buckets were needed. An additional problem was that on rare occasions a skylight tube would become loose and fall to the floor. Third, Wright concealed slim incandescent light bulbs around the tops of the petals when the company had insisted on artificial lighting in the space. The bulbs, however, were located between two layers of tubes and there was no practical way to change them. The company kept a fifteen-foot high, wheeled scaffold, nicknamed the "Trojan Horse," in the Great Workroom from which workers could unwire tubes to change burned-out bulbs.

To end the leakage the company replaced the top layer of tubes with rooftop skylights composed of angled flat sheets of fiberglass in a built-up aluminum frame. In 1957 Halama also removed the bottom, more visible tubes in some of the skylights, and replaced them with corrugated plastic sheets. Halama sent Wright photographs of them, and a disturbed Wright responded, "I am sorry to say that the elimination of the tubes has cheapened the building utterly. For God's sake, isn't there some way of using a heavier (thicker) half-round reproduction of the tubes with an opalescent concealing of the mess of structural guts above it? . . . The corrugated glass you suggest is only a wave but if made deeper and sand-blasted on the under side or upper side or both, might be all right."[7] Wright viewed the skylights the next month and agreed to attempt to design a compromise solution. Eventually the company replaced the skylight tubes with specially molded sheets of plexiglass that precisely mimic the profile of the tubes, painting dark lines on them to resemble the original joints between tubes. The layer of fiberglass above interfered with transmission of sunlight through the skylights so four mercury vapor streetlight bulbs were installed in each one. Today the workroom is far easier to maintain, but it has lost the brilliant, mysterious quality of light visible in historic photographs.

The complex's innovations in structure, on the other hand, have held up almost flawlessly. The only failure was the Administration Building carport's roof, which sagged until beams were mounted on top of it in 1941. However, the mushroom columns and the Research Tower have shown no sign of weakness, and the thin, unsupported floor slab beneath the advertising department dome displays virtually no deflection[8] (see fig. 140).

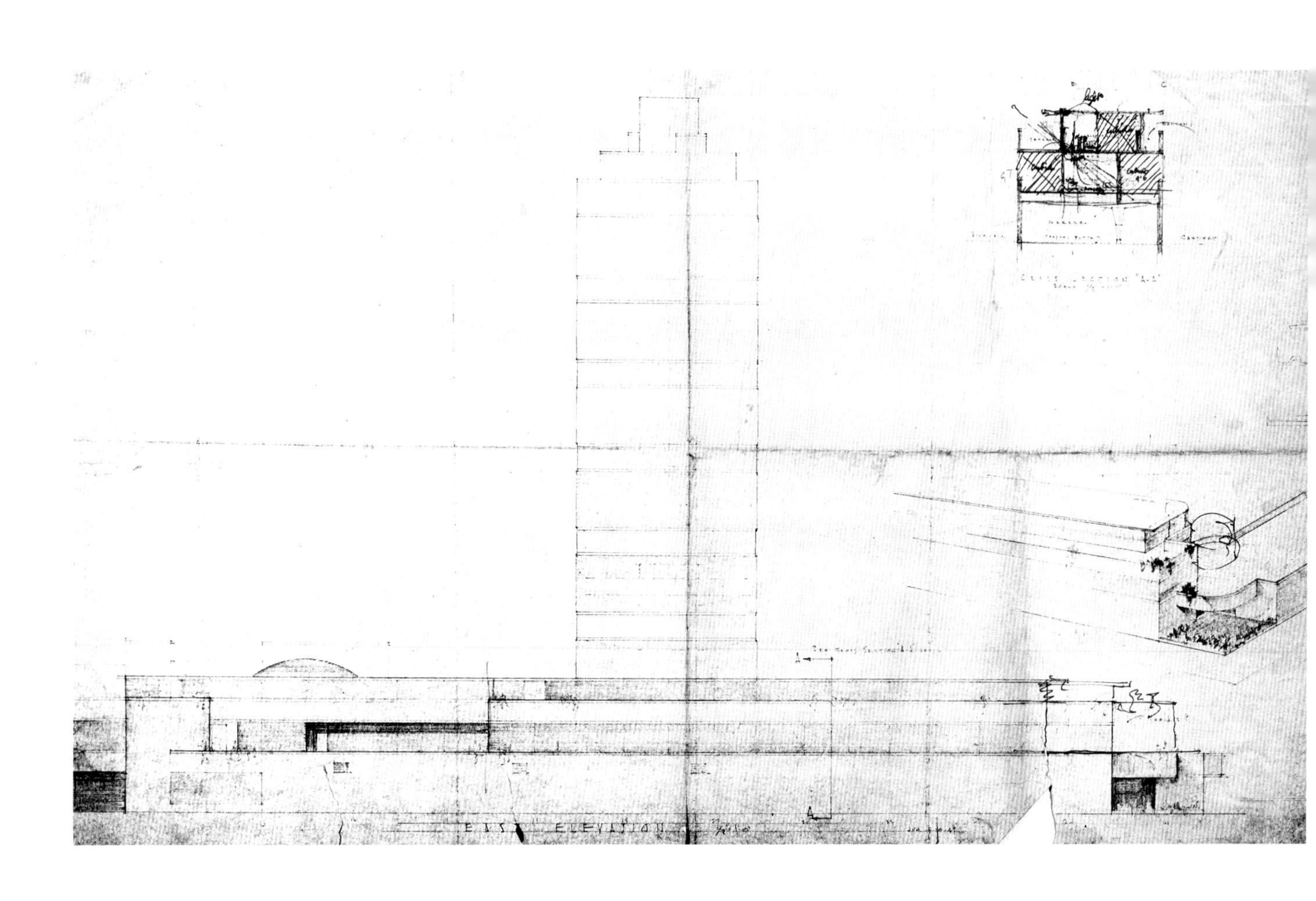
EAST ELEVATION
CROSS SECTION "A-A"

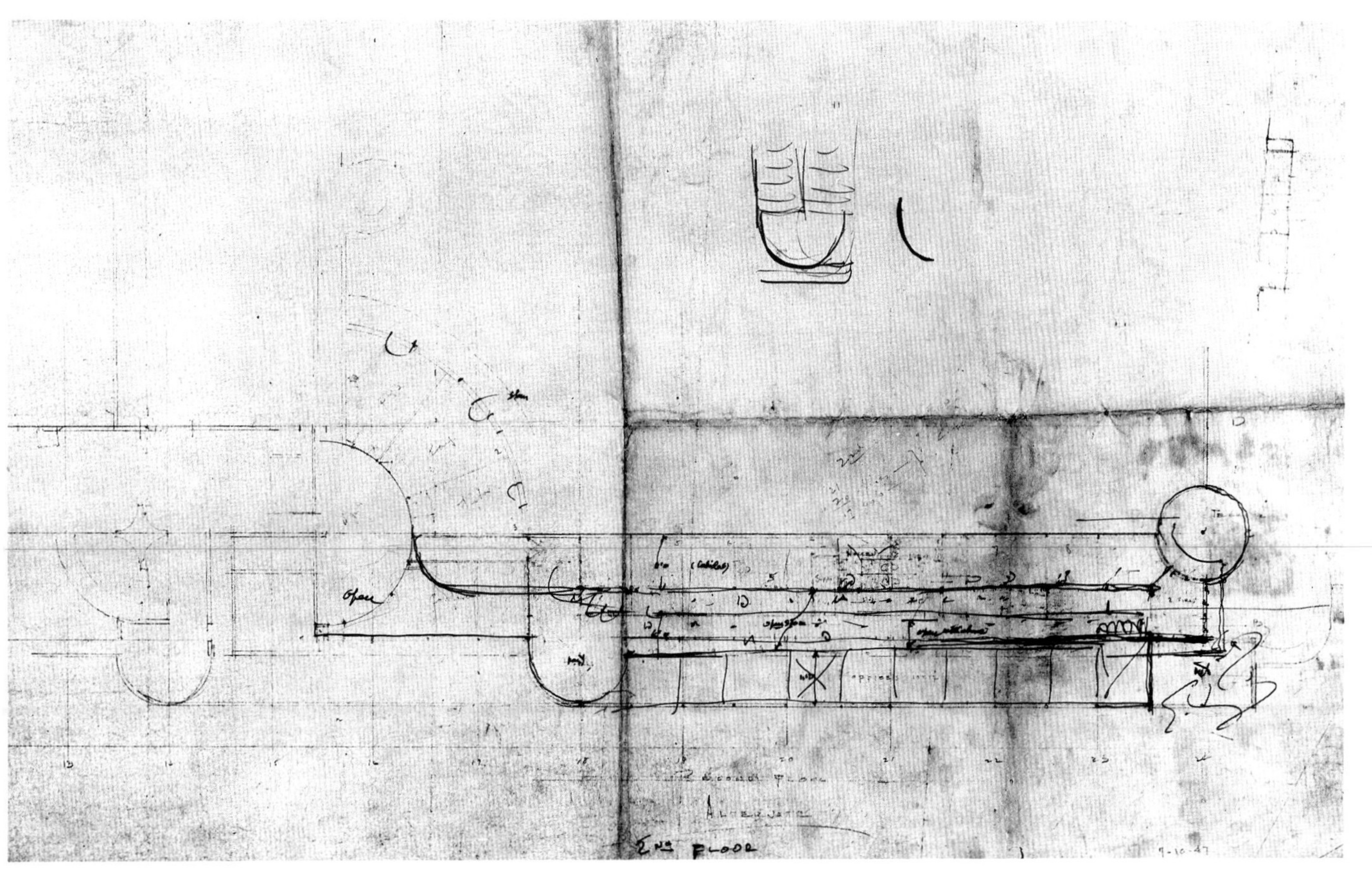

Fig. 152. East elevation of Research Tower complex showing a preliminary design for the second- and third-story addition to the east wing of the courtyard. The dark (inked) alterations are in Wright's hand and include the diagram of a two-story light well at the top of the section drawing (upper right) and a round conference room added onto the end of the building in the axonometric drawing (center right). Scale: 1/8″ = 1′–0″. Blueline copy of drawing, signed J. P. H. [John Halama], 36″ × 24″. (Courtesy of the Frank Lloyd Wright Foundation)

Fig. 153. Plan of preliminary design for office addition to the second floor of the east wing of the Research Tower carport in which Wright has reworked the drafted plan. Scale: 1/8″ = 1′–0″. Blueline copy of drawing, signed J. P. H. [John Halama], 36″ × 23″. (Courtesy of the Frank Lloyd Wright Foundation)

Fig. 154. Second- and third-story office addition over the east wing of Research Tower courtyard, designed in 1961 by Taliesin Associated Architects. Pleading austerity, the Johnson Company insisted on substituting corrugated sheets of plexiglass for the Pyrex tubing. The remainder of the exterior was executed in the same materials as the original buildings. (Courtesy of Johnson Wax)

In the 1960s the S. C. Johnson Company's huge growth necessitated yet another major expansion of its factory facilities. It was impractical to expand in its built-up urban setting, so the company did just what Wright had urged twenty-five years earlier: it built an entire new complex several miles outside of Racine. The irony is that it did not abandon its downtown plant, and will probably never do so, largely because the Frank Lloyd Wright buildings, now a worldwide symbol of the company, are there. The company had also outgrown its office and research buildings and began to debate how to expand them, now that Wright had died. Over a decade it hired four architectural firms, including Taliesin Associated Architects, to design proposals for a major addition to the Wright complex, but the company failed to accept any of the schemes. In 1977 a nearby hospital vacated its quarters, a seven-story building one block east of the complex (visible in fig. 124). The Johnson company purchased and remodeled it, and constructed a skylit tunnel from the new building to the Wright complex, moving some of its office departments, as well as the entire greatly enlarged research department, into it in 1982. The solution is a happy one, as any new building erected next to the buildings, designed without Wright's touch, would have risked damaging their delicate scale and massing.

The company's facilities needs change as it continues to grow, and its executives often debate new uses for the buildings. However they are used they are secure, because the chairman of the board, Samuel Johnson, appreciates them and regards them as a memorial to his father. The company still consults Wes Peters, today a senior architect with Taliesin Associated Architects, on contemplated alterations. They have kept the buildings surprisingly close to their original state.

The Administration Building remains the international corporate headquarters of the company. Concessions have been made to today's higher standards of quiet and privacy: the area under the mezzanine is now completely divided into private offices (still without locks), and Cherokee-red carpeting covers the Great Workroom floor. Some of the long since corroded pipes for the radiant floor-heating system are now used as under-floor conduits to connect the word processors that now sit on Wright's desks. Various divisions have moved in and out of the Great Workroom over the years; but its constant use attests to its flexibility. Herbert Johnson's original penthouse office serves today's president of the company, Raymond F. Farley, and the Executive Committee still meets in the penthouse conference room.

Major maintenance problems have been associated with the buildings, the inevitable cost of construction techniques that Wright himself considered experimental. In one respect, of course, attending to the problems has proved to be valuable research for a company in the maintenance business. But most important, the buildings, which continue to be toured by thousands of visitors every year, have had huge intangible benefits to the company. Sam Johnson has said:

> We became a different company the day the building opened. We achieved international attention because that building represented and symbolized the quality of everything we did in terms of products, people, the working environment within the building, the community relations and—most important—our ability to recruit creative people.
>
> When we get a really good person, he or she walks in that building and . . . suddenly comes to the conclusion that . . . this organization is interested in innovation, in new ideas and in the people who work in that enclosure. Over the years, we have been able to employ the most creative people who respond to that building. It's been a very favorable thing for the company.
>
> The tower, in a really positive sense, became a symbol of our commitment to innovation as a company. I remember Mr. Wright saying something like this to my father: "You can raise it like a torch—the tower—to inspire your people around the world." And it did, and it still does.[9]

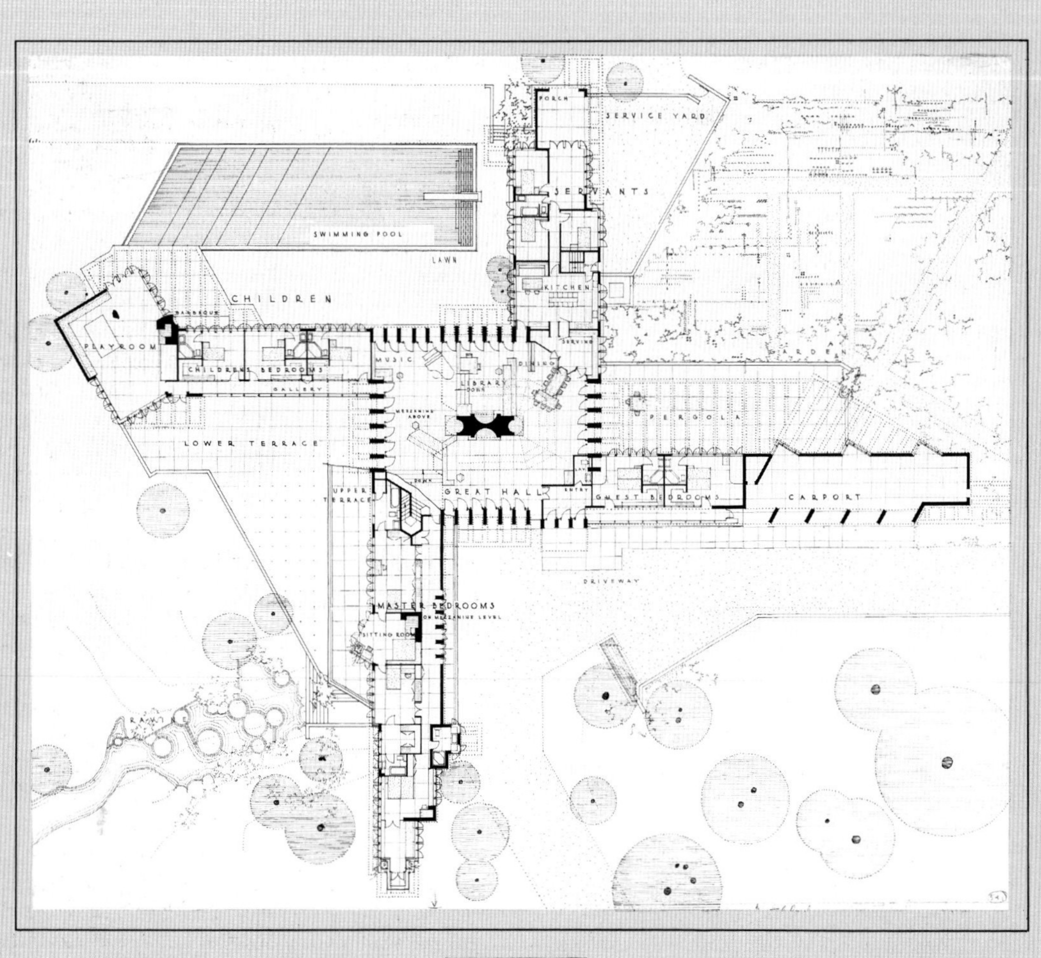
PORCH
SERVICE YARD
SERVANTS
SWIMMING POOL
LAWN
CHILDREN
KITCHEN
PLAYROOM
CHILDREN'S BEDROOMS
GALLERY
MUSIC
DINING
SERVING
GARDEN
PERGOLA
LOWER TERRACE
UPPER TERRACE
GREAT HALL
ENTRY
GUEST BEDROOMS
CARPORT
DRIVEWAY
MASTER BEDROOMS
SITTING ROOM

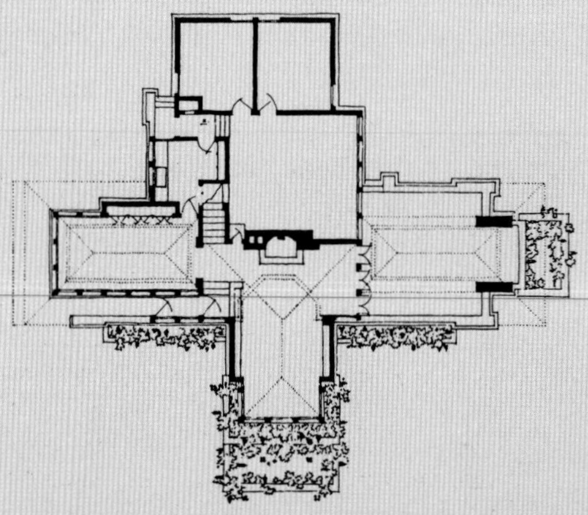

APPENDIX 1

WINGSPREAD AND RELATED COMMISSIONS

Fig. 155. Plan of Wingspread. In plan, Wingspread is a simplification and purification of Wright's earlier Prairie houses, which are composed of four wings pinwheeling slightly around the central chimney core. This off-centering is taken to its extreme in Wingspread. In the earlier houses, such as the Isabel Roberts house, one of the four wings is the main communal space—the living room—and dominates the other wings by being two stories high and fronting on the street. In Wingspread, the public living and dining areas occupy the forty-by-sixty-foot central tentlike space surrounding the massive chimney. All other functions are combined in the four wings nearly equal in height. Only the master bedroom wing, elevated one story, disrupts the uniformity of height. 26″ × 30″. Ink on tracing paper. (Courtesy of the Frank Lloyd Wright Foundation)

Fig. 156. Plan of the Isabel Roberts house, River Forest, Illinois, 1908. Lithograph.

Wright designed several other buildings that were linked to the Johnson commissions. Most notable was the house he designed for Herbert Johnson.[1] Johnson, who had been divorced in 1934, married Jane Roach in 1936 and they each brought two children to the new marriage. In the autumn of 1936 Johnson and his wife took Wright to see a large tract of virgin prairie and forest they owned just north of Racine. Johnson had kept it for years as a nature preserve, and was considering building a house on the property for his large family.

In mid-January of 1937, Johnson called Wright from the Drake Hotel in Chicago. The upper lobby of the hotel featured a freestanding central fireplace. Johnson thought that this arrangement might lend itself to the living room of a house. On a visit to Taliesin, he brought Wright a sketch he had drawn of a four-winged house, with a large room at the intersection of the wings and a freestanding fireplace in the center of the room. Wright applauded Johnson's scheme, and in a quick sketch turned Johnson's Greek cross plan into a pinwheel by shifting each wing to one side of the large room.[2] One of the wings—or zones, as Wright chose to call them—would house the master suite, another would house the children's rooms, another the servants and kitchen, and the fourth guests and a carport. The central chimney, containing five fireplaces on two levels, divided the central room, which Wright dubbed a wigwam, into an entry space, dining area, library, and family living area. Wright named the house Wingspread (figs. 155 and 157).

Construction of Wingspread began in May. Ben Wiltscheck agreed to build it on a cost-plus basis, and Wright assigned apprentices John Lautner and Edgar Tafel to draft and oversee the job. The job proceeded slowly and far exceeded cost estimates. Jane Johnson died in 1938 while the house was still under construction and Herbert Johnson contemplated leaving it unfinished. Urged on by Wright, he had it completed in 1939, when he and his two children moved into it. However, he never proceeded with two auxiliary projects Wright designed for the property: a group of farm buildings (fig. 161) and a gatehouse (fig. 160). Johnson lived in the house until 1959 when he gave it to the Johnson Foundation, which uses it as an educational conference center.

In his autobiography Wright called Wingspread "the last of the prairie houses." Some of the earlier Prairie houses, designed between 1900 and 1910, such as the Isabel Roberts house of 1908 (fig. 156), feature four wings extending from a central chimney core. One of the wings contains the entry area, one a two-story living room, one the dining room, and a fourth contains the kitchen. The family's bedrooms are located on the second floor. Wingspread may be seen as a new interpretation and the culmination of this morphological type.

Wingspread is a brilliant anomaly among Wright's work. Detailed like a Usonian house but based in plan on his earlier Prairie houses, it bridges his two great residential periods. It was one of the few houses he built in which he had to pay little attention to cost, but unlike his ornate Susan Dana House (1902), in Wingspread the materials and detailing are restrained and do not create the appearance of lavishness. The money went into subtleties: Wright wrote that Wingspread had the finest brickwork he had seen, and that the woodwork and furniture showed unusual craftsmanship. In many of his houses Wright had to rely on techniques of scale and proportion to give a sense of spaciousness, but in Wingspread no tricks were needed: the central room is in fact enormous. Through devices such as a mezzanine, built-in cabinetry and furniture, and steps, he caused the room to seem to be composed of four smaller, flowing spaces, each with a different function. The 14,000-square foot house is the largest Wright

Fig. 157. Aerial view of Wingspread, circa 1950. As in the Johnson Administration Building, the house's base is of cream-colored Kasota sandstone, and the walls are built of Cherokee-red brick with horizontal joints raked deeply and vertical joints flush and tinted red. The other materials, however, differ. The upper exterior walls are stuccoed; the fascias and the exterior doors and the window trim are made of unfinished cypress boards, and the roof is covered with red clay tiles with copper flashing. Cypress pergolas, now covered with grapevines, project beyond the body of the house. Extensive plate-glass windows open the interior to its surroundings, which Wright had lushly landscaped with arborvitae and pine trees. (Courtesy of Johnson Wax)

ever built, but it floats serenely on its semi-wooded site.

Wingspread bears a curious relationship to the Johnson Wax buildings. The Administration Building and Research Tower seem to have been subjected to a centripetal force: slick walls wrap compactly and seamlessly around the central tower and columns. Wingspread, however, appears to have been subjected to a centrifugal force. Its four irregular wings spin out like nebulae from the central core. The two approaches reflect Wright's opposing attitudes toward the sites. In one case he turned his back on the surroundings and imploded a building behind hermetic walls. In the other case the natural surroundings invited him to extend the building into the site. One can only wonder what Wright would have designed for the Johnson Company had Herbert Johnson accepted his appeal to build his office building in the countryside.

In the mid-1950s Wright transformed his notion of a great mushroom column-filled space into two more schemes, one small and one enormous. In 1954 he drafted his first version of the Freund y Cia department store project in San Salvador, El Salvador. All six versions of the building are composed of a two-story columniated sales floor filling the site. Offices are located in a mezzanine overlooking the room, and two circular ramps provide access to a parking garage in the basement. In some versions third-story offices surround a rooftop garden court (figs. 162, 163).

The next year Wright designed an expandable tentlike headquarters for the Lenkurt Electric Company in San Mateo, California. The six-hundred-foot-long structure was to be supported by three-story-high mushroom columns, twenty-four feet on center. The ground floor was entirely open for parking, and the huge two-story partitionable workroom was lit by pyramidlike skylights. The project was canceled when the firm was purchased by a larger corporation (figs. 164, 165).

Fig. 158. Central room, or "wigwam" of Wingspread, 1941. The twenty-five-foot-high ceiling is tiered, pagodalike, with three rows of clerestories. Radiant heating is located beneath the four-foot square concrete slabs, which are tinted Cherokee red. Wright also designed some of the furniture for the house. He based two barrel chairs on his earlier Darwin Martin house chair (1904). (Photo by Samuel Gottscho; courtesy of Gottscho-Schleisner)

Fig. 159. Perspective view of Wingspread. Pencil and colored pencil on tracing paper. 42″ × 33″. (Courtesy of the Frank Lloyd Wright Foundation)

Fig. 160. Gatehouse for Herbert F. Johnson, designed in 1938. This gatehouse was not built, although a far more modest building with small framing walls was. Unlike Wingspread itself, the walls in both designs are streamlined, composed of low, curved Cherokee-red brick walls, similar to those of the Administration Building. Pencil and colored pencil on tracing paper. 39″ × 14″. (Courtesy of the Frank Lloyd Wright Foundation)

Fig. 161. Group of farm buildings for Herbert F. Johnson, including a farmhouse, outbuildings, and zoo, designed in 1937. Ink and pencil on tracing paper. Original drawing missing. (Courtesy of the Frank Lloyd Wright Foundation)

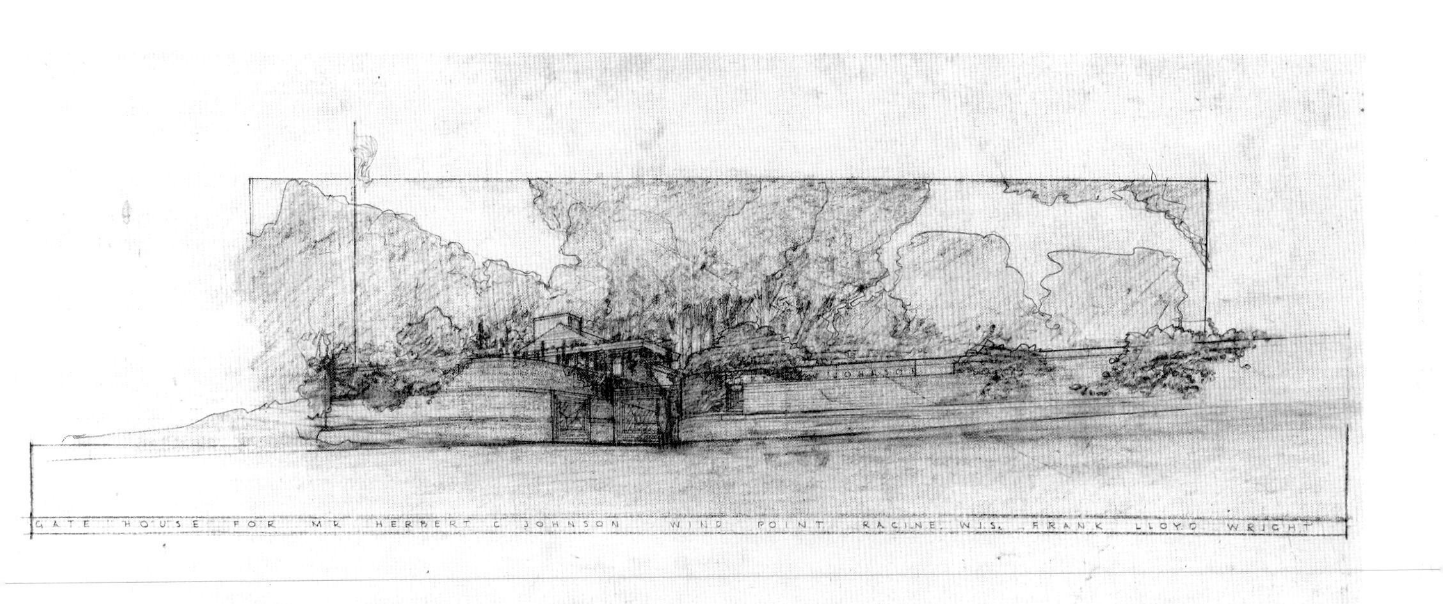
JOHNSON
GATE HOUSE FOR MR HERBERT C JOHNSON WIND POINT RACINE WIS. FRANK LLOYD WRIGHT

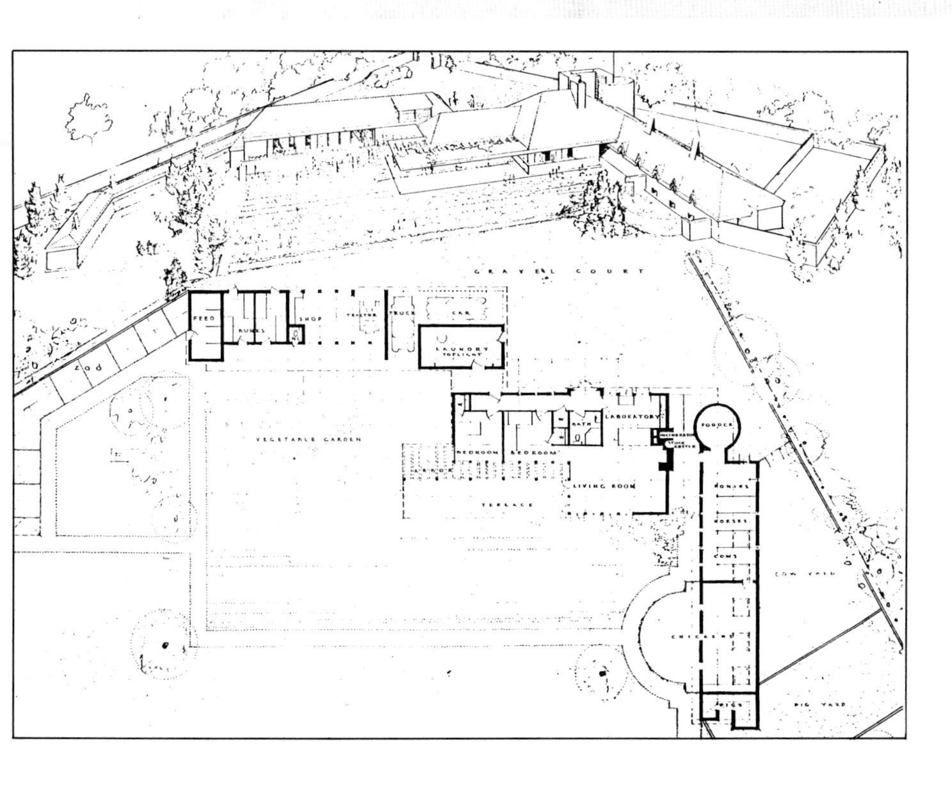
GRAVEL COURT
FEED
SHOP
TRACTOR
TRUCK
CAR
LAUNDRY
TOPLIGHT
VEGETABLE GARDEN
BEDROOM
BEDROOM
BATH
LABORATORY
FODDER
LIVING ROOM
TERRACE
PONIES
HORSES
COWS
COW YARD
CHICKENS
PIGS
PIG YARD

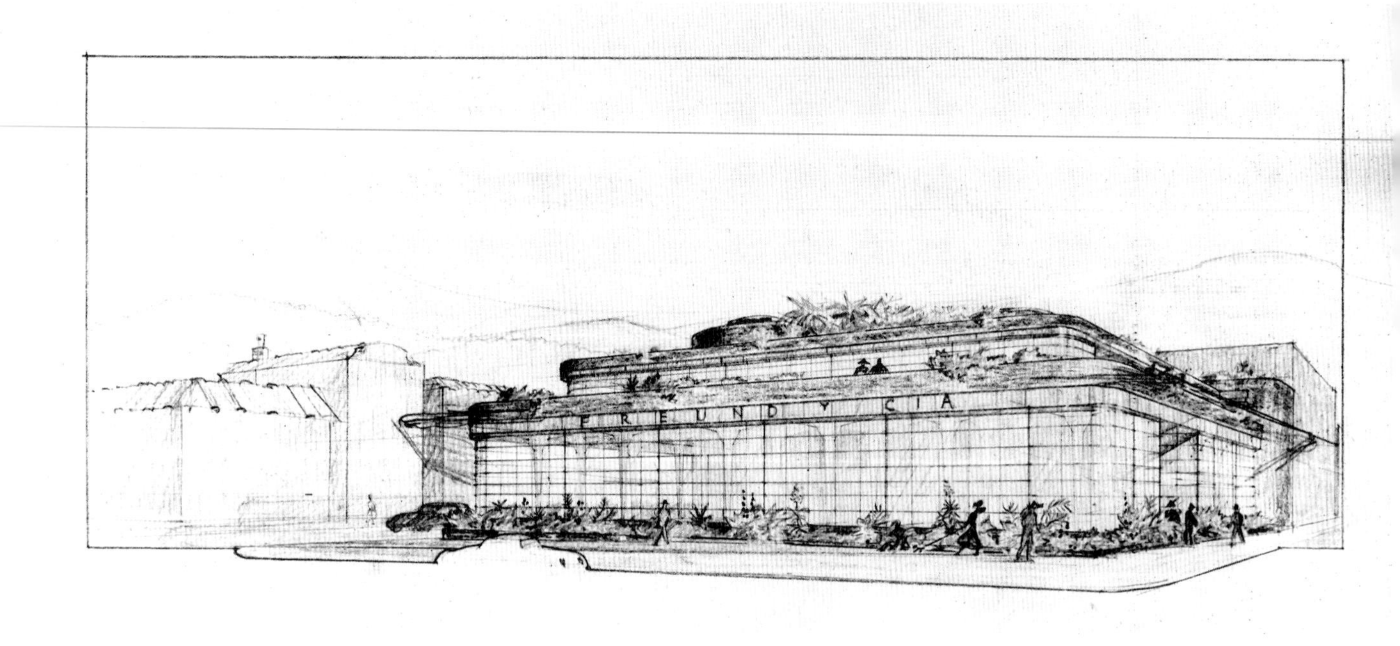

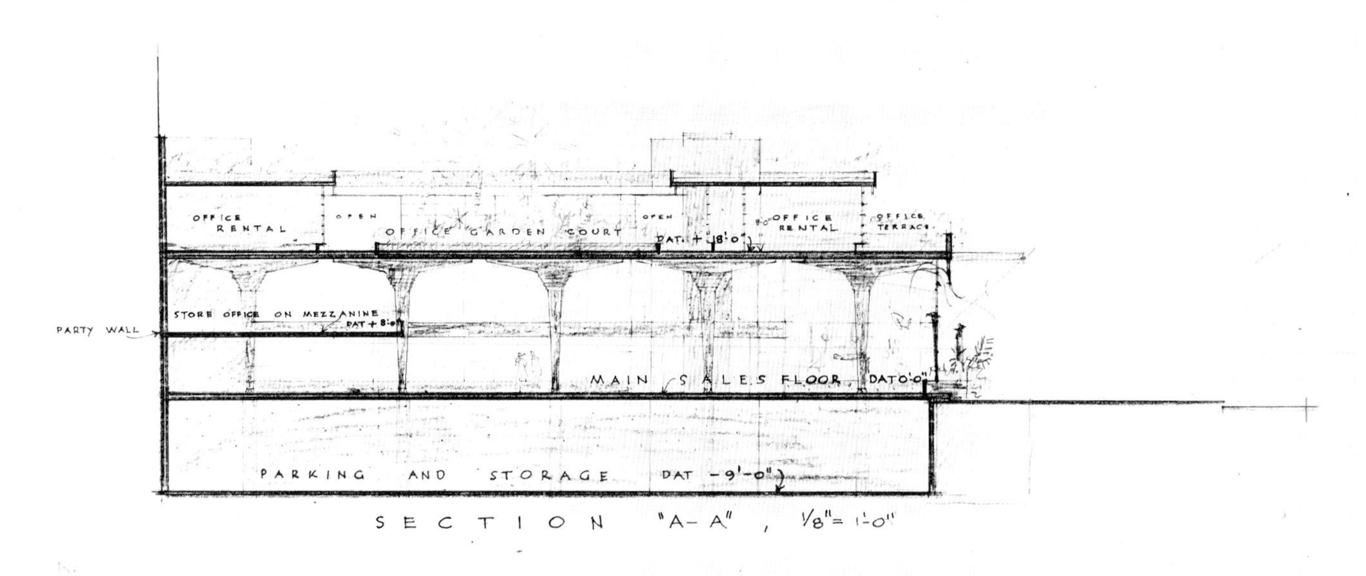

Fig. 162. Exterior perspective of Freund y Cia department store project, San Salvador, El Salvador, 1954. A reworking of Wright's 1931 Capital Journal project. Pencil and colored pencil on tracing paper. 27" × 22". (Courtesy of the Frank Lloyd Wright Foundation)

Fig. 163. Section through Freund y Cia project. Pencil and colored pencil on tracing paper. (Courtesy of the Frank Lloyd Wright Foundation)

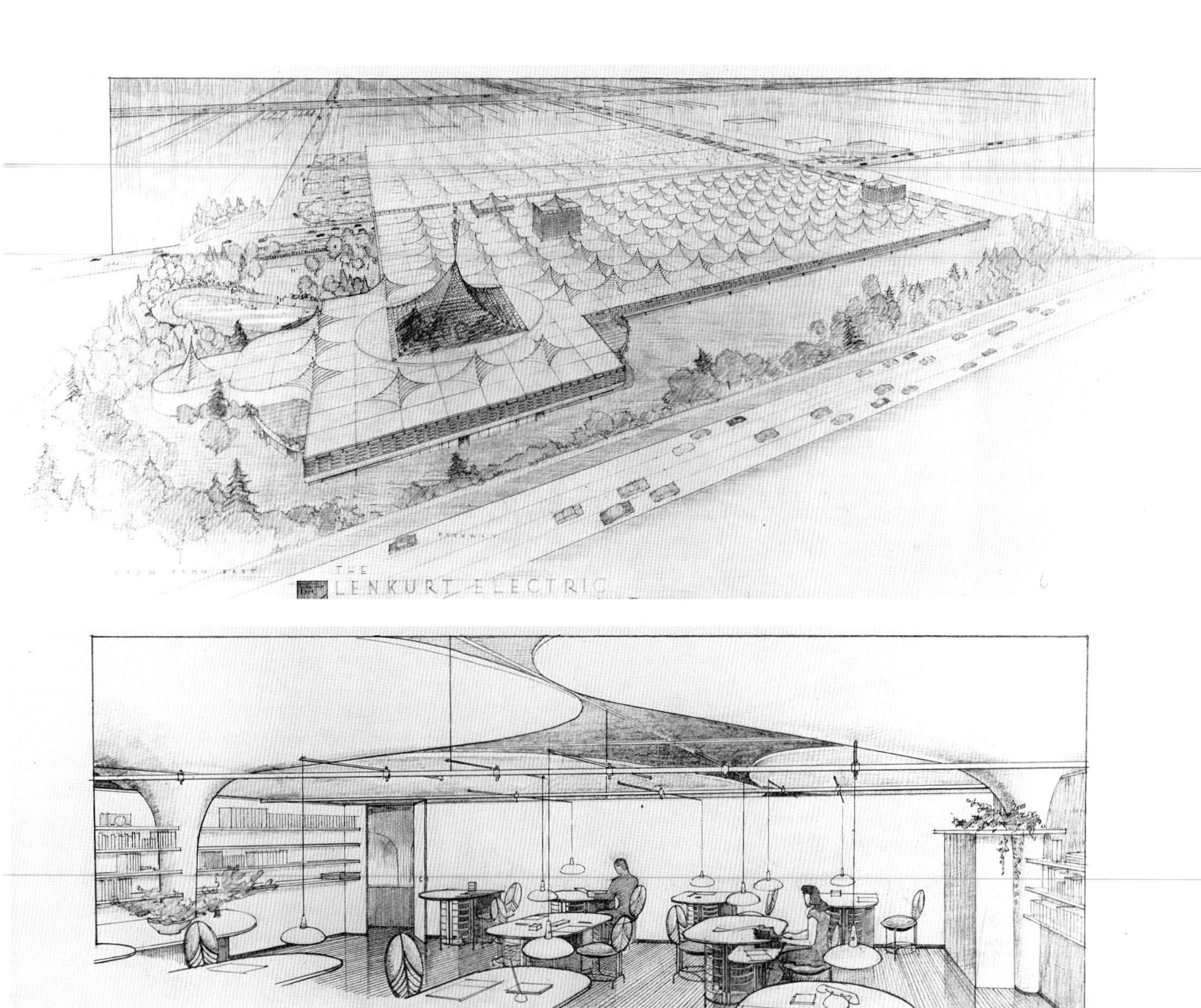

Fig. 164. Exterior perspective of Lenkurt Electric Company Administration Building project, San Mateo, California, 1955. Pencil and colored pencil on tracing paper. (Courtesy of the Frank Lloyd Wright Foundation)

Fig. 165. Perspective of mezzanine office, Lenkurt Electric Company project. Furniture is based on Johnson company office furniture. Pencil and colored pencil on tracing paper. (Courtesy of the Frank Lloyd Wright Foundation)

APPENDIX 2

"THE NEW BUILDING FOR S. C. JOHNSON & SON, INC."

This document was written by Wright, shortly after he designed the Administration Building, in response to a request by the Johnson Company for a statement that could be released to the press on the project. The completed building differs in a number of minor ways from this early description.

"The New Building for S. C. Johnson & Son, Inc."

Everyone interested in building uses the term "Modern Architecture". Usually the term means something "streamlined" from the outside—that is to say something smooth and flat, all ornament omitted, the corners cut out for window openings and gas pipe railings put on wherever they will ride. The thought in the building does not change. "Modernity"—so called—is achieved as the new look of something old rather than new look of something really new. Nevertheless, there is a type of thought-built building that is modern because it is better in every way than the old building. A higher ideal of what a building should be is behind the conception, and a more complete science is behind the execution of the building. The ideal is organic character throughout; the suitable thing in the most suitable way, all considered.

A branch to the left proceeding from this original ideal took the slogan "Form follows Function" with which to rationalize its irrational acts and succeeded in making thin buildings that look as though cut from cardboard with scissors, the cuttings folded into opposing planes without ornament.

A branch to the right got to making thick buildings that carried ornament too far—"Function following Form."

The parent stem kept on making buildings that had whatever virtues each branch possessed, and only the implication of their vices. In short, the parent stem kept on making buildings wherein Function and Form are made one.

The Larkin Administration Building of Buffalo, built in 1906, is the predecessor of the building for the "S. C. Johnson Wax" being built in 1936. The Larkin Building was the first "air conditioned" building in America: the first steel furnished and absolutely fire-proof building wherein simplicities like the wall-water closet and suspended water closet partitions, cushioned floors (magnasite as a building material), etc., appeared for the first time. And the building itself was a fireproof filing cabinet. The Larkin Building said the first word in the world for building as the same direct expression where materials and purpose are concerned that you may see in any battleship or an aeroplane. That administration building is a corner stone of what must be recognized as "modern architecture". Now comes another expression more gracious: a more highly developed synthesis of form and idea because it is a building more completely moved away from windowed walls. The building consists of [a] great work room breathing from above through nostrils where the air is fresh, deriving comfortable warmth from the floors beneath the occupant—climate rather than heating—and economy of heat: a building having dignified character and appropriate proportions, so complete in itself for its own sake that it is in no way inferior in harmony to the ancient cathedral.

This office building for the S. C. Johnson Wax Company—memorializing in a pioneering way the pioneering of a grandfather and a father—is simply and sincerely an interpretation of modern business conditions, and of business too, itself designed to be as inspiring to live and work in as any cathedral ever was to worship in.

Brick and glass work together with modern appliances in order to create this effect out of the nature of the building itself. The effects are not something put on nor are they ever added merely for effect.

All comes out of the way the whole thing is made to grow toward the purpose for which it was intended out of the way it was built.

In other words, the building will stand as an authentic example of Modern Architecture true to the traditions of that Architecture as they actually exist. That means a new center line for American culture no longer a senile provincial imitation of the great styles in any sense.

For example, the building is laid out upon a horizontal unit system 20′ o.c. [on center] both ways and a vertical unit of a brick course of 3½″. Glass is not used as bricks in this structure any more than bricks are used as glass. The building becomes crystal where crystal—transparent or translucent—is most useful and appropriate. The exterior enclosing wall material appears inside wherever it is sensible for it to do so in order to make the structure as monolithic as possible. The construction throughout is a simple setting up within the brick enclosing walls of slender concrete monolithic shafts with shallow wide-spreading tops—the shafts standing tip-toe on metal crowfeet bedded at the floor level: earthquakeproof, and fireproof construction.

Work itself is correlated in one vast room, the room to be air conditioned summer and winter, day-lit by the walls and roof becoming crystal wherever light will be most useful.

The officers are grouped together in a kind of pent-house on the roof slab of this big room. The pent-house, at the center, is open to the big room below in order to preserve intimate connection between work and officials; the unity of the whole. This effect of spaciousness is especially seen and felt at the main entrance.

The building stands within three rather narrow streets in unimpressive surroundings. So the main entrance is made interior to the lot; the motor car taken into account and provided for as a modern indispensable. Ample facilities for parking are made within walls and under cover at the entrance. All being provided for on the building premises. And the main building is set back from the street fronts 14 feet on all sides and this space is treated as a parterre planted with low shrubs and perennials. This colorful band of growth divides the walls from the sidewalk.

This parking entrance area becomes a playground, above.

A small cinema for broadcasting, for daytime lectures, entertainment and instruction is placed at mezzanine level at the middle of the whole arrangement where it may be open to the big work room and be connected to the playground over the parking area. An enclosed bridge connects the penthouse with a squash court rising above the garage.

Herbert Johnson's offices are at the center of the penthouse; the other officers grouped about him in proper order, his right bower, Jack Ramsey, at their head. Also, there is a spacious room for directors' meetings. Below, disposed in proper order in the great work space, are the office workers. The heads of various departments function in a low gallery, mezzanine to the big room, where direct vision and prompt connection with the workers in the big room is had directly at convenient points by spiral stairways dropping down to the lower level wherever convenient. All enclosures within the big workroom are glass and screened wherever desired by Aeroshades preserving thus the sense of the whole stimulating to various parts.

The automatic electric elevators from main floor to roof are simply iron baskets moving in the open but safely screened in with Pyralin.

The ½″ horizontal brick joints where elevator enclosures and stairs are concerned issue as iron rods to give the necessary protection to elevator and stairs with light horizontal lines.

The brick used is a special brick 2¼″ × 3″ × 9″ shale brick grooved on the back. Vertical joints are kept close, horizontal joints raked ½″ deep.

Where glass is used cork is always next to it. The lengths of glass tubing are set in mastic secured to internal joints by copper wire wound to a slight interior frame of steel which is not itself in contact with the glass. All glass walls and skylights are of the same tubing in the same units and all are hollow and doubled. Cork insulation is also used in all exterior walls and roofs.

Artificial lighting is introduced by way of neon tubes between these glass walls and skylights. No fixtures of any kind are visible in the building except office furniture.

The advertising features themselves are architectural, entirely, including the firm name across the top of the wall at the rear lot line.

A large illuminated globe placed at the center of a terraced pool on the axis of the main entrance way and across the side street is such a feature. There are large glass murals dividing the cinema from the main work room. These are equally effective seen from cinema or from the big room.

The toilets, locker accommodations, rest rooms, etc., have been provided directly beneath the work space where small spiral iron stairs lead directly down to them. The lower rooms are porcelain lined and are great sanitary features as a whole.

There are no corridors in the building—no dead spaces—no waste motion anywhere. All space is not only alive and working but so treated as in someway to contribute to the sense of a well organized activity in harmonious circumstances. A consistent whole.

Thus, unnecessary commitments and inhibitions aside, I take it, is the sort of thing architecture must be to be called modern.

Frank Lloyd Wright
TALIESIN: SPRING GREEN: WISCONSIN
October 11, 1936

NOTES

CHAPTER 1

1 Herbert Johnson interviewed by Edward Wilder, 1940.
2 Karen Boyd interviewed by the author, September 23, 1981.
3 Johnson apparently "inherited" Matson (1890–1963), who had been hired in 1924 by Johnson's father to remodel his home, a late Victorian Gothic house built for Samuel C. Johnson in 1903. Herbert Johnson hired Matson to do additional remodeling to the house in 1934. Matson was an eclectic architect whose work included a 1928 Racine Gothic Revival church, and the Racine, Wisconsin, City Hall, designed in a neoclassical style in 1931.
4 Though drawings of the design do not survive, the Henry Mitchell Elementary School in Racine, designed the following year, stands as an example of Matson's design. It is a simple two-story brick building with limestone Art Deco ornamentation.
5 Letter from Jack Ramsey to Herbert Johnson, July 19, 1936.
6 *Inland Architect*, August/September, 1969, p. 18.
7 *The North Shore Bulletin*, October 1925, "World's Largest Floor Finishing Plant in Racine, Wisconsin." pp. 9–10.
8 *Milwaukee Journal*, March 24, 1946, "Johnson's Bonus & Benefits Plan Brings Industrial Peace."
9 *Inland Architect*, August/September, 1969, p. 18.

CHAPTER 2

1 Frank Lloyd Wright, *An Autobiography* (New York: Duell, Sloan and Pearce, 1943), p. 468. Apparently Wright's quotation compresses events, as Johnson did not actually accompany Ramsey on his first meeting.
2 Edgar Tafel, *Apprentice to Genius*, (New York: McGraw-Hill, 1979), p. 175.
3 *Inland Architect*, August/September, 1969, p. 18.
4 Tafel interviewed by the author June 16, 1979.
5 In interviews with the author, Wright's former apprentices did not reach a consensus as to whether Wright referred to the Capital Journal project in this first meeting.
6 In a conversation with the author on September 27, 1985, John Howe stated that Wright told him that this was his reason for using the columns and shoes in such a fashion.
7 Letter from Jack Ramsey to Herbert Johnson, July 19, 1936.
8 Henrietta Louis interviewed by the author, May 27, 1981.
9 Letter from Ramsey to Johnson, July 19, 1936.
10 John Howe interviewed by the author, November 30, 1980.
11 Olgivanna Lloyd Wright, interviewed by the author, January 19, 1980, recalled, "He came at Mr. Wright's lunch time. We ate in the Hillside [Home School] upper-level dining room and we had a Russian dish, which we called *galupsi*. Herbert Johnson put it in his mouth and said, 'What is this awful stuff? It's terrible!' I said, I admire you for your sincerity, but that's all you're going to get.' 'Well,' he said, 'I drove all the way up here dreaming of a steak. 'Oh,' I said, 'You'll have to reduce your dream to the food in front of you.' He ate it. He was hungry!"
12 Herbert Johnson interviewed by Edward Wilder, 1940.
13 Olgivanna Wright interviewed by the author, January 19, 1980.
14 John Howe interviewed by the author, November 30, 1980.
15 Letter from Johnson to Wright, July 23, 1936.
16 Letter from Wright to Johnson, July 24, 1936.
17 Karen Boyd interviewed by the author, September 23, 1981.
18 Tafel interviewed by the author, February 5, 1982.
19 Letter from Johnson to Wright, July 30, 1936.
20 Olgivanna Wright interview.

CHAPTER 3

1 In a conversation with the author on September 27, 1985, John Howe did not recall Wright ever saying that the form of the Larkin Building was an influence on the Johnson Company's Administration Building. In his autobiography, however, Wright refers to the Larkin building as the Johnson Administration Building's sire.
2 Frank Lloyd Wright, *An Autobiography* (New York: Duell, Sloan and Pearce, 1943), p. 469.
3 Wright used the Larkin Building/Johnson Administration Building parti throughout his career for his major urban nonresidential buildings, in particular Unity Temple (1904) and the Guggenheim Museum (1943).
4 John Howe interviewed by the author, November 30, 1980.
5 Wright, *Writings & Buildings* (Cleveland: The World Publishing Company 1960), pp. 284–86. Edited transcript of an address to the Junior Chapter of the American Institute of Architects, New York City, 1952.
6 Robert Mosher interviewed by the author, April 23, 1981.
7 John Howe interviewed by the author, November 30, 1980.
8 William Wesley Peters interviewed by the author, April 22, 1979.
9 Howe interview.
10 Peters interviewed by the author, April 22, 1979.
11 Edgar Tafel interviewed by the author, October 1, 1979.
12 Letter from Wright to Herbert Johnson, August 15, 1936.
13 Letter from Johnson to Wright, August 18, 1936.
14 In a conversation with the author, Serge E. Logan, Director of Corporate Social Responsibility for the Johnson Company, noted that Johnson recounted this fact to him in 1961.
15 Howe interviewed by the author, September 27, 1985.
16 Edmund Teske interviewed by the author, January 10, 1980.
17 Letter from Johnson to Wright, August 21, 1936.
18 Letter from Wright to Johnson, August 24, 1936.
19 Letter from Wright to Jack Ramsey, August 24, 1936.
20 Olgivanna Lloyd Wright interviewed by the author, January 19, 1980.
21 Speech by Olgivanna Lloyd Wright, June 24, 1961, published in *Dedication of Wingspread*, by the Johnson Foundation.
22 Wright, *Unconnected Notes on the Jacob House* (transcript of speech in the Art Institute of Chicago's Jacobs Collection, undated).
23 Olgivanna Wright interview.

24 Wright, *Writings & Buildings*, ed., Edgar Kaufmann and Ben Raeburn (New York: New American Library, 1960), p. 281.

CHAPTER 4

1 Frank Lloyd Wright, (typed statement in Johnson Company archives, October 11, 1936).
2 J. Vernon Steinle interviewed by the author, December, 1979.
3 Wright, *An Autobiography* (New York: Duell, Sloan and Pearce, 1943), p. 242.
4 Letter from the Industrial Commission of Wisconsin to Herbert Johnson, November 21, 1936.
5 Robert Mosher interviewed by the author April 23, 1981.
6 Henry-Russell Hitchcock & Frank Lloyd Wright, *In The Nature of Materials* (New York: Duell, Sloan and Pearce, 1942), pp. 127–129.
7 Letter from Wright to Jack Ramsey, January 22, 1937.

CHAPTER 5

1 William Wesley Peters, interviewed by the author March 8, 1980.
2 Carl W. Condit, *American Building Art: The Twentieth Century* (New York: Oxford University Press, 1961), p. 174.
3 The author is indebted to Edgar Kaufmann, Jr., for bringing this point to his attention.
4 Peters, interviewed by the author March 8, 1980, Peters mentioned to the author that building materials' manufacturers' representatives often came to Taliesin to tell Wright about new products—knowing that if he used them the products might receive profitable exposure.
5 Letter from George McVicker to the author, October 12, 1979.
6 Herbert Jacobs, *Frank Lloyd Wright: America's Greatest Architect.* (New York: Harcourt, Brace & World, 1965). In an interview with the author on April 22, 1979 Peters stated that he recalled that the test column was left fully loaded for twenty-four hours before being knocked down.
7 Frank Lloyd Wright, *Writings & Buildings*, ed. Edgar Kaufmann and Ben Raeburn (New York: New American Library, 1960), p. 286.
8 Edgar Tafel, *Apprentice to Genius* (New York: McGraw-Hill, 1979), p. 180.

CHAPTER 6

1 Letter from Frank Lloyd Wright to Jack Ramsey, undated.
2 "Office Building Without Precedent," *Engineering News-Record*, December 9, 1937, p. 958.
3 Talk given by George Nelson at the New School, 1980.
4 Letter from Wright to Herbert Johnson, December 30, 1937.
5 Letter from Johnson to Wright, January 6, 1938.
6 Letter from Wright to Johnson, undated, but marked received January 12, 1938.
7 Edgar Tafel, interviewed by the author, June 16, 1979 and June 6, 1981.
8 Memo from Ben Wiltscheck to Wright, July 15, 1938.
9 Olgivanna Lloyd Wright interviewed by the author, January 19, 1980.
10 Letter from Wright to Jack Ramsey, August 31, 1938.
11 Letter from Ramsey to Wright, September 1, 1938.
12 David Hunting, an executive of Steelcase, Inc., who worked closely with Wright designing furniture for the Johnson building, interviewed by the author on January 12, 1982.
13 Karen Boyd interviewed by the author, September 23, 1981.
14 Edgar Tafel, *Apprentice to Genius* (New York: McGraw-Hill, 1979), p. 185.
15 Wright was actually seventy-one at the time. Apparently he began subtracting two years from his age thirty years earlier. Letter undated.
16 Letter from Ramsey to Wright, January 17, 1939.
17 Letter from Tafel to Wright, January 30, 1939.
18 Letter from Wright to Ramsey, February 11, 1939.
19 John Lautner, interviewed by the author, January 11, 1980.
20 Tafel, *Apprentice to Genius*, p. 187.

CHAPTER 7

1 Letter from Frank Lloyd Wright to Jack Ramsey, December 10, 1936.
2 Letter from Ramsey to Wright, December 11, 1936.
3 Letter from Ramsey to Wright, January 20, 1937.
4 Letter from Wright to Ramsey, January 21, 1937.
5 Wright submitted a slight variant on the first desk and chair to the U.S. Patent Office in applications dated December 20, 1937. According to a private agreement, Wright assigned 49 percent of any royalties to the Johnson Company. However, Steelcase never built the furniture for anyone else, although David Hunting of Steelcase told the author that his company was approached by "a couple of people."
6 Warren McArthur (d. 1961) participated in the construction of the Arizona Biltmore Hotel, designed by his brother Charles H. McArthur and Wright. During World War II the Warren McArthur Corporation built award-winning aluminum and magnesium aircraft seats. (obituary, *The New York Times*, December 18, 1961, p. 35.)
7 David Hunting, interviewed by the author, January 12, 1982.
8 Wright's presentation drawing of this chair is illustrated in David Hanks, *The Decorative Designs of Frank Lloyd Wright* (New York: E. P. Dutton, 1979), p. 151.

CHAPTER 8

1 Gustave Pabst, "An Office Building, or The Story of Two Men," *Milwaukee Journal*, April 27, 1939, p. 2.
2 "Frank Lloyd Wright Designs The Office of The Future for S. C. Johnson and Son, Incorporated," *American Business*, May 1939, p. 41.
3 Wright, *The New Building for S. C. Johnson & Son, Inc.* (unpublished press release, October 11, 1936, Johnson Company Archives).
4 In "Transcendency In the Light Court of Frank Lloyd Wright's Larkin Administration Building," Jack Quinan argues convincingly that Wright designed the Larkin Building according to Transcendentalist ideals and claims, "Wright's Larkin light court represented an analog to Emerson's

belief in the aspiration of all matter to a spiritual ideal and in the unity of all things in nature" (Typescript. Buffalo, N.Y., p. 18).

5 Employees' opinions assessed from interviews conducted by the author with Julia Jarie, Elsie Dostal, Robert Gardiner, J. Vernon Steinle, Edward Wilder and Raymond Carlson, all of whom were employed by the company at its Racine plant when it moved in to the new building in 1939.

6 Ralph M. Barnes: *Motion and Time Study*, 2d ed. (New York: John Wiley & Sons, Inc.).

CHAPTER 9

1 J. Vernon Steinle interviewed by the author, December 31, 1979.

2 In an interview with the author, Robert Mosher noted that in the late 1930s Fallingwater client Edgar Kaufmann, Sr., visited the partially built Administration Building, where Johnson complained to him of the trials of construction. Mosher recalled Kaufmann saying, "Building a Wright building is like having a baby: it takes nine months and then you have a bouncing boy, but you swear you'll never have another one." Ironically, both Kaufmann and Johnson hired Wright several times.

3 Letter from Herbert Johnson to Wright, December 7, 1943.

4 Letter from Wright to Johnson, undated (apparently December 8, 1943).

5 Letter from Johnson to Wright, December 9, 1943.

6 Letter from Wright to Johnson, December 13, 1943.

7 Letter from Wright to Johnson, December 14, 1943.

8 Letter from Wright to Johnson, December 16, 1943.

9 Undated letter from Wright, received by Herbert Johnson, December 22, 1943.

10 The company had bought up the remaining lots on the west side of the block on which the Administration Building was located, but had not bought the row of lots on the east side. Steinle's scheme used all the lots on the west side of the block north of the Administration Building. Johnson may have hoped to save some of that land for future expansion with his suggestion that Wright design a tall building. However, Wright's scheme filled up both sides of the block, necessitating that the company buy several additional lots.

11 *Jonwax Journal*, November, 1950, p. 4, quoting Wright's remarks at the opening of the Research Tower, in which he recounted his first conversation with Johnson about the research building.

12 The author wishes to acknowledge Edgar Kaufmann, Jr., for pointing out to him the possible influence of Fuller's project on Wright.

13 Transcript of speech by Johnson, November 17, 1950.

14 Wright was a Japanophile, and his first trip outside the United States in 1905, was to Japan. Its influence on his Prairie houses has often been noted. For example, see Grant Manson: *Frank Lloyd Wright To 1910, The First Golden Age* (New York: Van Nostrand Reinhold, 1958), pp. 34–40. The famous Horyu-ji is the oldest temple in Japan. After spending over three years in Japan Wright was almost certainly familiar with it.

15 Brought to the author's attention by Neil Levine.

CHAPTER 10

1 Memo from J. Vernon Steinle to Herbert Johnson, December 30, 1943.

2 Memo from Steinle to Johnson, December 30, 1943.

3 Ibid.

4 Letter from Frank Lloyd Wright to Steinle, February 6, 1944.

5 Letter from Steinle to Wright, February 8, 1944.

6 Letter from Johnson to Wright, February 15, 1944.

7 Letter from Steinle to Wright, March 10, 1944.

8 Letter from Wright to Johnson, May 22, 1944.

9 Memo from William Connolly to Johnson, Ben Wiltscheck, and J. J. Babb, September 6, 1944.

10 Interoffice memo from Johnson to Babb, October 2, 1944.

11 Telegram from Wright to Johnson, November 27, 1944.

12 Letter from Steinle to Johnson, December 1, 1944.

13 Letter from Ben Wiltscheck to Johnson, June 8, 1943.

14 Letter from Wiltscheck to Johnson, June 30, 1944.

15 Letter from Wright to Wiltscheck, June 2, 1945.

16 Memo from Wiltscheck to Johnson, June 11, 1945.

17 Steinle, interviewed by the author, December 31, 1979.

18 Letter from Wright to Johnson, November 16, 1944.

19 Letter from Johnson to Wright, November 20, 1944.

20 Letter from Wright to Johnson, October 25, 1946.

21 Information about this project received from the late Robert Whittaker of Kenosha, Wisconsin, a real estate developer who attempted to help Johnson raise money for the building program (interviewed by the author, July 29, 1982).

22 Letter from Johnson to Wright, April 10, 1946.

CHAPTER 11

1 Most of the architectural drawings were signed and dated by Frank Lloyd Wright in April 1946.

2 Jacob Stocker, interviewed by the author, April 4, 1980.

3 John Halama, interviewed by the author, July 1, 1985.

4 "Winter Weather Doesn't Stop This Job," *Construction Methods and Equipment*, March 1950, pp. 51–55.

5 Stocker, interviewed by the author.

6 Transcript of speech, probably delivered by Ben Wiltscheck at the opening of the Research Tower, November 17, 1950 (Johnson Company Archives).

7 Letter from T. H. Truslow, General Sales Manager, Technical Products Division, Corning Glass Works, to Wright, October 5, 1948.

8 Transcript of speech by Wiltscheck (see note 6).

9 The documentation of the Administration Building and Research Tower differs in part because fewer people involved in the creation of the earlier building were still living when the author conducted his research interviews.

CHAPTER 12

1 "Wright's Core-Supported Tower Unveiled in Photographs," *Architectural Record*, December 1950, pp. 11a–b.

2 "Speaking of Pictures," *Life*, December 11, 1950, pp. 8–10.

3 Eugene Kitzke, interviewed by the author, October 2, 1985.

4 J. Vernon Steinle, interviewed by the author, December 31, 1979.

5 In 1955 Frank Lloyd Wright remodeled the photography laboratory, which occupied the former squash court, into a two-story library to house the company's large collection of books and articles on wax.

6 Interviewed by the author over the telephone in 1985, John Halama said that he had nothing to do with the addition. The blueline prints of the preliminary design, however, are signed with Halama's initials.

7 Letter from Wright to Halama, August 24, 1957.

8 Conversation with William Wesley Peters, who is engaged by the Johnson Company to examine the building periodically, August 7, 1984.

9 "Mr. Wright and the Johnsons of Racine, Wis," *AIA Journal* (January 1979) p. 65

APPENDIX 1

1 Frank Lloyd Wright also designed the Karen Keland house in 1954, built in Racine for Herbert Johnson's daughter Karen Boyd. Also, in 1941 he designed the never-built Roy Peterson residence in Racine. Peterson was a staff photographer for the Johnson Company.

2 William Wesley Peters, interviewed by the author, April 22, 1979.

FLOOR PLANS

The following floor plans, section, and elevation represent the completed Johnson Wax complex as it appeared in 1950.

Opposite: First-floor plan of Administration Building and Research Tower. (Drawing by Gerald Wilson)

Overleaf: Second-floor (mezzanine) plan of Administration Building and Research Tower. (Drawing by Gerald Wilson)

SECOND FLOOR

1. Roof deck
2. Legal department
3. Exhibition dwelling (causerie)
4. Greenhouse
5. Roof garden
6. Photographic studio (former squash court)
7. Marketing department
8. Wax display
9. Library
10. Terrace
11. Theater
12. Mezzanine (open to Great Workroom)

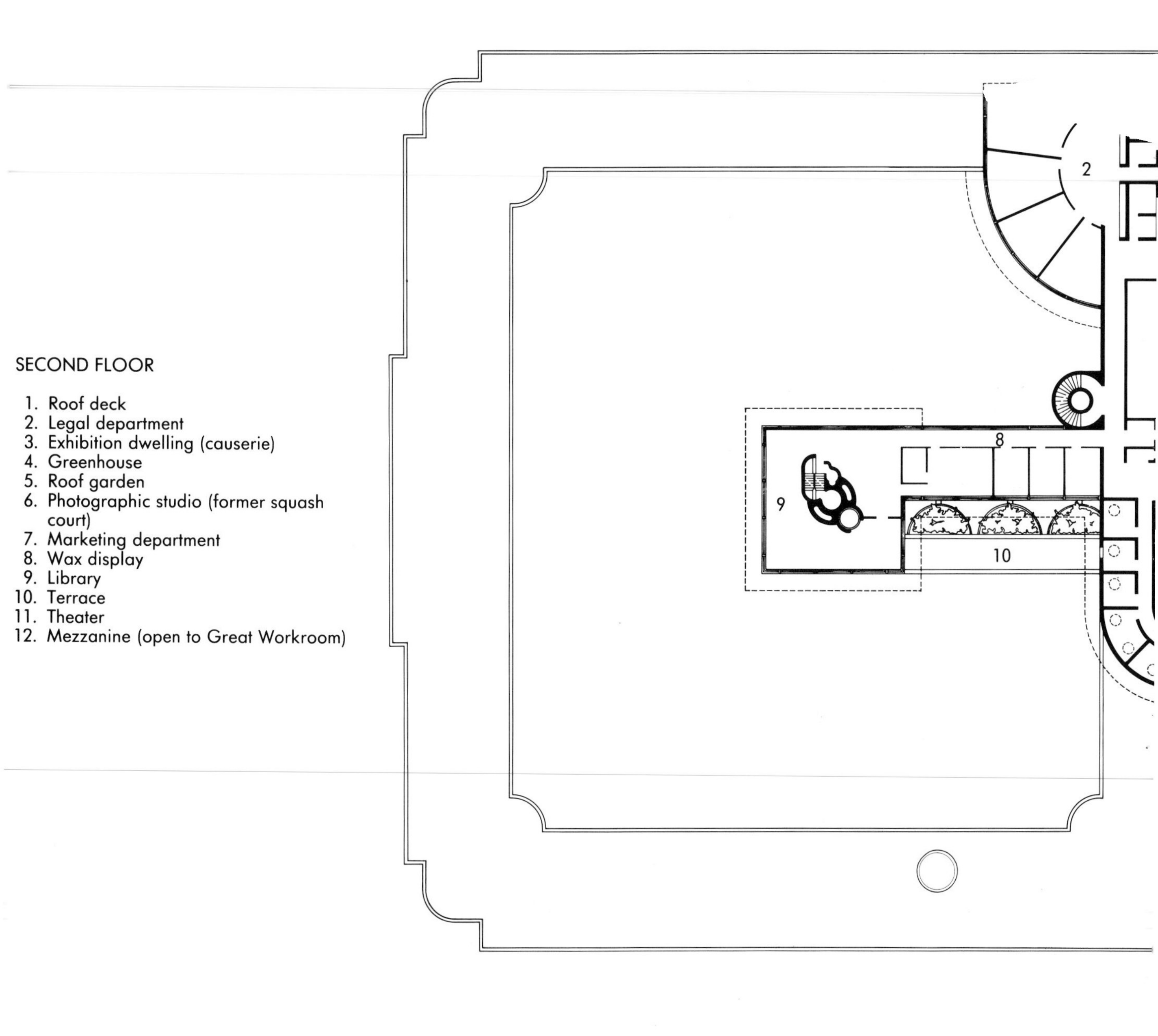

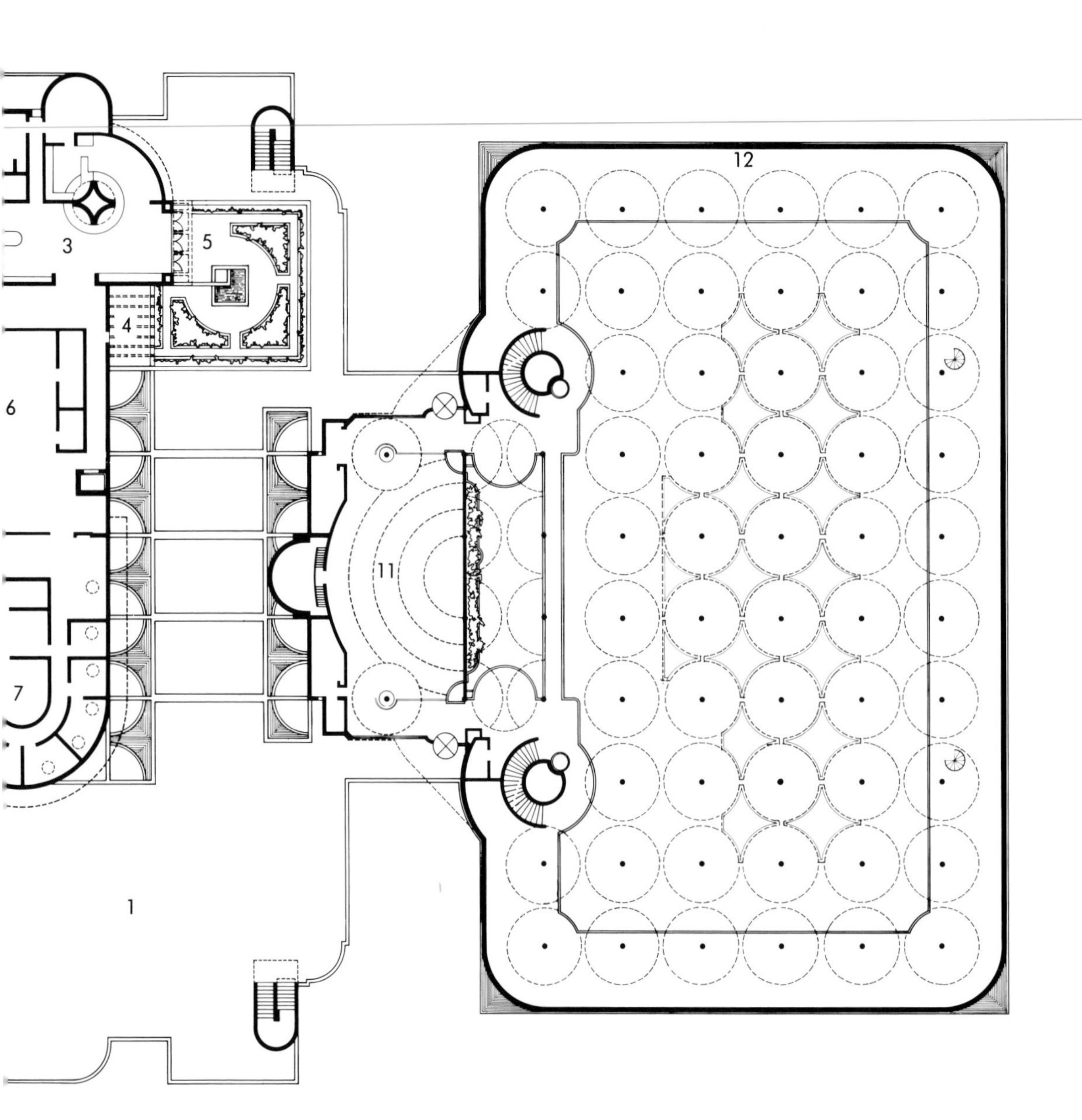
12
3
5
4
6
11
7
1

SECTION AND ELEVATION

Opposite: Third-floor (penthouse) plan of Administration Building and Research Tower. (Drawing by Gerald Wilson)

Overleaf, above: Longitudinal section through Administration Building and Research Tower. (Drawing by Gerald Wilson)

Overleaf, below: West Elevation of Administration of Administration Building and Research Tower. (Drawing by Gerald Wilson)

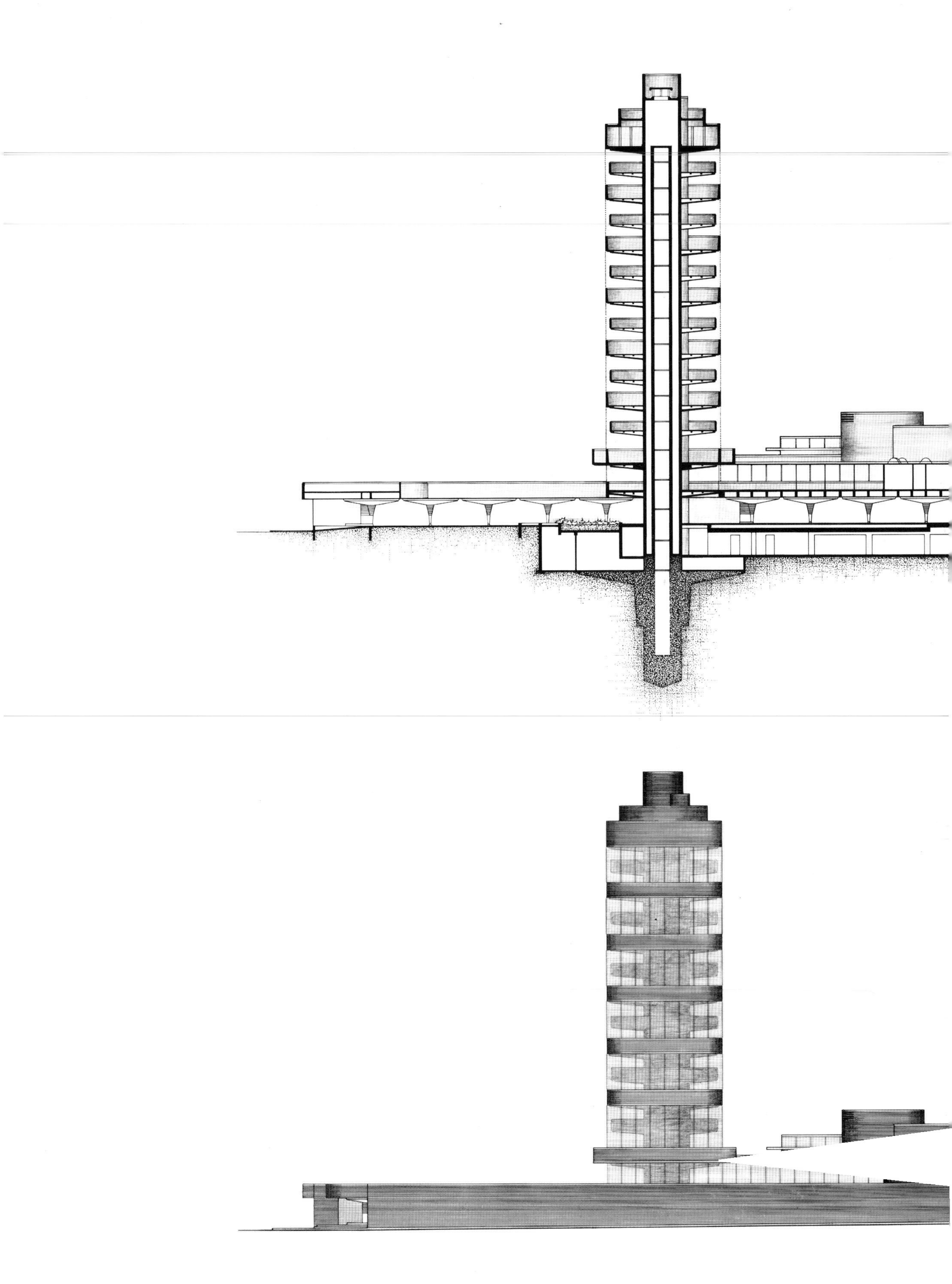

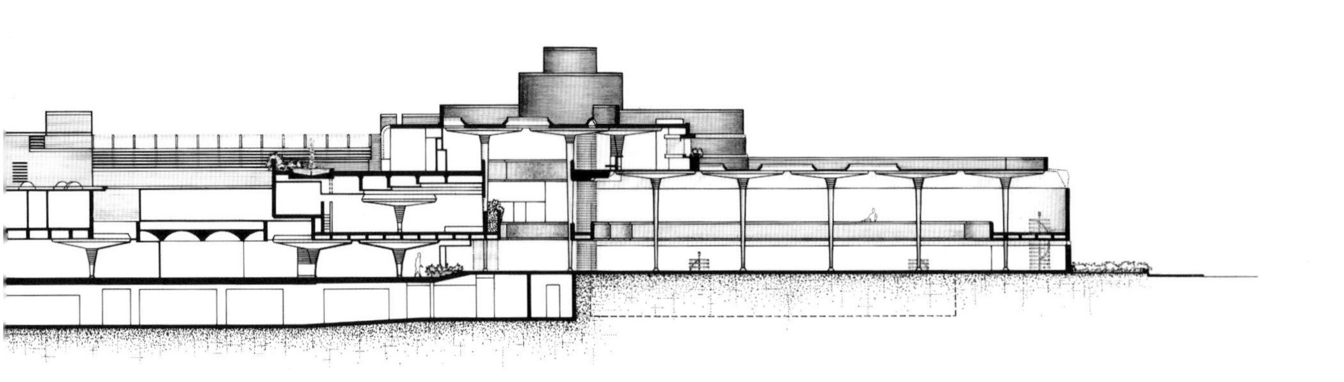

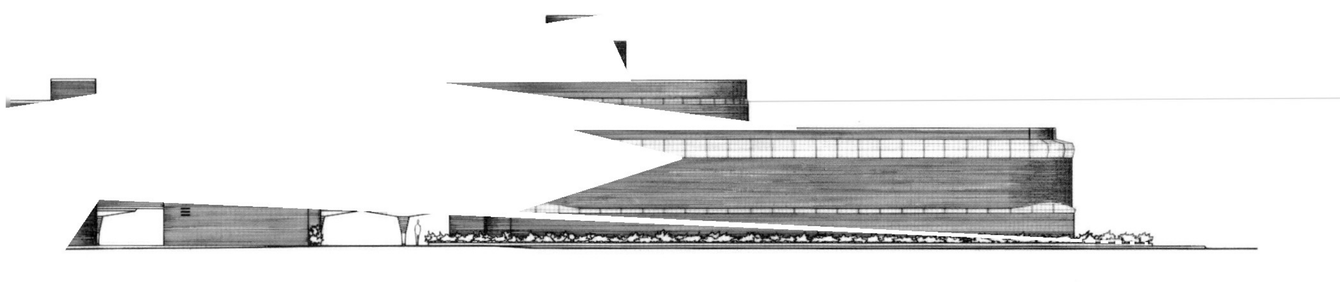

INDEX